# PRINCESS
## MORE TEARS
## TO CRY

*My life inside one of the
richest, most conservative
kingdoms in the world*

NEW YORK TIMES BESTSELLING AUTHOR
# JEAN SASSON

ISBN 978-1-939481-27-6

Cover photograph © Mohamad Itani / Trevillion Images

Jacket design by Natanya Wheeler

Book design by Judith Engracia


Printed in the United States of America

This book is a work of nonfiction. In some cases names have
been changed to protect the privacy of others.

# Other Works
# by Jean Sasson

**Nonfiction:**

*The Rape of Kuwait: The True Story of Iraqi Atrocities
Against a Civilian Population*

*Princess: A True Story of Life
Behind the Veil in Saudi Arabia*

*Princess Sultana's Daughters
(Daughters of Arabia in UK market)*

*Princess Sultana's Circle
(Desert Royal in UK market)*

*Mayada, Daughter of Iraq:
One Woman's Survival Under Saddam Hussein*

*Love in a Torn Land:
One Woman's Daring Escape from Iraq*

*Growing Up bin Laden: Osama's Wife and Son Take Us
Inside Their Secret World*

*For the Love of a Son:
One Afghan Woman's Quest for Her Stolen Child*

*American Chick in Saudi Arabia*

*Yasmeena's Choice:
A True Story of War, Rape, Courage and Survival*

**Historical Fiction:**
*Ester's Child* (to be re-released in 2015)

For additional information about Jean Sasson
and her books, please visit:
http://www.JeanSasson.com
Blog: http://jeansasson.wordpress.com/
Facebook:
http://www.facebook.com/AuthorJeanSasson
Twitter: http://twitter.com/jeansasson
ASK: http://ask.fm/jeansasson

*This book is dedicated to Amal,
a tiny girl who knew only fear and terror
at the hands of her brutal Saudi father,
who raped his five-year-old daughter to death.
Most shocking, Amal's father
claimed that he was a religious cleric.*

*May God forbid such a heinous death
to any young girl.*

All that is written here is real.
Some of the stories are happy and some are sad,
but all are true.

Names have been changed to protect all people
written about in this book, so as to keep them from
harm from family members or those who will take
offense at their true stories' becoming public
knowledge.

—Jean Sasson and Princess Sultana Al Sa'ud

# Table of Contents

# Map of Saudi Arabia

# Introduction
# by Princess Sultana Al Sa'ud

I am a princess who can never be queen. This is because in my country only the men and the wind are completely free. Under the current circumstances, never will a woman be elevated to the highest rank in our Saudi monarchy.

More than twenty years have passed since I first revealed the dark secrets of my land in the book *Princess: A True Story of Life Behind the Veil in Saudi Arabia.* I have returned to tell you much more. For those who have already read about my life, this book will bring you into the present day. For those who have not read the first three installments, please allow me to introduce you to my story, as well as provide information regarding the fate of women born in Saudi Arabia.

I will tell you what life is like for many females in Saudi Arabia in this the year AD 2014 of the Gregorian calendar, and AH 1435 of the Islamic calendar.

Men are allowed to have four wives and limitless concubines. My mother was the first of my father's wives, but she gave birth to only one son, the chief measure of a woman's respect and status in my country. My father soon married other women, which was a permanent anguish for my mother.

I was the youngest of my mother's eleven children—one son and ten daughters. Although I am a royal princess and was repeatedly told that I was a child of privilege, this was not my reality. Once I was able to fully comprehend our lives, I understood that my status was, in fact, very low. I lived in a luxurious palace, where beauty and wealth surrounded me. Yet these trappings of royalty meant little because I was a child who wanted nothing more than the love of both my parents. Although my darling mother adored me with her whole heart, my father attributed no value to females—in particular a female child as obstinate and bold as I was from the moment I was able to voice my thoughts. I knew that my father was capable of great love because he provided affection in abundance when it came to my brother, Ali. But, despite my overpowering desire to win my father's love, I never achieved my objective.

Although our four palaces were filled with servants to grant his every wish, Ali was never satisfied. He demanded that all who lived in the palace pander to him, including his mother and siblings. But I never did perform as my brother ordered. I was the youngest of the daughters and small for my age. As the baby, I was greatly pampered by my nine sisters and my mother, who treated me like a little doll to dress in frilly dresses. Thus Ali was not the only spoiled child in our home. Feeling myself the equal of my brother, I was comfortable pestering him daily with high-spirited disobedience.

But the day came when I first grasped that outside of our family circle of women I was not considered the little treasure they had led me to believe. A vivid memory grieves me today, many years later. It is of the day when I first grasped that my father did not love me as he loved his son. On that miserable day it was demonstrated to me that my brother would rule over me, at least until I was old enough to outwit him.

The incident occurred only because I declined to give Ali my apple. Rather than bend to his will, I ate the apple as quickly as possible, causing my brother to burn in fury. The moment Ali was able to speak through his rage, he shouted for Omar, who was our Egyptian driver, and who reported only to our father. Suddenly Omar's huge hands lifted me into the air and I was taken to confront my stern-faced father, who glared at me with true exasperation. I, a mere female, had dared to refuse a wish voiced by my brother, a male child who was born to rule. I was to pay dearly that day for nothing more than eating my own apple. After my father slapped me in the face, he told Omar that Ali was my master: Ali was to be given all my toys; he was to hold the power to say what I could or could not do, including when I might eat my daily meals. How my brother gloated! I was tortured by him for many weeks until he became interested in other pursuits.

From that day forward, Ali and I were devoted enemies. Although he bested me when I was very young, as I grew older I discovered that Ali was not as clever as his little sister, and he would fall for any deception. I soon surpassed my brother's wit, and this has never changed—even today, there are many times when I cannot contain the urge to dupe my brother on trivial issues, silly matters that cause him much embarrassment, for he lacks a sense of humor; he is iv

a man who is as arrogant and overbearing as the child he once was.

The saddest moment of my life came when my mother passed away, dying far too young and leaving her shattered youngest without a mother. My older sisters took over my care, all of them promising my mother on her deathbed that they'd look after her little Sultana. Mother feared for my future safety, she said, for Saudi Arabia was not a country that reacted favorably to defiant females.

She was right to worry. Everything was enormously difficult for females in those days. Although the rush of oil wealth introduced modernization to our desert kingdom, we were still living in the ninth century when it came to female freedoms. Social and legal restrictions against women were numerous. Many women still lived in purdah, isolated in their homes. All women had a male guardian, a man in the family whose duty it was to regulate behavior in every circumstance of that woman's life. Few girls attended schools, and those who did were solely of wealthy families and their education was confined to limited fields of study. All girls were veiled at puberty. Many young girls even married at puberty or shortly afterward. Those young girls married whomever their families dictated they would marry. Most girls wed a first or second cousin, a cultural tradition that created many genetic health issues for the children of such unions. Women were not allowed to drive. When girls graduated from school, their families would not permit them to work, even if appropriate jobs were available. Truthfully, everything in normal life was kept distant from females. Men ruled by fear, but they were also fearful of what might happen should any hint of individuality be expressed by women. Severe punishments were routine for the most innocent of behavior. Should a girl speak to a boy not of her family, the punishment could be life-threatening. I personally experienced the true horror of this when a good friend, who was so bold that she met with foreign men, was put to death on the orders of her father. She was drowned in the family swimming pool, a favorite method in those days, when fathers were able to murder wayward daughters. Indeed, for this heinous deed he received congratulations from all. Another girlfriend was married to an old man in a small village for the same act of youthful rebellion.

But as I matured from a child into my teenage years, there were hints of the changes that were coming. I was the first in my family allowed to meet my husband prior to marriage. Despite our being closely supervised by the females of both families, the occasion of our meeting was an astounding triumph. Perhaps this was indicative of positive changes, for during this same period of time more girls gained access to schools, an astute decision enforced by my own family of royal men. Not surprisingly, the crusade to further female education was fought fiercely by many men in the kingdom, a campaign led by the clerics and religious radicals. Those men demanded that the role of the female remain in the dark ages. Suddenly the heat of the Saudi desert no longer came from the sun, but from the fiery clash of ideas regarding the opposing views about women's lives.

I am pleased to have been a spark in this fire.

Education has become the impetus for women's ambitions. With education, new ideas stimulate female brains.

I have observed that as Saudi women become educated, Saudi men too are becoming more enlightened as to the contribution educated women can make to Saudi life, both private and public. Education benefits us all, for once women possess a voice that can be heard by their men, they boldly fight for their daughters. While change has been painfully gradual, once started, it has consistently moved in a positive direction.

During these years of struggle, I became the mother of three children—a son and two daughters. Once I was the mother of daughters, I fought even more aggressively for the humanitarian issues that affected the children of all Saudi citizens. I believe that if our daughters are unhappy, our sons also will feel the wind of unhappiness in their own lives. New social and cultural gains for women are equally beneficial for the men of Saudi Arabia.

Twenty-two years ago, I took a dangerous step and collaborated with my American writer friend Jean Sasson so that my story, and those of other women in my country, might be revealed to the world. Two further books followed. It was the first time that a female of the royal family had dared to speak out, to alert the world to the fact that a princess was being denied personal freedom. In publishing those books, I made a bold move, changing my life and the lives of many other women. My story was a bestseller in many countries, and I have been told that my spirited fight against discrimination has mattered greatly to women of nearly every nationality and religion. I have learned that many thousands of young women have taken up the fight, inspired by my life story. For this I am happy, despite the fact that I suffered greatly for my audacity, baffling my sisters, provoking my husband, and enraging my father and my brother. But I have no regrets, for I am a woman who will not be bullied into silence. I stand proud that the three books written about my life reveal the positives and negatives of my people and my land, both of which I love greatly.

I believe in open dialogue and know that without education, awareness, and the right of every citizen to live in dignity, no country can advance. But even as I speak these words I must admit a painful truth: while some change has come to my people and my country, many challenges remain to be met.

So, what gender reforms have occurred in Saudi Arabia since the time I was a strong-willed young girl who boldly battled blind favoritism for males and unfairness toward females? The answer is complicated.

True advances have been made for Saudi females, principally in education. My family's royal embassy in Washington, D.C., acknowledges that Saudi Arabia's education system has gone through an astonishing transformation, making education available for all Saudis who choose to attend school.

This makes it clear that the men of my family have made education for every Saudi citizen a prime goal. Nothing has changed the face of my country, and the men and women living there today, more than access to education. Like other royals, I have made education a favorite charity and have spent a great deal of money to assist in educating our young, as well as young girls in other Muslim lands. The only Saudi Arabian citizens who do not receive education are the female children of the ill-informed. My government does not become involved should a father refuse offers of education for his daughters. This is something that I hope will change in the years to come.

Other factors, such as travel and the Internet (linked together with education), are making Saudi Arabia a very different place from the desert kingdom of my youth. Many Saudi citizens are financially independent. With access to money, large numbers of Saudis travel the world. Travel has opened their minds to other worlds, where women have rights to live in freedom. Access to the Internet has increased the pace of change. Most young Saudis are equipped with computers and iPads and other electronic equipment that fosters awareness through access to news from many other countries. With education, travel, and Internet access, the young people of Saudi Arabia realize that their country and their personal freedom are imperiled by men who wish women to remain slaves.

Despite these positive points, I must sadly confess that even after years of toiling to create change in the lives of women in Saudi Arabia, the results are erratic and unpredictable. No rules are clearly set when it comes to females. All decisions pertaining to female behavior still remain in the hands of the men ruling a family. If the men in a woman's family are educated and fair-minded, females have the opportunity for happiness. If the men in a woman's family are unenlightened and cruel, females suffer due to male ignorance.

When I was a child, life was routinely brutal for most women of Saudi Arabia. Now that I am an adult, *some* women have benefited from change—but still the quality of life for a female in Saudi Arabia is dependent on males, who have the power to refuse freedom.

My friends, here is what life is like for Saudi women in the twenty-first century:

- I live in a country where I know a woman who graduated at the top of her class and is a respected physician.

- I live in a country where I know of a young child whose mother was not allowed legal custody after a divorce, even though the child was only a baby. This baby girl was brutally raped to death by her father, a Saudi Muslim cleric.
- I live in a country where I know a woman who successfully manages her own business and who is creating havoc for her male competitors in similar businesses.
- I live in a country where a cleric has ruled that a ten-year-old girl who is sexually abused on a daily basis by her thirty-five-year-old husband must remain in that marriage. The clerics ruled that it is unfair to take the chance of marriage away from any young girl.
- I live in a country where most girls are being educated and those girls take their education very seriously.
- I live in a country where only 15 percent of the workforce is female, because most fathers and husbands still insist that a woman's sole place is in the home, even if the woman is highly educated and wishes to work.
- I live in a country where women are still not allowed to drive an automobile.
- I live in a country where clerics ruled that a woman should be lashed for daring to drive her young son to school.
- I live in a country where women must still gain permission from a male guardian to work and to travel, where female rebellion can still cost a woman her life.
- I live in a country where a number of women defy the men who rule them, yet the men in

their families have *not* called for the women's deaths.

- I live in a country where most females obey their mother and father as to the selection of the man who will be their husband. Although it is said that women have the right to say no, few will do so, as they feel such disobedience will dishonor their parents.
- I live in a country where women can reach great heights in their careers and where many women live in happy marriages.
- I live in a country where many women live miserably and are confined to their homes, unable to make the simplest of personal decisions, such as the right to take their young children and leave their husbands, whether from personal unhappiness or brutal abuse.
- I live in a country where any man is free to emotionally abuse, beat, or even murder the women of his family without facing communal condemnation or legal penalty.
- I live in a country where most men and women frown upon such behavior.
- I live in a country ruled by a king who came to maturity at a time when women's feelings and rights never enjoyed consideration, but this king, King Abdullah, has made the cause of women a priority.

Greater reform is urgently needed, for nothing is predictable when it comes to women's lives in Saudi Arabia. And so now we push for the kind of change that brings guarantees: we need to make it illegal for a man to abuse any woman. We must push for the kind of change that gives an adult female the right to make personal choices.

Happily, I am no longer alone in my quest to bring change to my country. There are many Saudi women who are pushing for positive transformation. Members of my family know some of these women. I believe that the world would like to hear their extraordinary stories. For this reason, I have once again ventured beyond my safety zone to tell the world the truth about Saudi Arabia. I want to tell you all that is happening in my land.

In this book I will reveal changes in my personal life. There is much to tell about members of my family, the lives of my children and grandchildren, and my sisters and nieces and nephews. Due to his annoying personality, there are additional surprising stories to share about my brother Ali. My father is still with the living, but he has aged poorly. Sadly, he is still a man who believes that males should rule and females should obediently submit.

Nothing is more important than knowing about the lives of brave women, however. I believe that readers want to know what is happening to ordinary Saudi women, those who do not have the opportunities brought about by wealth. These women face many challenges unknown to royal women, and for that reason I hold them in the highest regard.

I have selected ten women out of the many who have a story that should be told. The Saudi women you will meet in the following pages are real— brave women who are forging a path that will open up a new world to all in Saudi Arabia.

Although the years of my life have passed too quickly, positive change in the lives of women in my country has moved much too slowly. But I thank God that I lived to see the day when a large number of Saudi women have the opportunity to achieve their dreams. I also thank God that I am in a unique position to tell you about these extraordinary women.

Meanwhile, the women of Saudi Arabia, whether royal or not, are pushing against two thousand years of history. Our only hope is to push together. We are reaching out for your help. May God guide your hand to our hands. If all women come together under the blessings of God, perhaps one day there *will be* a queen of Saudi Arabia.

*With heartfelt good wishes for all who so kindly care about me, and other women in Saudi Arabia,*

*Princess Sultana Al Sa'ud*

# Chapter One
# For the Love of Daughters

"Surely it must be death!" one of our Indonesian maids breathlessly called out from the butler's galley.

I froze in place listening to the sounds of high-pitched female voices resonating from our main family sitting room. I shivered in dismay when I recognized the heated voices as belonging to my two daughters, Maha and Amani. My easy stroll turned into a speedy gait as I moved rapidly to find them.

What were my girls fighting about now?

My oldest daughter Maha has claimed Europe as her home for the past seven years, returning to Saudi Arabia for annual visits only. Although Kareem and I often visit Maha, Amani had not seen her sister in more than a year. Yet even after a long absence from the other, from the moment Maha returned, my girls became instantly enthusiastic with their verbal sparring, returning once more to their repetitive arguments, disputing nearly every aspect of daily life for women in Saudi Arabia, something they have done since their teenage years.

# 2

Only a moment was needed for me to understand that their current fight revolved around the lack of Saudi females' right to drive automobiles, a topic that fuels many heated conversations in my country, and abroad.

Maha's voice was filled with contempt as she told her sister, "Amani, you should join the protests and drive! Otherwise, my little sister, you can go only as far as your feet can take you, and not one step further!"

Amani returned her sister's hateful glare but said nothing.

Longing for a response, Maha reminded Amani that all Saudi girls are not wealthy. "You are selfish, my sister. You know that very few Saudi women have full-time drivers. What do those women do when they need transportation to university or to go shopping? How should they get to their destinations? If they do not have access to a hired driver, or are not brave enough to take a bus or taxi, they will have to use their two feet to take them where they need to go!"

Knowing my daughters as I do, I knew that their angry spiral of accusations would expand, and I was right.

I had little time to ponder before Amani bounded into action, her face flashing dark red with anger as she leapt like a desert gazelle toward her elder sister. If I had not been in attendance, my two adult daughters would have certainly exchanged blows, possibly grappling to the floor to physically fight as they had once done as children.

I seized Maha by her upper arm and pulled with all my strength. As it was, Maha tumbled into me, as Amani stumbled and collided with Kareem, my husband, who had entered the sitting room in pursuit of the explosion of female cries.

My darling husband is a long-suffering father. Our daughters' continual battles exhaust him. Prior to this latest visit, Kareem had announced that he would no longer tolerate Maha and Amani conducting themselves as children. After all, both daughters are grown women. Amani was now a married woman and mother, while Maha lives as a single adult in one of Europe's major cities. Maha was working as an executive in one of her father's businesses, enjoying a normal social life with her friends. Time and again, Maha has demonstrated her ability to easily manage most adult situations, but her maturity forsakes her when she is with her younger sister.

Kareem fleetingly gazed at me in disbelief before raising his voice to shout, so as to be heard over the sputtering protest of Amani and the wrathful squawk produced by Maha. "This will cease! Now!" Kareem commanded.

Although my daughters have often ignored their mother's demands, they rarely fail to respond suitably to their father's orders. I felt myself the spectator to a miracle as their cries and insults silenced instantly.

At that moment my sister Sara walked soundlessly into the room. She had arrived early for the planned family party to celebrate Maha's visit. Sara's expression was as usual appealingly composed, but her big black eyes grew significantly bigger when she observed our outlandish scene.

Sara's lips curved into a smile. "My dear nieces, does fighting still hold such charm for you, even after two broken bones and a chipped tooth?"

Sara was recalling the most violent of my daughters' battles, after nine-year-old Amani had foolishly strung a thin trip wire across the back hallway that led to a special room holding newly born kittens. Amani believed her kittens to be such treasures that she endlessly obsessed that someone might attempt to steal the animals and sell them in the animal souk.

As fate would have it, Maha had been the unintended victim after rushing unsuspecting along the hallway. After tripping over the wire, Maha's violent fall had resulted in two broken wrists. When Amani heard the noise, she had raced to discover the identity of the kitty thief, only to find her sister writhing in pain. Amani angrily accused her sister of planning to steal all the kittens.

When Amani was a teenager, our family traveled to Mecca for the pilgrimage. During the religious event, Amani's religious faith was transformed; once a child whose faith was dormant, she emerged a determined young woman who wished to embrace all aspects of our Islamic faith with unnerving intensity. Since that life-changing religious experience, Amani had had the unfortunate habit of throwing a shadow of doubt on everyone's behavior, often accusing those around her of moral or criminal deeds.

When Amani tried to peer underneath Maha's body to make sure there were no kittens flattened there, an enraged Maha elbowed her sister in the face, breaking a tooth.

While the event was not amusing at the time—as Kareem and I had had to explain to our family physician the embarrassing nature of our daughters' injuries—Sara's comment and her cool nature were the perfect anger antidote. Kareem and I exchanged a look and laughed loudly at the memory of that time long ago when our daughters' behavior too often resembled that of wild beasts set loose in our home.

A humorless Amani did not approve of our laughter. She eased herself away from her father, brushing her dress's bodice with her hand as though nothing more worrying than a spill had occurred. She then greeted her Auntie Sara with a routine exchange of kisses, changing the subject by inquiring about Sara's sick grandchild, whose little life had recently been threatened by a serious bout of whooping cough. Maha, as triumphant as a conquering warrior, touched her favorite auntie's shoulder in a gesture of affection before retreating to pour a cold drink made of freshly squeezed lemons.

She and Amani then chose to occupy opposite sides of the room, portraying the perfect role of strangers to one another.

I love my two daughters as much as any mother can love their children, but even as adults they continue to test my patience. Years ago I had clung to the hope that adulthood would bring maturity, but I was sadly mistaken. Staring at my daughters, I saw that both wore an expression of haughty satisfaction. I fought the strongest desire to smack those faces.

Even as I made small talk with Sara and Kareem, I was questioning our life, wondering why two daughters of the same parents could not find one thing to agree upon. From their teenage years, our daughters have clashed on everything.

Maha was born a strong, free-spirited girl who took vigilant notice at a young age of the cultural and social constraints placed on Saudi females. Over the years, her rage festered at the unfairness of our country's social customs regarding gender; she grew to detest every restriction and often voiced her resolve to test each one. Amani embraced the most conservative, traditional beliefs of our land so long as they were directed at females. There were times when it seemed to me that Amani believed the shackles confining females were not harsh enough.

After years of traumatic episodes and incident, tranquility came to our home only once Maha had persuaded us, her parents, that she would never know true happiness while forced to live in Saudi Arabia. Kareem and I felt real concern that she would indeed purposely test every stringent social and tribal law regarding women if compelled to reside in the kingdom. Our Maha is fearless and unflinching when it comes to authority. Perhaps she would commit an act considered so culturally serious that there would be a chorus of communal disapproval followed by a clamor for our uncle, the king, to make an example of our daughter.

After many extended conversations, Kareem and I arranged for Maha to attend university in Europe. Happily, our daughter's aggressive personality lightened considerably after moving away. She was so content in Europe that we later accepted that she would always make her home far from our desert kingdom. From that time on, Maha made only rare trips to Saudi Arabia, although we often visited her.

Unlike her sister, Amani cherishes female life in Saudi Arabia, often stating that there is no country so good for women as our land. She believes herself to be lovingly protected from the vices of the world, rather than being inhibited from making personal choices without the input of her father, who was, and still remains, her male guardian. Prior to arranging Amani's marriage, Kareem insisted upon the legal stipulation that he, her father, remained her guardian. My husband could not abide the thought of any man holding such power over his child. According to these legal documents, at Kareem's death, Amani's eldest son will be her guardian, regardless of what age he might be at the time of his grandfather's demise. So it may come to pass that a child might be named Amani's guardian. For me, this is a ridiculous concept, one I believe women should fight with all their might, but my daughter claims she will bear no grudge should the day come when she will be an adult woman ruled by a guardian who is her male child!

Few people outside the kingdom understand that every Saudi female is born into the most rigid, male-dominated system, where a male will be her guardian. This is the case even in the year 2014 (AH 1435 in the Islamic calendar). This appointed male guardian has complete control over the female, from her first moment of birth to the last second of her death. Although the obligations of a guardian are not written in Saudi law, the guardian's rights to rule might as well be carved in stone. Saudi courts recognize obedience to the guardian as law, even if the female is a full adult. A woman needs authorization from her guardian before she can attend school, marry, divorce, open a bank account, seek employment, or even have many medical treatments including surgery. I have known personally of four occasions when a Saudi woman has died because her guardian has been traveling and was unavailable to provide permission for emergency surgery.

No woman in Saudi Arabia can escape the guardian's mantle, wrapped tightly around her body, keeping her a permanent prisoner of her guardian's every wish. The male guardian is her personal king, there to decide every aspect of her life. Such a guardian can rule that a woman has sullied the family honor and should be put to death, should he so choose. There is no one in the land to intervene, not even the police or members of government security. I am speaking the truth. I will admit that it is unusual these days for a guardian to rule that his wife or daughter should be put to death, but should he decide to do so, death will come to that woman. Such is the life of a Saudi female existing under the rule of a guardian. In fact, several cases have appeared in the international news recently, though others go unreported. Horrifying crimes of murder will be revealed in a later chapter.

Even I, a woman capable of caring for myself, have never lived a day without a guardian. My father was my guardian until I married Kareem. For me, my father was a very unkind guardian, although I am alive today because he never considered murdering me when I brought shame and disappointment to him. At the time of our marriage, Kareem accepted the mantle of guardianship over my father's youngest daughter. Should my husband pass from this earth before me, my son Abdullah will be my guardian.

Admittedly, my situation is safer than that of most Saudi women because my husband and I truly love each other. Many have been the times that my husband claims he would not wish to live if I were dead, so I have always reasoned that he would never kill me. Kareem's loving feelings for me give me a formidable power and a sense of security. So, since I left my family home, guardianship has posed only a negligible personal dilemma for me.

Actually, my husband lovingly spoke about guardianship early on in our marriage. I remember that day as if it were only a few weeks ago. My handsome husband swore upon our most holy book, the Koran, saying, "Sultana, we are guardians in trust. I am your guardian. You are my guardian. We will look to the other for help in every problem of life."

Only once did Kareem break his vow, and that was when he foolishly attempted to force me to accept a second wife. That plan did not go well for my husband. Those who know me personally, or who have read my story, know that I was the victor in that marital struggle. This, I believe, is because I am willing to die if I feel strongly enough about a situation, while my husband carefully guards his own life, as well as my own.

But now I had more problems than guardianship to contend with, for I heard Maha continue to speak under her breath, insulting Amani's Saudi education.

I was happy that Amani was college educated. In fact, during her high school years Amani had expressed little desire to attend university, asserting that a good Muslim woman needed nothing more than a husband and children. I was shattered by my child's resolve to avoid a full education. Kareem handled the situation wisely when he pointed out that there were important steps she had not taken, namely a university education. The subject of a husband could only be raised once Amani had earned her university degree, he told her.

After speaking with religious authorities, Amani became satisfied that education was not at odds with our Islamic faith. Once placated thus, she enrolled in the Arabic language and literature department of the Art and Humanities College at the Riyadh University for Women, later renamed the Princess Nora bint Abdul Rahman University after the most beloved sister of our grandfather, the first king, Abdul Aziz Al Sa'ud. To our surprise and parental glee, Amani slipped easily into continuing education, admitting that she relished her classes in the Arabic language and literature department. She earned high marks in all classes and graduated after four years of study.

I dreamt that Amani might be a teacher of literature to other girls, for she was very passionate in her learning, but soon found myself sighing with sadness when Amani announced that she would never work. There were too many possibilities of meeting men not of her family to chance entering the world of the working woman. She would never talk with, or work with, any man other than her husband, father, brother, son, or other close male relative. Amani claimed that her learning was undertaken so that she might better represent her religion, faith, and Islamic values, and also, most important, to be a better mother to her children.

Kareem told me not to protest: "Sultana, do not forget that 58 percent of college students in Saudi Arabia are female, yet only 14 percent of those girls can find jobs. It is just as well that Amani does not fill a position truly needed by another Saudi girl."

I grimaced at his words, yet I could not deny that Kareem spoke a woeful truth. While Amani would never need a salary from a job to provide life's necessities, our country is filled with educated girls who are anxious for much-needed employment. Certainly I am delighted that so many Saudi girls are being allowed to attend school, which was not always the case in my country.

Yet, for women in Saudi Arabia, as soon as they overcome one obstacle, another appears. While education of females is becoming accepted by most men, many fathers balk at the idea of their daughters' working; they want to ensure that men who are not members of the family do not have physical access to their daughters. Additionally, many husbands refuse permission for their wives to work, although most promise otherwise during the engagement period. Furthermore, many businesses do not like females' working in their establishments, dreading that the mix of men and women will create problems with the religious establishment. Angry-hearted clerics often assert that females and the devil walk hand in hand when women mingle with men who are strangers to them. Pity the poor Saudi woman who wants to use her intellect and her education to work in her chosen profession, for there are many barriers placed in her path.

Within months of graduating from college, Amani pressed for us to arrange a marriage with a suitable royal cousin. She did not name someone specific, asking only that he be a man from a known good royal family, of good character and a believer. She steadfastly rejected the opportunity to view a photograph of her groom-to-be, so charitably provided by his sister. Amani became incensed when her brother Abdullah taunted her with hints that her cousin was pleading to see his future bride's face, and that he, Abdullah, might relieve the young man's anxiety by displaying a photograph of Amani. She became so distraught that she tearfully entreated her father to intervene, and he did, forbidding our son from disturbing his sister any further on the matter.

Abdullah is a joyful soul who relentlessly teases his sisters, but only Maha shows the occasional sign of humor at his antics. If only my two daughters shared the pleasing and outgoing character of my son, I would be a mother filled with joy. Kareem, too, acknowledges that our son is trouble-free and has often said to me, "Sultana, God chose to reward us with an agreeable son and to challenge our endurance with Amani and Maha."

During the times he was personally frustrated with me for one thing or another, he delighted in adding an insult and laying blame on my head by saying: "My daughters have inherited their mother's propensity for generating bedlam." Certainly both daughters arrived on this earth preprogrammed with the most exhausting dispositions.

But as an opposite character to her mother and sister, Amani holds dear everything to do with being a woman ruled by men. She is also a poster girl for strict obedience of everything religious. From her teen years, she wore the full black veil with enormous satisfaction, believing it immoral for any woman to expose her face in public. She still covers her delicate hands with black gloves, and her feet and legs with thick black stockings, regardless of the sweltering heat in the kingdom—in fact, even when we visit Jeddah, the port city known for its drenching humidity.

I have always said that such a costume is extremely dangerous in the heat of Saudi Arabia, and my concerns were substantiated when a heavily pregnant Amani was visiting us at our Jeddah home. As she was not familiar with some of our newly employed male staff, she tended to wear her heavy veil from the moment she woke until she slept. My poor daughter feared that one of them might catch a glimpse of her uncovered face, although these men are trusted and accustomed to being around the females in our homes.

One morning she walked down the stairs fully veiled, annoying me and even surprising her Auntie Sara, who generally accepted the contrasting behavior of my two daughters with a smile. I started to voice my thoughts, saying I found it ridiculous for Amani to fully cover when at home. Besides, I enjoy having a conversation with someone I can see, and most particularly get pleasure from looking upon the faces of my children. At that moment Sara gave me a warning look and I bit my lip, asking instead, "Would you like some cold juice, my precious?"

Amani brushed past, saying, "No, Mummy. I feel like a stroll in the garden." One of our Indonesian maids opened the heavy wooden and glass door so that Amani could enter the special women's garden Kareem had so carefully designed for the females in our family. The garden is unusually large and studded with numerous enormous plants and lots of ferns; the effect was meant to be reminiscent of a rain forest. Overly protective of my pregnant daughter, I called out, "Don't get lost in all that greenery, sweet Amani." My daughter did not respond.

Soon Sara and I became distracted with a game of komkom; this is a fun game we often play when at Jeddah because the game requires seashells that the children can sometimes find on the Red Sea shoreline. Two of Sara's eight grandchildren played with us. The gaiety of watching the children toss the seashells on the floor was fun and I momentarily forgot the time. When Abdullah came into the sitting area and inquired about Amani, I suddenly realized that she had been in the garden for nearly an hour.

I jumped to my feet and dashed out of the door and into the garden, calling for my child. I gave a terrified scream when I saw her sprawled on the ground, the black cloth of her abaya draped over a small fern and fluttering in the sea breeze.

"Amani!" I shouted out.

Abdullah quickly followed, as well as several of our drivers, who had heard my cry and came running into the garden, normally forbidden to them.

For a moment, I thought my precious child was dead, finally smothered to death by all that heavy black fabric, her black stockings and gloves. Amani's costume probably weighed more than she did herself, as she had always been delicate in size. Even though she was pregnant, she weighed only forty kilograms, less than ninety pounds.

Abdullah and one of the drivers lifted Amani and carried her into our air-conditioned home. While they struggled to hold her carefully, for she was noticeably pregnant, her veil was accidentally pulled from her face and her long black skirt was hoisted above her waist.

At that moment I did not care, although Amani's black stockings only stretched to her knees, leaving her white thighs visible for all to see.

My daughter was placed upon the largest of the five sofas in the sitting area and I began to remove her heavy black cover. When I pulled back her veil, I caught my breath at the sight of her face, which was dark red, almost bruised in appearance, her eyes rolling back, exposing the whites of her eyes, a most alarming sight.

By this time one of the servants had located Kareem in his office and my husband was by my side, calling out for cold wet cloths to be placed on her face. On Kareem's instructions, Abdullah drove at speed to the home of our family physician, a very experienced Palestinian doctor who lived only a short distance from us. Abdullah was told to bring him to us to tend to our daughter.

By this time I felt myself going mad. Amani lay like a corpse. Kareem was pointing out that our daughter was breathing steadily, so there was no need for me to yank at my hair, something I did not even know I was doing. (Though when I pulled my hands away from my head, I saw that dozens of long black hairs were dangling from my clenched fingers.)

I looked around to see that every housemaid, driver, and gardener was packed tightly into our large sitting area, but before I had time to order them all to leave, our doctor arrived. I've never been so happy to see his big ruddy face and short chubby body, although in the past he had sometimes irritated me with his habit of folding his hands behind his back and pacing in circles, muttering incoherently while deep in thought.

I have always wanted to know instantly every aspect of a medical problem concerning my children. As the doctor hurried to hover over our daughter, asking that everyone step back to give her space to breathe, he seemed very concerned. I clung to Kareem's arm, staring at my child at the exact moment Amani opened her eyes. She unexpectedly saw the big face of the Palestinian doctor studying her face, then gasped loudly and fainted.

Amani was eventually returned to good health. The doctor announced that the heat was the problem and spoke in a low but firm voice to Amani, telling her that she should not wear such heavy black clothing in the heat and humidity of Jeddah. I knew from her expression that she would never follow doctor's orders and that I must remember to cease traveling to Jeddah during the hottest of the summer months. Our family would remain in Riyadh, where the air is dry, making life more tolerable for veiled women, or perhaps stay in Taif, our mountain retreat known for its cool breezes.

Amani's painful psychological ordeal was far from over. She was most scandalized when she later discovered that many employed in our Jeddah home had caught sight of her uncovered face, and that three of the drivers had even glimpsed the flesh on her legs. My child became so overexcited that her father and I had to promise that we would rotate all the employees from Jeddah to Riyadh when we were visiting our Jeddah palace. When we returned to Riyadh, those same employees would be sent back to Jeddah. It was going to be a merry-go-round of employees, only because Amani was too embarrassed to be in the company of those who had seen her face and legs.

Everything required for Amani's peace of mind seemed ridiculous to me, but there was nothing I would not do to ease the stress of one of my children, and most especially my pregnant daughter. And now time had passed and Amani was the mother of a son.

My two daughters had not seen each other in more than a year, yet fireworks had quickly erupted between them. In fact, Maha had arrived back in the kingdom only three days earlier, but already my two girls were fighting endlessly.

Kareem left to refresh himself for the night's company, advising Maha, "Daughter, please retire to your room and prepare yourself for this evening. The time will soon come for our guests to arrive."

I smiled, happy that Kareem reminded Maha of the entertaining evening ahead. After all, a large number of guests were expected to see Maha. Since the day we received notice that she was coming for a rare visit, a welcoming party had been planned. Nearly all the family had arranged their busy schedules so that they might be part of the celebration.

Sara and I had spent many hours planning the evening. We had decided to serve Maha's favorite Arabic foods, including al-kabsa, tahini, and tomato chicken. Kareem had arranged for separate food to be served in the men's gardens so that our vegan daughter Amani would not catch a view of the whole stuffed camel with lamb, chicken, eggs, and rice. We were afraid that our animal-loving Amani might destroy such a dish if it was spotted. Once in the past, Amani had discovered a cooked baby camel and had conducted a funeral and buried it in our garden before our guests even arrived. Therefore great secrecy surrounded the camel dish, a specialty our guests could savor and enjoy.

There would be plenty of French delicacies as well. Sara's French chef had been busy for the past few days, making his delicious bisque, salmon terrine, and pot-au-feu. A private airplane sent to France had returned with all the special French cheeses and baguettes.

I looked to see if Maha might obey her father. She nodded but didn't move a muscle away from her perch on the sofa.

From the moment Kareem exited the room, Amani resumed her disagreement with her sister. Attempting to bring Sara into the discussion, she asked, "Auntie Sara, what are your thoughts on women driving?" Then before Sara could consider a response, Amani's words continued to bubble from her lips: "Do you agree that if Saudi women drive, their veils will create visibility problems, causing accidents? Once an accident occurs, she would be forced into an illicit conversation with the other driver. What if he was a male driver, a stranger to her?"

Sara was caught in an awkward place, so I entered the conversation, saying, "Sweet girl, please do your mummy a favor and leave such controversial topics for another more appropriate time."

Before Amani could react, Maha made an angry grunt, but left the room in a hurry. I hoped she had taken her father's advice to use the time to repair her hair and makeup.

Before the tension could evaporate from the room, however, Maha returned. I saw that she had retrieved her international driving license and was flashing it at Amani in an aggressive manner, saying, "My little sister is one of those fools who has a college degree but is uneducated!"

Nothing could stop Amani: "The driving of automobiles by women is a source of undeniable vices. Women driving leads to that, and this is self-evident."

Amani often quoted fatwas issued by various Saudi clerics, and I recognized her words as having come from Sheikh Abdul Aziz bin Baz, a Saudi cleric who was the Grand Mufti of Saudi Arabia from 1993 until his death, at age eighty-eight, in 1999.

Baz was not very intelligent in my opinion and had proved his mental deficiencies by announcing many controversial rulings, one of which was that the earth was flat. He had said: "The earth is fixed and stable and has been spread out by God for mankind and made a bed and cradle for them, tied down by mountains lest it shake." After his statement, he was ridiculed by many journalists. My father once told Kareem that his older (half) brother, King Faisal, had become so enraged that Baz had mortified all Saudis through his ignorance that he had ordered the destruction of any papers or books that reported Baz's words. Later Baz declared that the sun rotates around the earth, though he retracted that statement after my cousin, Prince Sultan bin Salman, spent time aboard the space shuttle *Discovery*. When he returned to Saudi Arabia, it was said that he swore to the cleric that he had seen the earth from space, and that the earth was rotating and was not still.

Other rulings Baz made had to do with keeping all women in purdah, or isolation, and for this I always disliked the man. Others disagreed with me because he was loved by many. He was one of Amani's favorite clerics, although he had died when Amani was still a child.

Amani knew Baz's fatwa by heart, about women being forbidden from driving, and she proudly quoted, "Depravity leads to the innocent and pure women being accused of indecencies. Allah has laid down one of the harshest punishments for such an act to protect society from the spreading of the causes of depravity. Women driving cars, however, is one of the causes that lead to that." Now Maha was dancing around the room, singing her words in a loud voice: "I am free, Amani, while you willingly wear chains!" She leapt into the air like a ballerina, holding her driving license like a trophy.

My daughter is really too dramatic.

Maha continued her rant. "I am free! My sister wears chains!"

"Everything you do is haram, Maha," Amani announced self-importantly, with the greatest certainty.

"Listen, Amani. You are in the dark ages. You could be smart, but you seek ignorance and you appear to like portraying weakness and ignorance, to have men making all your decisions, when you are fully capable." Maha was smothering. "I am free, Amani, to live. I am free to think for myself. I am free to drive. I am free to have thoughts about anything I please. I am a woman freed from this madness you embrace so lovingly!"

My head spun like the earth at Maha's next statement, and even Sara gasped. "Today I tricked all those silly old men. I dressed as a man and took Abdullah's new Mercedes for a drive around the city."

"Maha!" I cried. "Maha, please tell me this is not so! You will humiliate your parents if you are caught dressing as a man and driving an automobile."

"Oh, Mother," Maha giggled, "I was never in danger. I wore no makeup. Abdullah painted a most realistic pencil mustache on my face. Abdullah did all the talking in the shops, so no one heard any feminine voice."

My voice went high in pitch. "My son knew of this?"

Maha's lips turned down in frustration. "Your son agrees with me, Mother. He is of the opinion that all these antiquated rules against women should disappear, just like this," and she snapped her fingers. "I hope a good future is waiting when one of the young princes like Abdullah is selected to be king. If it is my brother, he will put an end to this nonsense. Then, and only then, will I return to live in my country."

I was about to say a lot more, to tell Maha that I happened to know that Abdullah had no desire to be king of Saudi Arabia, as my son is not a man who has that spark of desire to rule others, but just then I heard the voices of various family members as they made their way down the long corridor to the sitting area. Our company was arriving. The hour of the long-anticipated family party had arrived.

"We will talk more later, Maha," I promised with a stern voice, as I scurried from the room to greet our guests. On my way I turned to Sara: "Dear sister, please organize my daughters and bring them to the party."

Sara nodded in agreement. "Do not worry, Sultana," she said. "We will join you soon."

I kept a confident look until I walked from the room to make my way up the long corridor. That's when my shoulders slumped in despair and exhaustion; I had witnessed another very unpleasant scene between my two beautiful daughters.

In recent years I had often found myself engrossed in wonderful daydreams of how my family would finally come together in harmony. I had hoped that my dreams would come true that night.

Mainly, I wished to impress my father with my well-kept home and obedient children. Over the years I had sought an agreeable relationship with the man who had given me life, despite the years he had spent inflicting pain on me, his youngest daughter. Before the horrible scene between Amani and Maha, I was delighted that my father had finally accepted an invitation to my home. But now, with Amani and Maha in such uncompromising moods, I knew if disorder erupted in his presence I would never see my father again. In his old age he had unwaveringly avoided conflict, and I knew he would certainly not tolerate an unpleasant scene between these two young women. Indeed, it would reflect badly on both myself and my husband if such a scene took place.

The thought passed through my mind that I should forget the party and seal myself behind the impenetrable steel door Kareem had recently installed.

This precaution was taken after Kareem had met with one of his cousins, an important official in Saudi intelligence in the Ministry of the Interior. Kareem's cousin revealed alarming information about the interrogation of a young Saudi man who had crossed over from being a law-abiding citizen to one who had caught the dangerous fever of radicalism. The young man had recently spent time in Syria while fighting in that civil war. During his interrogation, he had divulged troubling intelligence, reporting that Al Qaeda operatives were slipping across our border with Yemen to move into small villages in our own kingdom. From those villages they had plans to set up raids against the members of the Saudi government. One of their favorite schemes was the plot to bring death to members of the Saudi royal family, people like Kareem and me and our children.

I kept walking down the long corridor to my fate, whatever it might be. I attempted to refocus my mind on the coming hours, praying to Allah that the evening before me would bring merriment and enjoyment.

# Chapter Two
# The Party

Like a siren song, diamonds call out to most females. I no longer hear that call. I lost my desire for expensive jewelry the moment I discovered the immense joy one derives from helping others. Now when I am shown exquisite jewels, I do not envisage the glittering gems draped around my neck, hanging from my ears, or clasped upon my wrist; instead, I contemplate what the value of those gems could procure. Perhaps it would allow an eager child to take lessons in a good school, or a sickly mother to feel the glow of calm, knowing she will live to return to her children after receiving high-priced medical care.

I was walking into a situation where I would have such an opportunity, as lively voices animating the corridor led me to believe that members of my family were already enjoying the pleasure of an exciting reunion. But I was wrong. Expensive jewelry was the cause of much of the commotion.

As I entered the largest of our sitting rooms, I heard the distinct voices of three of my older sisters. Dismay washed over me when I looked to see my sisters, Tahani, Dunia, and Haifa, clustered in a circle breathlessly exclaiming over Dunia's new looped diamond necklace, which was hanging nearly to her waist.

Sara had described the piece of jewelry to me a few days earlier, but I was startled when I saw that the long-stringed necklace could be wrapped round Dunia's neck three times. Many hundreds of diamonds had been used to make such a substantial piece. It was much larger than I could ever have imagined. I stood staring and assessing that necklace. Each diamond was worth a small fortune. Each diamond could educate a child. Each diamond could support a poor family for a year. The blinding glitter of Dunia's diamonds held no appeal for me.

Sara had mentioned that our sister had paid many millions of dollars for the necklace. As a woman who only cares for the frivolous things in life, Dunia had devoted many hours to searching for the most extraordinary jewels and seeking to acquire them all.

We did not understand the seriousness of Dunia's obsession until Sara purchased a special coffee-table book, *My Love Affair with Jewelry*, as a gift for her. It featured the jewelry collection of the legendary American actress Elizabeth Taylor. From her youth, Sara has always tried to encourage our family to read books, even picture books with few words. She believed that the "guided tour" by Elizabeth Taylor would bring Dunia many hours of pleasure. Actually, the book brought on a bizarre illness that created a crisis.

Dunia became hysterical, a woman without clear thoughts, crying out that she must have the Krupp diamond, a 33.19-carat stone that had been a gift from Taylor's husband, the actor Richard Burton. Dunia wept for hours over a second diamond, a

69.42-carat stone Burton had also purchased for his wife.

Dunia's physician was summoned. After prescribing sedatives, he ordered a month of total bed rest, with curtains drawn, so that his patient would not think of the world outside her palace and all the jewels that might be had. He called in Dunia's daughters, telling them that there was to be no discussion of jewels.

To our everlasting amazement, the doctor diagnosed Dunia's illness as the first known case of "the Elizabeth Taylor Jewelry Virus"! While Dunia was recovering, one of her daughters sensibly slipped the jewelry book away; in fact, she burned it so that her mother would not be tempted to once more suffer envy to the point of infirmity.

Hopefully Dunia had recovered from her Elizabeth Taylor angst now, and she appeared very content with her diamond rope necklace. I overheard her say in a clear voice that was meant to be heard, "Do not tell, but this necklace is more costly than the most fabulous pieces Uncle Fahd purchased for Jawhara."

By Uncle Fahd, Dunia was speaking of King Fahd, who was a half brother of our father and a favored uncle we had all loved very much. His death on the first day of August 2005 was a dreadful blow to my immediate family, for that was the day that the hub of Saudi power moved to another unit of our large family.

Our grandfather, King Abdul Aziz, had many wives from various Saudi tribes and those wives gave him many, many sons—and even more daughters. While all the sons *could* be considered in line for the throne, only twelve of my grandfather's sons were serious contenders for the crown.

Jawhara was our Uncle Fahd's favorite wife and is the mother of his most beloved son, the youngest, Abdul Aziz bin Fahd. In our world, the eldest son is the most important in the eyes of the father and of the community; but the youngest son is generally the most loved. Both positions, first and last, establish a certain favoritism.

Princess Jawhara is a unique woman. Even after our much-loved uncle passed from the earth, Jawhara kept the respect of our family. She was part of the entourage that accompanied her husband's half-brother and successor, King Abdullah, on trips out of the country. Such a thing rarely happens in Saudi Arabia. Once a husband passes from this life, the women generally retreat into the background, never to be seen or heard from again, other than within the tight confines of their immediate family.

I have always suspected that several of my sisters were jealous of Jawhara's beauty and of her favored status. But I always liked her, for a number of reasons, mainly because she came out in public to speak about education for girls long before other women were brave enough to do so. During those days, even the wife of a king generally remained invisible to the public. But Jawhara used her intelligence to better our land, making a good name for herself and for our country. And, despite her powerful position, I always found her to be a kindly person who did not hold herself higher than all those around her. The Kingdom of Saudi Arabia needs many such women to take us into the future.

Most likely Dunia was one of the sisters most jealous because, as the favored wife of King Fahd,

Jawhara had accumulated enormous wealth. She probably owned more jewels than most of the royal women combined. I gazed at my sister, a beautiful woman who had wealth, health, and the love of her family, yet none of these attributes quenched her thirst to acquire more of everything, particularly jewelry. Dunia is ten years older than I, yet has not learned during all her years of living that expensive baubles do not bring happiness. She has no comprehension of this important truth. I feel sad for my sister, for I fear she will never know true happiness.

At this point, Dunia proudly confided, "My sisters, I also participated in the necklace design. The designer claimed that my input made this necklace most unique."

Just then my attention shifted from Dunia because I saw my brother Ali appear in the doorway. Walking slowly, he leered at one of our maids, a very pretty Indonesian girl named Sabeen, meaning one who follows. Sabeen, who was new to our household, was an innocent girl, happy to be making a nice salary to send home to her parents to pay for the education for her two younger brothers. I reminded myself to warn Sabeen to stay far from Ali's reach. The dear girl was a lovely addition to our staff, and I meant to protect her from all lecherous men. This vow included men in my own family, as my brother and two of his sons were well known for their desire to bed every attractive woman who came into their orbit. I glanced at Sabeen and smiled encouragingly. She was carefully balancing a serving tray loaded with glasses of cold pineapple, apple, and cranberry juice.

I sighed deeply and scowled at my brother, who was so preoccupied observing pretty Sabeen that he failed to notice my displeasure. I continued to stare for other reasons. I had not seen Ali in more than a year and was surprised to see large bags drooping under his eyes and hanging jaw jowls swaying as he walked. Even his paunchy stomach jiggled with each step he made. He was a wiggling sight!

My brother is a self-indulgent man and, as such, he has aged more poorly than most. Since he was a teenage boy, Ali has made no effort to restrain his appetite for many vices, including excessive eating and smoking. Amani, who is close with one of his daughters, had recently reported that Ali had even begun to drink alcohol to excess.

As one who once told falsehoods and slipped unnoticed to drink prohibited alcohol, I know too well that such noxious liquids are bad for the human body, as well as for our human psychological well-being. I am pleased to say that I have not taken a drop of the forbidden liquid in more than seven years, although I admit it was very hard to break the addictive pattern of turning to alcohol each time I was stressed or depressed by the antics of my children, or angry at my husband.

Suddenly I heard my name and there was "Little Sultana" running in my direction. Ah, joy! My first grandchild—my only granddaughter and namesake—is a celebrated beauty. Her raven black hair reaches to her waist, her olive skin is flawless, and most unique to her appearance are her eyes, as black as midnight. Allah has blessed her with a rare and beautiful look.

While physical beauty is a great gift given to one without any effort on their part, it means little in comparison with the character of a person. I am most gratified because our Little Sultana came to this earth predetermined by God to possess an elevated intelligence, a sunny disposition, a good soul, and a generous spirit, one that instantly recognizes those less privileged. Even though she was only seven years old at the time, she was mindful to extend kindness and generosity to others. Since the very young age of six years, she frequently emptied her room of her favorite toys, games, clothes, and books so that her father could distribute the treasured items to the children's wards at local hospitals, or to the poor in the small villages.

I have never forgotten the time I discovered this charitable trait. I was visiting my son Abdullah's home when I witnessed Little Sultana's uncommon generosity. I had been in Europe visiting Maha, and on my return to Saudi Arabia had passed through London to shop at one of my favorite places, the huge department store Harrods. While there, I had selected some luxurious designer clothes for various members of my family, in particular for my grandchildren. At the same time, I had purchased some lovely trinkets for Little Sultana's long hair. Harrods carries a number of designer lines of the most unusual bows, ribbons, and shiny metallic barrettes for a girl or woman to glamorize her tresses. Of course, I also chose some special games and toys.

I was excited to deliver the goodies to my son's two children, Little Sultana and her younger brother Faisal, who was a mere babe, not yet even old enough to walk. Faisal was napping when I arrived, so I settled back to enjoy watching Little Sultana open her gifts.

At first my granddaughter was thrilled, carefully scrutinizing her dresses, miniature handbags, hair accessories, shoes, games, and toys. But then she became suspiciously quiet. Her small brow wrinkled and her full lips pursed, as though she was thinking of something much too serious for such a young child. My heart broke when she sat at my feet, clasped my knees and said in her baby voice, "Jadda [meaning grandmother], I have far too many beautiful things for a child."

"What?" I exclaimed, giving a questioning look to my daughter-in-law Zain, the mother of Little Sultana.

"Jadda, I heard about poor people from a teacher at school. I learned that there are people living in our country who do not have nice clothes, or books or toys. I want to share your gifts with a little girl who has nothing."

For one of the few times in my life, I was at a loss for words. To my mind, Little Sultana was too young to have such ideas and thoughts. Everyone knows that children are most often self-centered because they are children. I wanted all three of my grandchildren to enjoy being children without a care or a worry. Not knowing what to say, I waved my arms in the air and gave a questioning look to Abdullah's wife: "Zain? What is this?"

Zain, who is always conversational, was also at a loss. "This is new, for sure—something very odd to me."

I returned my concentration to my granddaughter, saying, "Darling, you are a little sweetie to wish to share. It is a good thing to do, for charity is one of the most important things expected of Muslims. So I agree that you should share. But why don't we go to your room and select some of your older dresses and toys?" I paused for a long moment. "Then you can enjoy the beautiful things your Jadda brought you from London."

Little Sultana thoughtfully stared at me with a hint of disappointment. "Jadda, do you mean that I should keep the most beautiful things for myself and give away the old things to others?"

"Yes. That is what I mean, my little doll," I said a bit too enthusiastically, for I longed to see Little Sultana wearing the clothing I had purchased.

My precious granddaughter looked at me for a long moment, then wisely replied, her words spoken very slowly, "Jadda, if I give something that I do not want, is that not the same as not giving at all?"

Stunned into shamed speechlessness, I nodded. I stood to begin gathering all the treasures I had purchased for Little Sultana, bagging them into the largest of the gift bags and placing them in a corner of the room. "Yes, darling, you are right," I said. "We will speak with your father to make certain to find some little girls who have nothing. Soon they will have many beautiful things."

I left knowing that from that time I would need to purchase two of everything in the hope that Little Sultana would be happy giving a set away and keeping a set for herself.

Later, when I discussed Little Sultana's reaction with my son Abdullah, he was not too surprised, telling me, "Mother, this tiny girl is teaching us all." He smiled with pride.

My son loves his daughter to the point of madness, at least measured against many Saudi fathers who are still firmly fastened to the vision of a son rather than a daughter. He has loved his daughter with a pure love since the moment she came to us.

My adult son is all that I ever dreamed he might become. He is intelligent, kind, and generous. Most important, my son believes with great certainty that females are as worthy as males. This is a rarity in my culture.

Sadly, others do not feel as Abdullah does, as, for example, the reactions of Little Sultana's maternal relatives—the parents, grandparents, siblings, and cousins of Zain. Even my son, who is a powerful prince, can do little with those who praise the birth and existence of his son Faisal, while ignoring his little daughter. Thankfully, Zain walks hand in hand with her husband and she, too, is disappointed by the behavior of her family. But in Saudi Arabia one must tread carefully; and besides, Zain's is a sweet and loving personality that avoids confrontation.

And so it has come to pass that despite the fact that my granddaughter was born a wealthy princess, her life is not perfect. Although to her father, mother, and paternal grandparents she is the moon and the stars, she must cope with the problem of being born a girl in this land, a child without true value.

But Little Sultana is meeting these prejudices with the wisdom of one much older than her years. Although she is as strong as her grandmother Sultana, she meets her adversaries with calm wisdom rather than following my method of reacting to sexism with hostility and aggression.

As a woman who has fought for her entire life to bring awareness to those who scorn and belittle females, such reactions to my precious granddaughter have not only saddened me but also created much disappointment and anger in me. Over the years I have learned that one cannot force someone to adopt another person's beliefs and values, however. Perhaps my granddaughter will succeed where I have failed, as she has a softer personality than her grandmother.

In my past, I fear I was too aggressive, which often turned people away.

A good moment had now come for Little Sultana, in attendance at the family party, crying out in joy as though we have not seen each other for months, when in fact I had spent hours with her the day before.

"Jadda! Jadda!" Little Sultana cried as she reached, beckoning me to lean forward so that she might kiss my face and offer her cute little cheeks for me to kiss.

As I nuzzled my face in her perfumed locks, Ali strode to my side, nudging me while saying, "Praise Allah, this little beauty will make some man a first-rate wife."

I whirled around like an angry tiger to my coarse brother, who was already thinking of my granddaughter as a slave to some man, perhaps to one of his unruly grandsons, who was bound to grow into a man such as Ali. I hissed in his ear so that Little Sultana could not overhear: "Your tongue curls in ugliness, uttering revolting words, my brother. This girl will serve no man." Ali, as usual, grimaced in astonishment at my stinging reply, for my brother had lived his entire life without adjusting his philosophies to advancing ideas. He has no clue about his ignorance of humanity. On the day Allah takes him from this earth, I fear that he will leave convinced that all women are born only to serve men in the bedroom and in the kitchen.

At that moment Little Sultana ran away to greet Maha, who was walking into the room with the confidence and stunning power of a woman who knows she controls her own destiny. Everyone turned to look at my dramatic daughter, who grows more physically exquisite with each passing year.

I silently prayed to Allah to allow Maha to leave her hostilities against our land and its traditions at rest until the evening was at an end.

My brother had noticed Maha's entrance as well. Ali had never enjoyed a good relationship with either of my daughters, possibly because Maha and Amani had a warmer, more lenient upbringing than his daughters. My daughters know they are loved, and that their feelings and opinions are valued by us, their parents; Ali's daughters live in fear of their father.

Ali has enjoyed the troubles I have endured at the hands of my daughters. "Ah, Sultana," he retorted with a satisfied smirk, as he glared at Maha, "my memory failed me until now. Maha has returned, so I assume misfortune is visiting your palace. I forgive your temper, my little sister."

My temper was surely rising, for I could feel my entire body flushing with heat. My tongue was about to deliver a spiteful rebuke when our sister Sara walked to our side, defusing the situation. "Ali, brother, we have your favorite Arabic dishes specially prepared just as you like them." Sara looked around the room.

"Tell us, where is Sita?"

Sita was my brother's latest wife, the eighth woman he had wed since he first married as a young man. Ali, like my father, is only allowed four wives at a time, according to Islam. But both men have a habit of divorcing wives who displease them so that they might marry young women.

Sita is a stunning beauty from a poor Sunni Syrian family. Salman, one of Ali's youngest sons, had met Sita's brother at a café in Damascus while on holiday in the area. Sita's brother had mentioned that his older sister was so beautiful that his parents were saving her for someone with enough gold to match her weight. When such a man came along, they would agree to the golden dowry. Salman, who had reached the age when young men yearn to marry, took an interest in a woman who must be more physically magnificent than a movie star. He asked to see a photograph. A picture was finally produced and Salman was instantly smitten. The young woman was lovely enough to trigger a young man's dreams. He left Syria with the photograph in his pocket, returning to Saudi Arabia, where he told the story to his father.

Ali was interested, but for the wrong reason. Once my conniving brother saw the glamor and beauty of the intended, he asked her age. Learning that she was three years older than his son Salman, my brother found his excuse. He insisted that the girl was too mature for a boy aged only twenty-one. Ali adamantly refused Salman's request for a dowry of gold, although the amount was no more than what my brother spent on trifles every month.

Despite his son's pleas, a week later the unfeeling Ali sent his representative to meet with the family to arrange his own marriage with Sita. Without negotiating, Ali paid the dowry requested, which was Sita's weight in gold coins. Her price was costly, because Sita is a tall girl, and, although not fat, neither is she skinny.

Sara had told me: "Oh Sultana, Ali's son left his father's palace in a rare rage and is refusing to return to the kingdom. He may never speak to his father again, and who can blame him?"

Unsurprisingly, Ali had laughed off the matter, according to Sara. "My brother is soulless," I had replied angrily. For sure, most men want to please their sons and make them happy, but Ali would always put himself before anyone else, even his own child.

In the beginning, I was prepared to feel sorry for Sita, for my heart aches for any woman married to my brother. But from my observations she was so happy to have married into wealth that she appeared not to notice that her husband was portly and more than thirty years her senior; he is even older in looks than his years. In fact, during a party for one of my nieces, Sita had pointedly told us all, "My family is still rejoicing, for their fortune is made. Ali insisted that they keep my dowry gold and they have built a nice home and are sending my younger siblings to one of the best schools. My good husband has hired three of my brothers and so now they can afford a marriage dowry, too. All are planning to wed within the year."

I could not imagine Ali showing Sita any tender feelings, although Sara said that she had noticed he was very attentive to his newest bride. I supposed that Ali's feelings for Sita were expressed because of the activity in their bedroom, but even Sita did not appear displeased, so I saved my sympathy for others—those who were truly suffering.

At this point, I heard a swell of noise and looked toward the entrance, where my aging father was making his way into the room. He was upright, but barely. Two of his manservants were holding his arms, one on each side, while a third stood behind him in case he stumbled backward. My father is nearing the end of his life and, despite our volatile history, my feelings have softened over the years, as every daughter yearns for affection from her father.

As he shuffled into the room, he was surrounded by nearly everyone at the party. Looking at his frail form, and remembering the strong and powerful male he once was, tears came to my eyes. Lately, I had endeavored to think of the good things about my father. I had tried to be charitable toward him and now believed that there was much to be thankful for. My father was the reason many good people were living on this earth.

Like Ali, my father was an expert at divorcing his least favorite wife in order to make room for a new one, and so it came to pass that my father had married twelve women over the course of his long life. Nine of those women provided him with children, twenty-seven daughters and twenty sons, of whom forty-five are still with the living. His daughters and sons gave life to many grandchildren, and now those grandchildren are producing great-grandchildren. It is a good thing that our family has accumulated great wealth, for there are many mouths to feed, many brains to educate, and many bodies requiring clothing and shelter.

Although he was never a loving father to his daughters, he was a man who provided well for his family and that counts for something, I suppose. His sons and grandsons love him with a great intensity, for he has never shown anything but affection to anyone born male.

Several years back, my children had given their father a dazzling throne chair covered with imitation jewels as a joke. Very touchingly, they said they knew he would never be king of Saudi Arabia but he was a king in their eyes. That throne has a golden-covered seat, and shimmering stones line the back and the chair legs. It's quite a magnificent throne and has created a lot of exhilarating talk with our guests, as many believe that the jewels and the gold are real, when in fact that is not true.

My father had never seen the throne, but now his eyes lit with delight as he spotted the alluring chair. He motioned to Abdullah that he wanted to sit upon it.

All the children smiled and clapped as my father took the seat of honor. There he sat, looking upon the sea of faces and bestowing smiles upon them all, like a benevolent ruler. He even gave a wide smile to his daughters, granddaughters, and great-granddaughters.

I felt happy, glad that my father was having a rare moment of old-age joy. I had heard from Sara that he was very bitter in his heart at becoming old and infirm, and was usually in a most cantankerous mood.

Then I noticed Abdullah and Amani leaving the room, before quickly returning with their two sons, to present them to their great-grandfather, who had never seen either child. Abdullah cradled his son Faisal, while little Khalid was cushioned happily in Amani's arms. I stood in watchful silence as my father smiled with gladness while nodding his approval of my two grandsons. All was well with the world until an excited Little Sultana rushed to be by her father's side. My heart plunged in fear that my father would insult my granddaughter, just as he had slighted me when I was a child.

But Little Sultana did not know to be wary of my father. She looked thoughtfully at my father and at the throne he was occupying, then, to everyone's delight, she gave a deep and perfect curtsy.

My father savored the moment, smiling with pleasure at Abdullah's daughter. I suppose for this instant my father believed he was a real king. He brushed his hand over Little Sultana's head and face, and said something complimentary. An expression of pure joy came to Sultana's little face and that joy was mirrored on Abdullah's face. My relatives began to applaud and cheer, for they had seen something none of us would ever have dreamed possible. My father had given his undivided attention and open admiration to a female child.

Just then Kareem stepped to my side and encircled my waist with his arm, giving me a gentle squeeze with his hand. My husband and I looked deep into each other's eyes, knowing that each of us was as happy as we could be. There are occasions in life when everything feels perfect, and this was one of those moments.

# Chapter Three
# My Father

Many times over the years I have experienced two contrasting emotions simultaneously—joy and grief. On that wonderful evening, family relationships were coming together beautifully, bringing me the rare joy of kinship. Knowing what I knew of my two daughters, I worried that before the evening was over they would create a scene that would spoil the party. Should that have happened, grief would have shadowed pleasure, although I hoped at the time that that was not to be the case.

Joyful outbursts ensued, however, as those late to the party made their entrances. Assad, Sara's devoted and ever-loving husband, popped in with a wide smile, his hand clasping that of their pretty daughter, Nashwa.

Nashwa is the second child born to my sister, arriving on the same day that I gave birth to my third and last child, Amani. Both our daughters were born with complicated and problematic personalities. Truthfully, as difficult as Amani has been, I prefer my exertions with Amani over Sara's challenges with

Nashwa. Nashwa tested Sara's well-known patience on more occasions than I can possibly tally.

It is tricky to portray Nashwa in her youth. How does one describe the power and force of a tsunami? In plain terms, Nashwa can best be explained as a loud child in her youngest years, a wild child in her teenage years, and then, like a miracle straight from Allah, on the exact date of her nineteenth birthday, Nashwa became a model daughter. The once loud and troublesome girl became a quiet and content young woman, and her intelligence shone through. The energy she had previously expended on the forbidden matters of female life in Saudi Arabia was channeled into her studies. As sudden as an unexpected and blinding sunburst that explodes onto earth, Nashwa changed from the naughty girl she was to the impeccable girl she became.

Nashwa's school grades were once so poor that no school in Saudi Arabia would have accepted her attendance had she not been a princess. But after that mind-boggling day, she began climbing to the top of her first-year college class. She soon surpassed all her classmates. Nashwa then expressed an interest in architecture, but since there was no university in Saudi Arabia to equal her ambitions, she had transferred to a prestigious university in the United States, graduating with a bachelor's degree in her chosen field, receiving the highest grades and honors in her subject. Upon graduation, she did not seek to remain abroad, as did my Maha. Nashwa was eager to return to Saudi Arabia to use her education and talents to help design various buildings in Jeddah, acclaimed for their unique designs. With a sense of wonder, Sara reported that her previously scheming, cunning daughter was serious and dedicated to her craft, always talking shop and interested only in work.

Yet there was one concern hanging over Sara's heart. My sister was becoming increasingly uneasy that Nashwa never expressed an interest in the possibility of marriage and children, even when her father Assad assured her that she could both have a career and be a wife and mother. Nashwa, like Maha, was exceedingly fortunate to be a member of the royal family and the daughter of a man who wanted his daughters to excel.

Sara and I are both blessed to have met the men we married, two brothers with comparable attitudes toward love, marriage, and children. There have been no sexist biases shown by Assad or Kareem when it comes to their daughters.

Since Amani celebrates the same day of birth as Nashwa, Sara has always felt that our daughters must surely share a rare understanding and natural intimacy. Sara, who had witnessed how wonderfully well Amani had embraced marriage and motherhood, began to dream that this happiness and contentment might influence Nashwa. "Sultana," she repeatedly suggested, "please do invite Nashwa to join your family on the days Amani comes over with little Khalid."

I failed to restrain my laughter at Sara's suggestion. My dear sister has misplaced the reality of Amani's history with Nashwa. Our two daughters have never really liked each other. When they were small children, they were playmates, but only because they were together time and again. Once Amani had experienced her life-altering religious encounter with God in Mecca, all pretenses of friendship came to an end. This was Amani's fault—my daughter began to almost stalk her cousin, the madcap, erratic Nashwa, doing her utmost to convert Nashwa to her purist manner of thinking and living. Nashwa resisted all of her attempts; in fact, she seemed to loathe Amani. Indeed, many members of the family also felt Amani could be unbearable because of the way she spoke and behaved. Even her siblings could not endure her loud, aggressive criticisms.

Never can I forget the dreadful day when Rana, my niece from my eldest sister, Nura, was nearly killed while trying to escape Amani.

I had taken Maha and Amani with me when I went to s e e Nura. Generally our girls entertained one another while Nura and I enjoyed a pleasant visit, chatting about the goings-on in our extended Al Sa'ud family. With thousands of aunties, uncles, and cousins, there are always fascinating stories to divulge and analyze. Other times my sister and I would be in a memory mood. We might spend hours reminiscing about those innocent times with our loving mother, recalling little stories about the extraordinary woman who gave us life, loved us, endeavored to teach us right from wrong and, most important, struggled to protect her ten daughters from our strict father.

This particular visit with Nura occurred about a year after Amani had become religious in the extreme. Nura, who is one of the world's calmest and gentlest women, congenially greeted us, calling out for her two youngest girls to join us for tea. When tea was brought out, we all exclaimed over those little finger sandwiches. They were made just like the sandwiches served in the most luxurious British hotels at afternoon tea.

Nura had taught her children lovely manners, so my usually rambunctious girls were subdued into goodness, sitting quietly, eating the delicious food gratefully since both had slept past lunch. The social visit had, therefore, started out well enough.

As we finished our little treat, all spoke the customary "*Alhamdulilah,*" meaning "Thanks be to God." Dear Amani continued on to say the words "*An'am Allah alaikum kather Allah kherkum,*" asking Allah to be generous to our hostess. Nura was pleased with Amani for those good wishes and flashed a smile.

I stroked my child on her knee, letting her know that I was pleased with her behavior.

Just then one of Nura's shy Sri Lankan maids came into the room to whisk away the plates and napkins. Another maid appeared with warm water to pour over and rinse our hands. The water flowed through our fingers and into a little porcelain bowl set down for that very purpose. We all dabbed our lips and mouths with that water, too. We were provided with small hand towels to dry the liquid from our lips and hands.

As is customary, a third maid entered the area swinging a small vessel of smoking incense, which we wafted toward ourselves with our right hands. Finally, a fourth maid poured sweet-smelling perfume into our hands.

We were all refreshed, with everything having gone perfectly, and now we were looking forward to several hours of visiting and sharing news.

Nura's youngest daughter, Rana, politely excused herself and left the room for a moment to repair her lipstick. When she returned to us, she was carrying a small jeweled compact in her hand, telling Maha, "Look at this compact. The stones look like diamonds, but they are not." She giggled, saying, "I am no longer purchasing real stones because Mummy says that it is better not to be wasteful with money, that the oil being taken from the earth will never be seen again."

"That is very true, Rana," Maha said with a nod.

From an early age, Maha had been aware of our earth and of the waste of so many resources. Maha has never been a girl who asked for more than she needed, and now she looked at Rana with a new appreciation—all of us like someone who shares our ideas.

Rana smiled brightly, feeling herself an important part of the afternoon. Her huge smile brought attention to her lipstick, which was a very bold, neon-glowing shade of lilac, something one did not usually see in conservative Saudi Arabia in those days.

Suddenly, the pleasant visit turned into a harsh nightmare. For no reason that I could imagine, Amani burst out with a cruel criticism of her cousin. Amani's voice was low, but her words were severe: "Rana, you are covered in sin with that ugly blue eye shadow on your lids and that ghastly lipstick on your big lips. Dear cousin, do remember, please, that you are a Muslim and that what you are doing is forbidden by God Himself."

"Amani!" I gasped in shame. "Apologize to your cousin." I glanced at Nura, who was in a state of bewilderment. "Nura, dear sister, I am sorry for my daughter's rude words."

"Do not apologize for me, Mother," Amani sputtered in irritation. "I am only trying to help my cousin live as it is commanded. You should join with me to help Rana live the life of a believer." Amani stood up and began to walk toward Rana to deliver additional condemnations. That's when poor Rana ran from the room, weeping tears, for she was piteously aggrieved by the unforgiving words of my daughter.

Nura looked at Amani in disbelief, for Nura has the good heart of a woman who would never harm the feelings of another. She had raised her children to be equally thoughtful. Nura used her hands to push from sitting to standing, then moved as fast as her heavy body allowed, calling out for Rana, "Darling girl, do not run away."

Maha stood up and shoved her sister. Maha is a tall and big girl, strong and forceful, while Amani is physically delicate.

"Amani!" Maha cried. "Are you crazy, or just mean?" Maha looked at me, "Amani is mean, Mother!"

I sadly nodded in agreement. I could not deny that Amani's words were often cruel. Yet despite how strongly she held her views, there was never any excuse for such hostility.

Still unsure as to what I might do to turn the afternoon back to one of pleasure and happiness, I stood helplessly. Then I heard Rana screaming loudly. That's when my heart plummeted in despair. All of a sudden I recalled Nura's telling me that Rana had endured many unhappy moments during the past year. First, the skin on her face had broken into big red boils, for what reason the dermatologist could never diagnose. Rana began wearing her veil every moment of every day and night. Her mother told me that she even slept in the veil to keep the maids who sometimes entered private rooms from seeing those red boils. And then before those unsightly boils could heal, she fell down the marble steps in Ali's home because she could not see clearly through the veil she was wearing to hide the boils on her face. The steps were steep and she fractured her nose. Since that accident Rana's nose had developed an unattractive bump; the poor girl disliked this new feature on her face so much that she had spent many unhappy hours sobbing, crying out that she was an ugly girl; she thought no man would marry her, even though she was a princess with much wealth.

I was devastated that Amani had chosen to inflict her personal opinions about what a female should or should not do when it came to personal appearance—and particularly when it involved a member of the family who already had serious concerns about the way she looked.

I quickly sent a sullen Amani home with our driver, not even bothering to warn my child that there would be consequences for her meanness. Kareem could not abide cruelty to others and he would be the one to deal with our daughter.

Maha and I would borrow one of Nura's drivers once we had properly apologized and reassured Rana that she was a very attractive girl and that her lipstick was a shade that even I might wear. As a matter of fact, I decided at that moment that I would purchase some of that color and wear it the next time I saw Rana.

But for the moment I was in the middle of a huge crisis. Rana could not be found. Nura and I both became nearly hysterical as a search was carried out in the house. Staff helped us look under every bed, in every closet and large cupboard, and every tub and shower, and even behind every bush in the women's garden, but without success. I was terrified that my sister's child might have brought harm to herself due to insensitive words from my own daughter. I would never have recovered from such a thing.

After three hours of frantic searching, Maha's booming voice could be heard in every corner of Nura's palace. "Rana is here! Rana is here!"

Nura and I looked at each other. "Praise Allah! Rana is found!" my sister cried.

But more grave news was to come. My heart really stopped, at least for a few beats, when Nura and I followed the sound of Maha's voice into a big room in a part of the palace I had never seen. It was the storage area for foodstuffs, with seven refrigerators and ten large freezers lined against the wall.

The poor girl had wrapped her body in a blanket and had stuffed herself into a large freezer that had recently been delivered but not yet filled with foodstuffs. The kitchen servants were waiting for the freezer temperature to reach the correct setting. Thankfully the blanket was fluffy and large enough to cover the oversized bed Nura's husband had built specially for himself. He happened to be one of the tallest and fattest of the Al Sa'ud men, so his needs were those of a large bulk of a man. A big section of that blanket had caught in the freezer door, keeping just enough air going into the freezer to save Rana from suffocating!

I gave a ragged sob when Nura unwrapped that blanket from the body of her child. The flesh on Rana's face and arms had turned an odd shade of blue from the cold. Rana's tears had turned into icicles, looking for all the world like some stalactites I had seen in a cave years before when Kareem and I were in Europe.

Looking at the nearly frozen face of that girl, and seeing the frightened expression on Nura's face, never have I felt so despondent. It was good that I had sent Amani home, for if she had been nearby I fear I might have beaten my child.

Maha and two of the servants carried Rana to her mother's bed. There, she was covered in five blankets, and hand-fed warm soup and given hot tea. When Nura eased herself in bed with her daughter, holding her child and covering her face with kisses, Maha and I took our leave, each holding to the other in our misery and grief.

I was in such a fog of despair that until this day I cannot recall the punishment Kareem meted out to Amani. But I do know that since that incident she has been more cautious in her verbal assaults. Rana, of course, avoided Amani from that day on, and who could blame the poor girl. None of Nura's daughters attended Amani's wedding, and I understood why.

I had never recovered from the shock of that day. Although my sister remained loving and kind until the second of her death, I was wrapped in shame. On Nura's deathbed I was still weeping and apologizing for that dreadful episode created by my child. I will never forget how my gentle sister took her finger and touched my lips, telling me in her own way to forget that long-ago day.

Nura has been dead for a number of years, and I miss her keenly. After the death of my adored mother, Nura became my substitute mother.

After a deep, sad sigh, thinking of my dead sister, my attention returned to the party and the night before us. I looked around the room, searching for my sister Sara. I knew that she would most likely use the night to encourage a closeness between Amani and Nashwa. Knowing Amani as I do, I was against such a scheme. Such a thing could never fulfill Sara's wishes. Nashwa and Amani had never strayed from the paths they had chosen. One was an independent woman elevating her career; the other wanted nothing more than to serve her husband and bear his children. Both our daughters were happy with their choices. Over the years I learned to do something Kareem has always claimed would be impossible, which is to still my tongue and not try to change the unchangeable.

I shook my head in disbelief when I saw Sara rush through a crowd of family revelers to reach her daughter so that she might entice a reluctant Nashwa into Amani's circle. My smiling sister reached for little Khalid and held him close to Nashwa's face, thinking to tempt her with the beauty of that little boy. I heaved a sigh of pure love for my sister. For sure, she would never stop trying to bring what she believed would be undeniable bliss to all those she loved.

I thank Allah daily that He chose to bestow such a one as Sara to me as my loving sister.

A chorus of female voices drew my attention away from Sara. Ah! There was a surprise visitor. Munira, my long-suffering niece, was making an unexpected appearance at the party. "Munira," I said, as I walked quickly to her side, "you are my most favored guest on this evening."

I nodded at her eldest son, a dear boy who was now my niece's guardian.

Munira smiled happily for the first time in many years, hugging and kissing me with abandon. "Oh, Auntie, thank you for inviting me. This is my first outing since . . . you know . . ."

My eyes met her eyes and I blinked with a yes. I did understand. I did not tell Munira that my sisters and I had actually celebrated when her husband Hadi had suffered a massive stroke and died. We rejoiced because we knew that finally, Hadi's female victims would soon be free. Four months previously, Allah had deemed that the time had come for life to end on earth for the hated Hadi, the most despicable friend of my brother Ali's. At Hadi's death, my dear niece was liberated from that tyrant.

Hadi had first come to my attention many years before when my family was holidaying in Cairo, Egypt. He and Ali had purchased a young virgin girl from her mother for the purpose of sex. Hadi had never amended his inhumane ways; in fact, he had become more malicious with each passing year. That vile man continued living his life as a man of twisted pleasures, fatally attracted to the violent control of all women in his sphere of influence.

I believe that is why he was so enticed by the idea of Ali's eldest daughter, Munira. She was a magnet he could not ignore. Munira was a shy girl whose father's actions brought her to a place of genuine fear of all men. From Munira's early teenage years, she had expressed a terror of marriage, pleading to be spared the one thing most Saudis believe is the only true path for a woman, that of a wife and mother.

And so it came to pass that Ali promised her in marriage to his most ferocious acquaintance: Hadi. Sara and I had pleaded with our brother to consider his daughter's unique temperament: she was the most timid girl any of us had ever known. But Ali laughed at Munira's fears, saying that Hadi would cure her of any fear of the bedroom. Hadi was a man who demanded all sexual rights at all hours of the day and night. Over time, such sexual assaults were sure to bring his daughter to a right way of thinking, he believed. Ali's mind was settled. Munira's body was owned by her husband.

Munira was doomed.

For years, she lived in misery and terror of her husband. He appeared excited by his wife's fear of him and terror of the sexual act. Although he married six women over the years, until the day he passed from the earth Hadi was most drawn to our precious Munira, a woman who spent most of her life hiding from her husband, then, once found, weeping and pleading with Hadi to leave her alone. Of course, her actions led to further abuse, including physical beatings.

At one point we believed that Munira would do something forbidden for all Muslims, which is to commit suicide. At her lowest point, she even wrote a most heart-wrenching poem and passed it to Sara.

I had memorized Munira's poem. Since the evening in the desert when I had first read it, I often found myself repeating the words—words motivated by pure wretchedness. The poem has brought me to tears many times, taking my mind to poor Munira, wondering if my niece was at that moment enduring a sexual assault.

### Buried Alive
by Princess Munira Al Sa'ud

*I have lived* and known what it is to smile
*I have lived* the life of a young girl with hopeful
   promise

*I have lived* the life of a young girl who felt the
    warmth of womanhood
*I have lived* the feeling of longing for the love of a
    good man
*I have lived* the life of a woman whose promise was
    cut short
*I have lived* the life of one whose dreams were dashed
*I have lived* knowing tremendous fear for every man
*I have lived* through the fears raised by the specter of
    an evil coupling
*I have lived* to see the devil in the guise of a man,
    ruling my every action
*I have lived* as a beggar to this man, pleading with
    him to leave me alone
*I have lived* to witness my husband have the pleasure
    of being a man
*I have lived* to be ravished by the man to whom I was
    given
*I have lived* only to endure nightly rapes
*I have lived* to be buried while still alive
*I have lived* to wonder why those who claim to love
    me, helped to bury me
*I have lived* through all of these things, and I am not
    yet twenty-five years old

Now those words no longer expressed Munira's nightmare reality. Munira, at last, was emancipated. Hadi was dead and in his sandy grave, and no longer free to rape girls and women. And Munira's poem has spread around the world in the pages of the books about my life. The poem always reminds me that my purpose in life is to help women who have nowhere to turn. And I hope her words prompt other strong women to never turn their back on a woman in need.

I watched as my sisters and nieces ran to Munira, to welcome her back to the world of the living and the happy. All of us laughed with the purest pleasure when Munira confided, "My children are taking me on a holiday, to Europe. I will go to London and to Paris!"

This was thrilling news for all of us. Hadi had never allowed Munira to travel with him and the family when they left the kingdom to holiday in foreign lands. I believe Hadi was frightened that his wife would run away to seek help from a women's organization in the West, had she the opportunity. But now she was going to travel to the wonderful places she had seen only in pictures slipped to her by her loving children. Munira, who had barely spoken for many years, was now dominating the conversation, sharing her thoughts with all around her. "And after I visit every gallery in Paris, I will go to London, and work my way through more museums."

"What a waste of a wonderful woman," I muttered under my breath, but now that Munira's chains had been broken she was free to enjoy the beauty of life. It was difficult to take my eyes away from Munira's glowing face and happy smile, but I did when thirty-year-old Mohammed, the jovial son of Reema, the second of my sisters to have passed from the earth, came walking toward me. I nearly fainted when I saw that Mohammed was holding a hugely enlarged photograph of my long-dead mother over his head.

Although she was young in the photograph, surely in the early days of her marriage, I would have recognized her under any circumstances.

I shouted so stridently that the hum of voices quieted. "Mother!" I sobbed loudly. "Mother!" There was an increased buzz of excitement, as few knew the cause of my shouts. But I had a good reason to exclaim. My beloved mother had been dead since I was a young girl. I had never seen a photograph of her likeness. I believed that no such photograph existed. During the days my mother was alive, images of human beings were looked upon as something forbidden. Certainly, few people ever took photographs of Muslim women in Saudi Arabia. I doubt my mother ever considered having her picture taken. She would have most likely hidden from anyone carrying a camera with the intention of taking her picture.

Kareem ran to my side. "Sultana, what on earth?" Then he saw what I had seen. Kareem turned to Reema's son, asking,

"Mohammed? What? What is this?"

Mohammed was very satisfied with himself. He was pleased with the big photograph he was carrying in his arms and thrilled by the commotion he had caused. He began laughing and gestured toward my father, who was still happily perched on Kareem's imitation throne. "You must ask my grandfather. He is the one behind this surprise."

My father? I stared mutely at my aging father, sitting in the midst of admirers, seemingly unaware that his daughters were circling the photograph of their mother. I felt a spark of curiosity as to where he had found the photograph. Then I was hit by a tinge of anger that he had never shown me the picture.

Almost instantly my resentment vanished, and instead I felt a rush of thankfulness that he had finally produced such a picture. I was in a turmoil of strong feelings.

By this time Sara and my other sisters had rushed to stand beside me. Sara's hand lightly brushed the photographed face of our mother.

"Mother," she whispered, her lips trembling with emotion. Despite Mother's young age in the photograph, all of her daughters had recognized her instantly.

"It really is Mother," Dunia said, with great certainty. She seemed to have forgotten her expensive necklace for the first time since the start of the party.

A weepy Haifa collapsed into the arms of her youngest son, who was a teenager. Haifa was unable to speak.

Tahani stood quietly, shaking her head before motioning for her eldest daughter to come. "You must see your grandmother!"

Maha, Amani, and Abdullah gathered round, as close as they could to me, and to the picture of my mother. "Is that really Grandmother?" my son asked in a voice filled with awe.

Finally, I could speak. "Yes, my son, that is your grandmother, the kindest and best mother to have ever lived."

Maha and Amani were brushing tears off their faces.

"Grandmother was magnificent," Amani whispered in hushed wonder.

"Yes, she was beautiful like a movie star," Maha murmured.

I stared silently, studying the striking image of my darling mother. When I was a child, I had never thought of my mother as beautiful. She was, well, my mother. But thinking about the exceptional beauty of eight of her ten daughters, I was struck by the idea that Mother's daughters had inherited her great beauty. I examined the picture even more intently. The years had taken their toll on my memory. I had forgotten that she had a small mole on the right side of her face, about an inch above the far corner of her lips. I no longer remembered how full her lips were, the kind of lips young girls today want so badly they are willing to undergo the painful procedure of having a needle pushed into their flesh. Then I was struck with awareness that Little Sultana had inherited Mother's full lips. I smiled widely, knowing that Little Sultana's lips would from that moment on bring my mother back to life in my mind.

I had also lost the memory of her large and expressive eyes—eyes that I saw nearly every day when I looked into the eyes of my sister Sara. Strangely, Mother's hair was uncovered in the photograph, and I realized that I had inherited her thick dark hair, lying in waves across her shoulders.

Mother was alive in all of us!

I stared and stared, knowing that the one thing I had never forgotten was the sweetness of my mother's smile.

Suddenly I was overwhelmed by emotion. I would have fallen to my knees had Kareem and Abdullah not lifted me and guided me to a chair. "Mother, Mother, Mother," I murmured. Never had I wanted to feel my mother's touch so urgently as at that moment.

Mohammed began to walk toward my father with Mother's photograph. I pushed myself upright, determined never to let that picture out of my sight. Kareem and Abdullah guided my steps, and my sisters and I followed Mohammed as he went to my father.

"Grandfather," I heard him say, "I brought the picture, as you said I should do. You said there would be a celebration, but I am afraid I have encouraged a flood of women's tears."

My father's head jerked upright and he looked upon his daughters, all of whom were weeping tears of joy mingled with regret, for their mother was long dead and far away from their touch.

My father looked through the crowd of women until his eyes rested on my face. "Sultana," he said, "come here, my child."

For the first time in my life, my father had called to me in a gentle tone.

Uneasy at being singled out, I tentatively walked toward him, shaking slightly. "Yes, Father, I am here," I said, as I knelt at his feet, due more to weakness than to subservience.

"Sultana," he stated in a calm voice, "I am coming to the end of my life. My child, for the past few years I have been thinking of all I did, or did not do, in my life."

I nodded, as I did not know what else to do.

My father glanced for some moments at the image of my mother, still held tightly in the hands of my nephew, Mohammed.

"Sultana, when your mother knew that she was dying, she called me to her deathbed. Of course, I answered her call. When I saw that she was indeed dying, I felt a deep sadness; she had been a good woman and the best wife and mother for all those years. Your mother asked very little of me for all the years we were married." He paused. "But she did make two deathbed requests."

My father paused for a mere moment. "Your mother loved all eleven of her children, Sultana. I do not believe that she loved you more than she loved any of her daughters or her son." At that, my father looked up and smiled at my sisters. "But, Sultana, I believe that your sisters, who are all mothers, will understand that she was most concerned for her baby daughter. And that child was you.

"Your mother asked that I take special care of you, my daughter. She had dreamed that you, Sultana, would carry a big grief with you for the rest of your life, for you were far too young to lose your mother. I know your mother also felt that you were an emotional child who needed the loving presence of a mother.

"Her second request was that I present you with the only photograph ever taken of my first wife, which I had allowed a foreign photographer, a man from England, to take a month after we were married. This picture has been kept hidden from all eyes but mine." Father's eyes closed, and I had the feeling that he was looking back in time, remembering the early days when Mother was his young bride and all things seemed possible. His old dreams were interrupted by a fit of coughing, which took him a few moments to clear. Several servants leapt forward with handkerchiefs in their hands, and another tapped him lightly on his back.

Finally, he finished his story. "I agreed to your mother's requests, Sultana. I gave your mother my word that I would not be too harsh on you. I also told her that on the day of your wedding I would present her photograph to you. She wanted you to keep her image in a special place so that all her children might feel the joy of seeing their mother when she was a young woman.

"Although I have felt some bitterness from you, my child, I do not understand why. I do believe that I kept my first promise, always being easy on you when you deserved reprimands for wayward behavior. I even allowed you to meet your husband before you married. I did not punish you severely for some of your conduct, only because of the promise I had given to your mother.

"But, Sultana, I failed to give you this picture of your mother. This was not intentional. I forgot it. After she died, the picture was taken from its secret place and packed and stored in a safe location. Only recently did one of the servants find the carefully s e a l e d crate and brought it to me, asking if it should be unsealed. I admit that I had no idea what might be in that crate, and when it was opened for me to view, a rush of memories came to me.

"I knew then that I had forgotten a promise I gave to your mother those many years ago.

"And so I have had the picture newly framed, and now, my daughter, it is yours to display in your home, and to have this image of your mother that you might greet her every day."

A hush was over the room, for everyone in our family knew that my father and I did not enjoy a close relationship. All waited to see my reaction.

But I felt a great calm, with all the anger and hostility I had harbored for so many years miraculously evaporating from my heart. I no longer disliked my father. Indeed, I felt a great sorrow that he was nearing death and we had never experienced a close bond, the kind of relationship Kareem and our daughters so enjoyed.

"Father," I finally said, "I am sorry I was not a better daughter." My father had had quite enough of sentimentality by then. He touched me on the shoulder and said, "Do not worry, daughter. Just remember your father as a good man who did not lock you in a room or beat you with a stick."

I blinked, knowing that in my father's eyes the absence of physical abuse had made him a good father.

For some reason I smiled, and for the first time in my life I felt a great joy and a love for the man who was my father. I rose to my feet and gave my father a heartfelt hug and told him, "I love you, Father."

I heard the applause of my relatives and I turned smiling, expecting to see approval in every eye. But I winced when I saw my brother Ali glaring at me with great hatred.

I had reached a promising place with my father, but I knew that the battle with my only brother would continue.

I ignored my brother, asking Abdullah to accept my mother's photograph from Mohammed. I then told my sisters, "This photograph of Mother belongs to all of us. We will decide together the best place to hang this picture so that all of you will see it when you first enter my home."

My sisters were pleased, with none expressing jealousy.

Soon our guests departed, with only Ali failing to bid me goodbye or to thank me for the evening. Although I felt that some unfinished business with Ali would result from the evening, I shrugged that idea away. I did not want to spoil my beautiful memories with worries of something that might never come to pass.

The evening had been one of the most lovely I have lived. Before sleeping, Kareem and I enjoyed a walk in our garden, speaking about our family and the joyful moments we had spent in their company.

For one of the few times in my life, I had nothing to complain about. A tranquil peace settled over me and I loved every moment of the gentleness surrounding me. I whispered a prayer: "Thank you, Allah," and wrapped myself in the beauty of the night, my restless soul temporarily at peace.

# Chapter Four
# Yes, Women Can Rule

Since I was a young girl, I have experienced many extraordinary moments, with the good and bad alternating in the blink of an eye. Many of my childhood problems came about because I was female and I fought to rule my own life. This is not necessarily a good thing in a male-dominated society: every male in my life, in particular my father and my brother, felt it his right to rule over me—with violence, if necessary. Regardless of the punishments they inflicted, however, I never stopped fighting. Why? The reason is simple: I wanted to be in charge of my own destiny and make my own decisions.

After I married and became the mother of a son and two daughters, my problems continued. In fact, the electrifying tempo of these ups and downs escalated: I am not a wife to easily accept her husband's rules. I demand a say in everything that affects my life, and the lives of my son and two daughters. Thankfully, Kareem is a man who is intelligent and knows that happiness will remain elusive if only one person in a marriage has power. Thus I raised my daughters to feel the power of personal choice and to know that they should rule their own lives as well.

My two daughters have never failed to put forward their points of view. Due to their particularly outspoken natures, and the fact that neither gives in easily, our lives have often been filled with turmoil. Even after Abdullah and Amani left our home to marry, and Maha moved far from Saudi Arabia, the havoc and general emotional chaos in our family life persisted.

These upheavals have, however, been well worth it, for each member of our family acknowledges that women's feelings are of value. Personal freedom produces upheaval. Females are quiet, passive, and unhappy when the males around them behave like tyrants. Kareem and I love Abdullah, but our affection for our daughters matches our love for our son. In our family, the women are assertive, the males relaxed. Kareem and Abdullah both make extensive efforts to avoid confrontation, while my daughters dance happily toward opposition. Due to these personality differences, many were the times when the wishes of our daughters overruled the desires of our son. This is not typical in a Saudi household, or even an average royal household, where men are bestowed with such elevated status that even the most pampered princess will bend her will to meet the demands of a prince.

Darling Abdullah often accuses us of allowing females to rule our home completely. Anytime our son feels outmaneuvered or outnumbered by his sisters, he sighs and mutters, "Women rule this palace!"

Although my heart feels his pain, I am happy that Kareem and I have created a democratic home, where females are as likely as males to be the victor in a family dispute.

But whatever the particulars behind our reality are, family disturbances create indisputable distress for my husband, who, with each passing year, grows more certain that he cannot bear the endless tumult brought about by our uncompromising daughters. There have been shocking moments when Kareem has considered running away from his children.

It was an episode featuring Amani that first brought Kareem to this surprising idea. The incident occurred when both Amani and Abdullah and their spouses and children were visiting us at our home in Taif. The Saudi government and most of our Al Sa'ud cousins flee the heat of Riyadh in summer and establish themselves in cool Taif. The elevation of the city is over 1,800 meters (6,100 feet), and the climate is so moderate that the area is known for its honey, figs, grapes, and other delicious fruits. Since I was a child, I have spent the hottest of the Saudi summer months in Taif, so as to escape the heat of desert Riyadh and the humidity of seaside Jeddah. The holiday is always pleasant and relaxing for us since Taif is a small city compared with Riyadh. There are more than five million inhabitants living in our capital city these days, while Taif has approximately half a million citizens.

When Amani is in attendance, everyone knows that our family will be observed vigilantly by my exceedingly devout daughter. Amani never misses any of the five daily calls to prayer; in fact, she adds three extra prayers a day to please God. As is her way, while in Taif one year, under the same roof as her family, she noticed that her brother, who has always had difficulty rising early, had skipped two mornings of the predawn prayer known to Muslims as the Fajr prayer.

By the second day Amani could not restrain her revulsion, which had been building for more than twenty-four hours. Finally, she erupted; indignantly rising mid-prayer from her prayer rug, she rushed to Abdullah's private apartment. My daughter shocked all those who were praying when she began to pound on the door with her fists, yelling loudly, "Abdullah! Brother! You shame yourself! Do you not know that prayer is better than sleep?"

Bedlam ensued when Abdullah's wife, Zain, burst from the bedroom, confused by the clamor and thinking some crisis was happening. My granddaughter, Little Sultana, woke from her sleep and began to sob, fearing something was wrong with her mother. A half-dressed and startled Abdullah then stumbled from their private apartments, looking wildly in all directions. When he saw Amani's angry expression and realized the cause of his family's distress, my son made it clear that he had had quite enough of his meddlesome sister. Easygoing Abdullah changed in an instant and for once in his life he glowered at his youngest sister, his face turning into an ugly grimace as he shouted, "Amani, may God paralyze your tongue!" My son turned away in a fine fury but not before slinging a second insult. "Tend to your own prayers, Amani," he snarled. "And I hope a fat fly lands in your big mouth!"

This is a serious insult, as all Muslims know it is important to keep a hygienic mouth and to keep our hands and feet clean, particularly during the time of prayer. This was a significant affront from my long-suffering son!

When Abdullah gathered his wife and daughter and slammed the door in Amani's face, I heard him shout, "No, Amani! You cannot always rule!"

On hearing this angry encounter, I was relieved that my kindly son would not be pushed forever by his domineering sister. While my youngest daughter is conspicuously insensitive to others, she is acutely sensitive to herself, and a loud scene erupted further when a weeping Amani ran to her father to claim that Abdullah had disrespected her for no reason. She was only trying to keep her greatly loved brother on a smooth path to Paradise, she claimed.

I listened carefully, sad that Amani was trying to manipulate her father in this way. This is something I have determined I will not do, believing that meeting resistance with authority and conviction is always the best thing to do to get results and gain respect. Unless the situation is extreme, and human life is not in danger, I do not use or rely upon my femininity. I do not cry or whimper. I know that there are times when women are in the wrong, too; certainly Amani had demonstrated this on more than one occasion.

Kareem listened carefully but could not be taken in by his youngest child, as he had been so many times in the past. "Please tell me what actions you took, or words you spoke, Amani, to bring such an outburst from your brother."

Amani's tears became genuine when she comprehended that her father was not going to take her side and reprimand her brother without question. Although it took many minutes for Kareem to calm the situation, never once did he question Abdullah about Amani's false charges. My husband and I know our children well.

After Amani returned to her prayers and Abdullah promised to join us for breakfast, my fatigued husband called me to follow him to our quarters. After closing and bolting the door, he whispered, "Sultana, I am going to plot our escape." With a solemn face he told me, "I am looking for a hidden harbor in a distant land. We will retreat from our troublesome children."

Confused, I asked, "What is this you are saying, husband?"

He reassured me, "Do not worry. We will see our children on occasion. Perhaps we will plan an annual visit on the seashore in France, for a holiday with the family. The rest of the year we will enjoy life without our children and their constant quarrelling." He looked concerned, and seemed very serious about this plan. "Make a list of the places you would like to live, darling, and I will purchase a nice home there. But make sure not to tell the children."

I do not disrespect my beloved husband, but I admit I laughed at his preposterous scheme. Regardless of my children's bad conduct, I cannot bear to be separated from them for more than a few weeks. I love my children and grandchildren with my whole heart. In this instant, I was determined that I would rule over Kareem.

I hugged my poor distraught husband, even as I destroyed his fantasy of tranquillity. "You are dreaming, husband," I said. "Until the day a white shroud is slipped over my still body and I am buried in the sands of our land, you and I shall always remain captive to the dramas of our children's lives."

Kareem sulked for several days, and I warned the children about their behavior. I told them that their father was too burdened by their constant clashes, that he was having irrational thoughts about abandoning them all. This revelation caught their attention, and for several months thereafter Amani was on her best behavior.

But the sibling conflicts started again within the year, most particularly between our two daughters. As parents, the battles created by our children still torment us, with one disturbance following another like a giant tsunami sending wave after wave crashing to the shore.

Yet it is not only our children who are responsible for the problems that arise in our family. Sometimes the extended family members play their part in causing strife and upheaval. It was, therefore, no surprise that what should have been one of the most pleasurable and rewarding evenings of my life ended in tears.

This particular incident involved my daughter Maha and my brother's daughter, Medina; they created one of the most outrageous scenes I have ever encountered—and it brought the wrath of my brother Ali on all our heads.

This upsetting situation occurred three days after the festivities at my home—and several weeks before Maha was scheduled to return to Europe. Maha and Amani had agreed to come together in a peaceful manner long enough for the three of us to confer with my sisters as to the ideal place and position in my home to display the beautiful photograph of our mother, the precious image that had been rediscovered after so many years.

My sisters and I, along with nine of our daughters, had settled upon the best time to meet and we planned to enjoy an afternoon tea party. This would be a memorial gathering in honor of our mother. Sadly, none of Mother's granddaughters was born soon enough to remember their wonderful grandmother.

The eagerly anticipated afternoon finally arrived. Sara and I sat alone, waiting for our sisters and their daughters, whom we had asked to arrive early. I glanced at the elaborate golden clock sitting on the side table before expressing my concerns: "I hope everyone arrives on time." (Saudis are notorious for being tardy for nearly every gathering, whether for business or pleasure. I have heard that foreign businesspeople complain bitterly about this trait.)

Sara reached for her mobile phone. "I will call my girls."

Sara had said that her daughters would arrive together, as all would be driven by the family's most trusted Indonesian driver.

Although Sara's phone was not at my ear, once she was connected I could overhear the girls' noisy laughter and enthusiastic chatter. Unlike my girls, Sara's daughters adore each other and their time together is generally full of merriment.

I watched my sister's face and began to worry when I saw her forehead wrinkle in a frown. After heaving a loud sigh, she disconnected the call, telling me, "They are sitting in traffic."

I clicked my tongue in annoyance. For as long as I have been alive, the city of Riyadh has been plagued with perpetual road work and traffic congestion. Why, I do not know, for there are many city committees specially formed whose members continually study and plan the best methods for traffic control, but nothing ever relieves the ghastly traffic jams of my country. Even the Al Sa'ud royals must endure the aggravation of dreadful traffic jams. Unless one is the king of Saudi Arabia, the crown prince, or one of the highest-ranking princes, there will be no specific measures taken to clear gridlocks to enable one to breeze through the traffic.

"Assad told me that it is the young people who cause all the problems," Sara announced with quiet certainty. "He says that he recently met with our cousin Turki bin Abdullah, who informed Assad of the scary news that our country has the highest rate of road accidents in the entire region."

"Well, our city has grown from a small village to a city of over five million in only a few generations," I reminded her. "Perhaps the high statistics come naturally because a few have blossomed into many."

Sara's mind was suddenly focused on the mind-boggling traffic statistics her husband had mentioned, so she paid no heed to me.

"And, even more alarming, Sultana, we have the highest death rates from road traffic accidents of nearly any country in the world, if you can believe it! It is the young men who are joyriders, who do those silly drifting and two-wheel driving stunts, that are creating many of the traffic problems."

"Well, surely Turki knows what he is talking about," I replied. Our cousin Turki, who is one of the sons of King Abdullah, was well placed to know about such matters, being deputy government minister of the Riyadh region. And I, like Sara, had heard about the joyriders and drifting stunts, all activities so dangerous to the well-being of young Saudi men.

"Boredom is killing our young Saudi boys," I said with authority. I shrugged and raised my hands. "What is there for them to do?"

"Yes, I have heard many sad tales," my sister replied.

"Oh, let us speak of something pleasant, Sara," I said, not wanting to think about all the Saudi mothers who would one day mourn their sons: undeniably good boys who after being bitten by boredom raced their cars on two wheels, almost guaranteeing that they would soon be lowered into a grave.

I asked one of our housemaids to refresh our tea before returning to my conversation with Sara.

"Let us talk about Mother," I enthused.

A happy expression returned to Sara's face. "How lucky we are that Father's servant found Mother's photograph."

"Yes, yes," I agreed.

From Father's physical appearance and behavior, we all knew that his time on earth was limited. Had he passed from life before the servant had discovered the mystery wooden crate, it is most likely that our mother's picture would have been forever lost to us.

"I had not realized Mother's great beauty," I said, thinking that out of ten daughters born to my mother only Sara matched her unique beauty. Yet Mother's splendid genetics had touched all of her daughters in some way; though my two deceased sisters, Nura and Reema, resembled my father more.

Sara smiled. "Oh? Well, you were young when she died, Sultana. Everyone looked old to you. I always knew that Mother was one of the most beautiful women in the extended Al Sa'ud family. I heard talk from several cousins that awareness of her beauty was widespread."

As I sipped my tea I thought about Mother's beauty, wondering how I had missed such loveliness.

Just as I opened my mouth to ask Sara how any woman could maintain her good looks after giving birth to eleven children, I heard the sound of my sisters' voices in the hall. Sara and I strolled arm in arm to greet them. Today was to be one of the most notable days of our lives.

I asked my housemaid Aisha to fetch Maha and Amani from their respective rooms. Despite Amani's marriage and Maha's move to Europe, both had spacious apartments in our home, to use whenever they desired. Only Abdullah had given up his apartment in our home, although his new home was very near to our own and he visited us daily, if he was in the kingdom.

Sara and I stood as one, happily greeting our sisters and nieces. Sara's excited daughters burst through the door, thrilled to have finally escaped the Riyadh traffic. The noisy greetings were pleasant for all.

When I saw Amani and Maha walk into the spacious hallway, I was pleased that neither appeared to be in a foul mood. At the sight of their amiable faces, my mood reached a peak of happiness. "Today is going to be a wonderful day," I announced to my daughters, sisters, and nieces.

After refreshments, we settled ourselves down to await the arrival of Reema's son, Mohammed, and my son, Abdullah. Both were due to appear very soon, as I had asked them to arrive after the girls; I did not want the event to be rushed, so I allowed ample time for the females in the family to properly exchange greetings and news, and generally catch up with one another. My son and his cousin would be supervising the placement of Mother's likeness, which sat in a corner of the room, covered with a cloth of green silk. I had shrouded the picture so that the unveiling ceremony would have even more significance. My sister Dunia declared in a loud voice, so as to be heard by all, "Praise Allah! No longer must I use my memory to conjure an image of Mother." "Yes," I agreed. "I want to spend many hours sitting gazing at her elegant beauty, remembering all that she was, and still is, to her daughters."

Ali's daughter Medina, born to his third wife, suddenly made a strange noise and I turned to stare at her, thinking that she might be choking. Rarely have I been in Medina's company, for she has made it known since her earliest teenage days that she does not care for me or for my daughters. I always supposed that she had believed her father's propaganda against me. And why not? Most humans defend what they have been taught in their childhood. That is the only reason I rarely feel anger at Medina; instead, I lay the blame upon the guilty party—my brother Ali.

Truly, I felt surprised to see Medina come to the gathering at my home, but I was pleased, hoping that she had matured and would reach out and enjoy friendly relations with me and her extended family.

Suddenly, Medina jumped up from her chair and shocked us all when she walked toward Mother's picture, which was still covered in the silk cloth. She grasped the cloth and pulled it away from the picture, and as we all watched in complete surprise she glowered at me—her eyes full of fury—and then cried out, "This photograph will soon be in our palace. My father says that he must have it. This picture belongs in the home of Grandmother's only son."

Little shocks ran the entire length of my body. I was truly stunned. Before this incident I had not realized how m u c h Medina physically resembled her father; but when she snarled at me, her eyes staring and her face marked with a menacing expression, she looked just as he did when angered.

Sara stood up and spoke in a loud and forceful manner, shocking all because my sister rarely speaks in anything but a soft, low tone: "Medina, still your tongue and close your lips!"

That's when I noticed Medina's big teeth, which in that moment looked pointed. I inhaled loudly.

"No, Auntie," Medina said, in a more subtle tone, for few in our family ever turn against Sara. "I came today representing my father. This picture belongs to him. He is the ruler of his sisters, and the only man of the family. He will keep this picture and will invite his sisters for an annual gathering so that they might look upon it."

To our absolute astonishment and alarm, Medina, who is physically large and has always been stronger than most—a girl who was known to beat her brothers in fact—lifted Mother's picture and dashed toward the door, holding the large framed photograph over her head.

"Quick, do something, she's running away with it!" one of my nieces shouted.

We all screamed, then I set off our very loud alarm system, which was surely heard far away. By catching us off guard, Medina had succeeded in escaping and was through the entranceway and out of my front door in a flash.

I chased after her, but Maha, who is a fast runner, quickly passed me. We were a train of excited women: I followed Maha, and my sisters and nieces followed me. Events moved so fast that I was soon witnessing a horrifying sight: my daughter in a physical struggle with her cousin.

"Maha! Take care for Mother's picture!" I shouted, terrified that it might be destroyed during their scuffle.

Maha listened to my warning and loosened her grip on Medina's neck, as the picture threatened to fall onto the hard stones of our driveway. It was then that Medina took the opportunity to cram Mother's picture into the backseat of her father's new Rolls-Royce.

Obviously she had instructed the driver to be ready to flee, for Ali's driver had failed to park in the usual area, with the rest of the cars. I heard the motor running. The driver was ready to bolt from our grounds. Medina made a single smooth move and leapt into the backseat of the car as it moved, slowly at first, before it sped off. My heart froze when I saw Maha make an attempt to catch the door handle. I was pleased to see that she was unsuccessful, although it was not pleasant to see my daughter lose her footing and fall to roll around on the grassy knoll. I was relieved that she was not hurt, thanks be to God.

But the unimaginable had happened. The vehicle carrying my Mother's precious photograph was gone.

As if this terrible incident had not been enough, as we gathered together on the drive, we suddenly saw Maha rush toward a Mercedes that belonged to one of my sisters or my nieces and leap into the driver's seat. With most of the drivers relaxing and drinking tea in one of the charming pavilions in our yard, there was no one to stop my daughter. Due to the safety of our home, which was behind tall fencing and gates, the drivers had left their keys in the ignitions.

One of Sara's daughters cried out, "Maha is driving away!"

In shock, I could not utter a single word.

Amani touched my arm, saying, "I will call Father." Then she dashed inside.

Before I closed my eyes in complete terror, the last thing I saw was my daughter doing that which is forbidden in Saudi Arabia— driving a car— and she was doing so at considerable speed.

"She is driving too fast! She will be killed in a crash," Dunia screeched.

"No, Maha is a very skilled driver," Sara murmured. "She is afraid of nothing. She will catch Medina and she will come back with Mother's picture."

Soon Amani rushed to my side, reporting the reassuring news that her father had left his offices and was on his way to Ali's palace, which was not a long distance from our own. I sighed, praying that Kareem would manage this enormous family crisis.

Sara encouraged our hysterical sisters and their stressed daughters to leave for their homes, promising that the moment Mother's photograph had been returned to its rightful place, they would all be notified and we would once more gather for our unveiling ceremony.

I restrained myself from declaring that I would make certain guards would be in attendance and provide protection so that neither my brother nor any of his children would be allowed on our palace grounds.

At that time Abdullah and Mohammed had made their appearance. Thinking we were so excited to see them that we had gathered in the driveway to greet them, they were startled to see our tears and hear our cries. When we told them about the catastrophe, both expressed horror yet showed an instant determination to right a terrible wrong. My son and my nephew ran to their vehicles. As he passed us by, Abdullah's head appeared in the open car window as he shouted, "Do not worry! We will meet Father at Ali's palace. We will bring Grandmother home!"

I thought that perhaps it was not a good idea to put Abdullah in the path of peril, but he was gone before I could stop him.

Sara, Amani, and I tried to reassure our frightened servants and drivers, who had by now gathered around us. They had heard our screams of terror and were, quite understandably, alarmed. Chaos reigned! The male servants and drivers were shouting, while the females were crying; some were afraid that our king had died, while others believed that the country was under attack.

Finally everyone understood that there was no national calamity, just a family crisis that needed to be dealt with fast.

We went back inside our palace to wait for information, although it was some considerable time before we heard any news.

Finally, our loved ones returned, but from one glance we knew that all was not well. Amani groaned in abject terror when Kareem, Abdullah, and Maha came into view. The three were covered in blood, or at least that is what we believed, based on the evidence before our eyes. What looked like blood was dripping from their faces and hands. Thinking all had been involved in a grisly car accident, I struggled to move, but I quickly discovered that my legs were incapable of supporting my body. Once again I was in shock.

When I managed to stand, not knowing quite what to do or who needed attention first, I looked at Kareem, who seemed to be stumbling. I pleaded with him, "What? What?"

Kareem was gulping for breath but held up his hands, his palms visible to me; they were a pinkish color.

Sara was equally concerned and wanted an explanation too: "What has happened?"

In a frightened voice, Amani then asked, "Father, are you wounded?"

"No, we are not injured," Kareem said finally.

I was very confused by this time and gestured at my son's body: "What is this blood, then?"

For a heart-stopping moment I was afraid that they had injured Medina, or possibly Ali had been hurt. Although I am a person who fights injustice, and have been known to pinch my children or twist their ears when they have misbehaved, I do not like violence.

Maha, whose entire body, from her head to her toes, was covered in red liquid, finally said, "This is not blood, Mummy. This is red paint. Your brother, his devil of a daughter, and several of his sons doused us all in red paint."

I could not comprehend what I was hearing. "Paint?"

Abdullah then explained all. "Yes, Mother. When we arrived, Maha had already taken photograph from Medina. We quickly placed the picture in Father's large trunk. Mohammed, thinking the crisis had ended, left. Then the three of us foolishly stood together in the drive discussing how to get Auntie Dunia's car returned without Maha driving and while we were talking that gang of thieves slipped behind the large bushes near the drive and came at us throwing buckets of red paint."

Such a scene I could not imagine. I was rendered speechless for one of the few times in my life.

Sara, who knows about every kind of paint, even house paints, due to her years of being an artist, puckered her lips and gently inquired, "Is this water-based paint?"

Sara's unanticipated query instantly created some relief, and all of us began to laugh hysterically.

"Water-based?" Abdullah questioned.

Kareem struggled to gain control of his senses. He was laughing so much that it took some time before he was able to ask his son one final question. "Abdullah, son, how could you fail to ask Ali if the paint was water-based?"

A snorting Abdullah, still laughing uncontrollably, finally collapsed on the floor, ruining my lovely white carpet, while Maha clung with her paint-soaked hands to the back of my favorite sofa, spoiling the exclusive golden fabric I had so passionately hunted down throughout all of Asia.

But I did not despair for one second: I cared only for the safety of the ones I love.

Thankfully, only their pride was wounded, for the paint *was* found to be water-based and so my three darlings were able, after a few days of multiple showers and lots of scrubbing, to remove the red paint from their hair and skin. We could not help but wonder where on earth Ali and his children had found cans of red paint for their attack.

Some months later, Medina telephoned Amani to brag about her role in the drama that day, revealing that Ali was in the process of building a dance hall for his new Syrian wife Sita, who had hired a dancer from Argentina to teach her how to tango. Sita, who likes garish decorations, had insisted that the large hall be painted a bright shade of red and it was that paint that was within easy reach when Ali and his children looked for something to use in an attack upon my family.

To our everlasting joy, Mother's picture was not damaged. Had it not been tucked into the trunk of Kareem's car, Ali and his family would have recklessly covered Mother's likeness with red paint, ruining the irreplaceable picture completely. The photograph of our mother, which her daughters considered to be a great treasure, would have been lost to us forever.

The fact that Mother's picture came so close to utter devastation brought my sisters firmly to my side, and for once all were keenly disappointed in their only brother, who obviously preferred to ruin Mother's picture than for it to be displayed in my home. To this day, my sisters and their daughters still feel a great fury toward Ali. They have all told him that their anger has reached such heights that neither he nor his family members are welcome in their homes. They all say that it is time to teach Ali a lesson: although they are not men, his sisters are *not* without rights. And so, for the first time in our family, women ruled.

Sara was so disappointed in her younger brother that she approached our father to expose Ali's and Medina's reckless behavior. Sara reported that even our father expressed anger at what Ali and Medina had done. Father said that they were going against our mother's wishes and the promise Father had given her upon her deathbed. For him, Ali and his children had brought shame upon the family.

Abdullah brought a smile to my face when he spoke of the situation, saying, "Mother, most people think Saudi women need a man for protection. But, in this case, it is a Saudi man, my Uncle Ali, who needs protection."

"If only that would remain so, my son," I replied.

But at least all now knew that it was Ali who had the evil spirit and not his little sister, whom he was always blaming for everything. And this brought me some small comfort.

The last I heard, Father was so annoyed that when he had occasion to see Ali, he refused his son's efforts to kiss his hand or to join him for a meal at his home. Ali, who had become accustomed since the days of babyhood to being treated as a golden child by our father, was so stunned to be the object of his father's disappointment and displeasure that he booked a trip abroad, planning to lie low and stay indefinitely at his palaces in France and Spain.

Ali was unrepentant, however, and it came as a big shock when I was told that my brother had asked all in his family to pray to Allah for me to lose my eyesight. My brother dislikes me so much he does not want me to enjoy the wondrous photograph of my mother.

His extreme antagonism was, and always had been, a big disturbance to Kareem and my children, for who knew how else his resentment might manifest itself in the future? To be sure, the knowledge of his vindictive prayers had caused me some anxiety, and I made several appointments with specialists to monitor any eyesight problems. I was greatly relieved each time I heard doctors say that my eyes were still the eyes of a young woman without any threatening diseases. Allah has not chosen to grant Ali his wishful prayer that I go blind. My brother's actions since the time he was a child leave no doubt in my mind that he is a very evil man.

After years of disagreements, and even fights with my brother, I believe that Ali will make a move against me and my family someday. Perhaps he will delay his intrigues until Father has passed from this life. There is nothing to do but to wait for my fate.

Kareem is so determined to guard the picture safely at our home that he hired knowledgeable experts, who make their living protecting the most expensive paintings in European museums, to come into our palace and devise an alarm system that will go off should anyone attempt to remove Mother's picture from our wall.

Despite my concerns and fears about Ali, I still know tremendous joy. Every morning in my home in Riyadh, I have the pleasure of greeting my mother's image. I feel the powerful love I have always felt for Mother, and her love for me. When looking into her beautiful face, I have the feeling that she is embracing me as surely as her loving arms used to enfold me when I was her baby. Although she has been in her grave for many long years, her picture gives me the sensation that she is once again by my side. Her kindly spirit has revitalized my strength to continue the arduous battle I have been waging since I was a young girl: to assist any female I encounter who might need a helping hand.

One lovely morning I gazed at my mother and smiled, telling her, "Mummy, in one short lifetime

Saudi women have started on a wonderful path to freedom. Many have begun to rule their own lives."

Unknown to me, as I spoke these words, my devoted son Abdullah had entered the room and was standing a few feet behind me. He smiled and looked at his grandmother's image, then clasped me in a heartfelt hug.

"Yes, Grandmother!" he cried out. "Believe your daughter, Sultana. Women rule!"

And so, with a heart filled with gladness and anticipation for better lives for all women, I continue my journey.

# Chapter Five
# Dr. Meena: The Wealth of Education

The greatest of all riches is education. While great wealth can be lost, education cannot be withdrawn, canceled, or recalled. Education multiplies like no other investment, because it encourages a hunger that is never satisfied. This is why I have spent much of my adult life spreading the idea that education is wealth.

The marvelous truth is that, while daunting challenges remain for females in my country, many improvements have been made in every aspect of a woman's daily life.

Our most important victory has been in the realm of education. The first girls' school in Saudi Arabia was established in 1956, and in only two generations education has become available for nearly all Saudi females.

When I was a child, education was mainly limited to the elite. My sisters and I were taught by a private foreign tutor, a woman who was specifically employed to teach the daughters of the royal family—but of course, only the truly wealthy could employ such a teacher.

Few ordinary Saudis considered learning essential for their daughters; the pivotal ambition of most families was to educate their sons. My uncle King Faisal and his wife Iffat, who enjoyed an unusually modern marriage, where the wife participated in decision making, set in motion a revolution of sorts when they worked together to make education for girls a high priority.

Yet despite my uncle's best efforts, few Saudi girls gained an education that advanced further than basic reading and writing. After King Faisal's assassination by one of his nephews in 1975, other matters of state took precedence and progress to make education available for females stalled. During my childhood, goals for female learning were so dismal that there was little opportunity for girls to gain the level of education that might lead to a Ph.D. or a medical degree.

I vividly recall the moment when I realized that a female could even work in the medical field. That was the day our family driver escorted Mother, Sara, and me for a dental appointment at the offices of a female dentist. The three of us had been suffering for some time from excruciating toothaches. Mother's back teeth were rotting. Sara's gums were red and swollen for reasons unknown to us. I had bitten a hard sweet with such enthusiasm that I had chipped a tooth nearly to the gum.

The delay in getting dental treatment was a result of there being very few female dentists in Riyadh. Father would never have allowed any male dentist to view his wife's uncovered face and look into her mouth, although, curiously enough, a male doctor was allowed to examine her naked body when she experienced pains in later life.

Mother later confided to her oldest daughter, Nura, that she had overheard Father's instructions to his assistant, whose job it was to oversee all aspects of medical care for the females in the family, and they were very precise and direct. He had dictated that while his wife was forbidden to take off her face veil, she could remove her clothing. So long as a male physician did not see her face, it was not shameful for him to see her body. Such things I find inexplicable about my own culture.

Surprisingly, other more stringent restrictions remain for some Saudi women; barely a month passes without news of some poor woman who has died only because her husband had refused to allow a male physician to examine her.

Once a female dentist established offices in Riyadh, my father's assistant made an appointment for us to be seen without delay. If my memory serves me correctly, the dentist was a woman from Lebanon, a country where education was not a rarity for every woman. I remember her calm expression, and how she was so attentive to our mother and her two daughters. Now that I have matured, I realize that she probably felt very sorry for my mother and her female children. Arab women from other countries always seem to understand that, despite our oil wealth, women in Saudi Arabia are tragically poor when it comes to personal freedom. While women from less wealthy Arab lands might envy our wealth, they have never envied the many difficult restrictions placed upon our lives.

Whatever that kindly dentist might have felt for us, Sara and I were in awe of her youth and her knowledge. Until that day, every woman we had encountered was without a career or a job outside the home.

I was very young at the time, but Sara was older and more confident. She asked the dentist so many questions—about this instrument or that machine, or where she had obtained her degree—and I recall how Mother flushed, embarrassed at her daughter's outspoken manner. In Mother's world, Saudi women were expected to be content with being a wife and mother, and any desire or ambition to work outside the home was met with dismay, even disbelief.

While we females had made tiny steps toward freedom in the 1960s and 1970s, everything changed for the worse in 1979. That was the disturbing year when the Islamic revolution in Iran occurred and the ruler of that country, known as the Shah of the Pahlavi dynasty, was overthrown. He was replaced by the Grand Ayatollah Khomeini, the leader of the Islamic revolution. From the beginning, Khomeini made it clear that he was a man who found females distasteful; this feeling was appallingly common for men of religion.

The men in my family were alarmed that something similar might occur in Saudi Arabia. This is because our country is filled with men who believe that Allah speaks only to them. With nearly every man believing he is the only person privileged to know Allah's truth, endless disagreements ensue.

My uncle, King Khalid, and his brothers came to believe Saudi Arabia was following in the footsteps of Iran. This belief came about in the latter part of 1979, when insurgents protesting against the rule of my family took hundreds of worshipping pilgrims hostage at the Grand Mosque in Mecca. The ensuing battle lasted for two weeks and cost the lives of many militants, as well as hostages and Saudi Arabian soldiers defending the Al Sa'ud rule.

I listened eagerly when my father repeated words our King Khalid had said, words that expressed his concerns and worries for our country, and for the rule of his family in this land.

Poor King Khalid. He was a devout man who took his royal duties more seriously than most, so it was understandable that he was distraught by the path so many Muslims were following.

After the Grand Mosque crisis had ended, and the surviving insurgents had been beheaded, the men in my extended Al Sa'ud family came together to devise a method to pacify radicals. That is when the men I know as relatives surrendered all Saudi female rights, saying that freedom for women would increase the wrath of the most religious men and would threaten the crown.

And that is when, as women, our baby steps to freedom were brought to a standstill. The long years of our personal freedom "drought" resulted in stagnation; no longer was consideration given to the advancement of females.

As the years passed, I heard talk of female doctors working in my country, but they were women who had come from other lands, mostly England, America, and Asia. For me, those women did not count, for they did not improve the opportunities of Saudi females. There were very few Arab doctors from neighboring countries.

But in the year 2014 Saudi women are again gaining ground. These days almost all Saudi girls are educated, at least to age sixteen or seventeen. And if parents agree, older girls are given permission to continue their education to gain work in high-ranking professions, such as medicine. More and more Saudi women are choosing to become pediatric dentists or physicians, and are also specializing as physicians for women.

The struggle has been so profound that I never fail to react with excitement anytime I learn that a Saudi woman has made her way through the many years of schooling to obtain a medical degree. Nothing pleases me more than to make an appointment with a female Saudi doctor; in fact, I go out of my way to locate the latest female physicians in Riyadh, Jeddah, and Taif, for these are the cities where I spend most of my time. I adore meeting women who have achieved their goals and I like to observe their working habits, to analyze how such women cope with professional life in the kingdom. I know that the difficulties here are still many. I have a need to understand how these women cope on a personal level and to assess exactly what it has taken for them to achieve such high professional goals.

Such personal research helps me to make better choices when I am determining how best to help women achieve their ambitions, or deciding which organizations to support in my efforts to improve the opportunities for women in general.

Only twice have I made female doctors aware of my ardent mission to spend much of my time and considerable resources to ensure that all girls get the best education. Admittedly, it is very difficult for me to keep my secrets when I am in the presence of a woman I greatly admire, a woman who has not only survived but also succeeded in maneuvering through one of the most arduous obstacle courses in the world in order to obtain a good education and become a medical doctor in the Kingdom of Saudi Arabia. There are generally three areas where I have been able to help Saudi women in the field of medicine. I have helped girls in need of an education, who may have gone on to study in that profession. Others were women who needed more practical help: either they were women who had appealed for medical assistance to the boards of various royal hospitals, who had then contacted members of the royal family— I have been called on in this manner on many occasions, for I am a high-ranking princess who is known for my generosity when it comes to issues affecting women—or they were young mothers who feared for the lives of their daughters, whose well-being was being threatened by their fathers, brothers, or uncles.

Of course, none of these people could ever imagine that I was Princess Sultana, known because of the books about my life. They only knew that I was one of several royal princesses who devoted much time and money to educating girls and to finding government resources to pay for necessary medical treatment for those who could not afford it.

But change is far from complete in the kingdom. Although some Saudi women are finding life less complex and dangerous than it was during my generation, there are many who must still battle alone to survive a system built by men to maintain total power over women. The struggles these women endure often serve to demonstrate that the problems I have personally faced are comical and trivial in comparison.

Having outlined how difficult it is for Saudi women to achieve a medical degree, I wish to share a

92

specific story about one special woman. My thoughts
often drift to this indomitable female, who was born
into one of the most tragic situations, yet through
willpower and education, brought herself out of the
darkness of servitude and into the light. I will refer to
her as Dr. Meena, a Saudi woman who has the desire
and ability to serve, and who I believe is triggering
some of the most needed and greatest changes for all
women of Saudi Arabia.

I met Dr. Meena in 2012, when I was invited, along
with approximately fifteen of my female cousins, to
attend a conference on the subject of education for
Saudi girls at one of the royal hospitals in Riyadh.
When I arrived, I gave instructions for my driver, a
nice middle-aged Muslim man from Indonesia named
Batara, to drive to the front of the hospital so that I
could make my way directly to the meeting room.
Batara has worked for my husband for many years
and has Kareem's complete confidence. As a result,
Batara is appointed as my personal driver when we
are in Saudi Arabia. He takes his job seriously and is
very pleased to be so trusted that he even travels with
us from city to city.

On this particular day, when Batara realized I
was going to enter the hospital without him by my
side, he respectfully objected, for he considers it a vital
duty of his job that I arrive securely at any
destination. He even goes so far as to try to inspect
a room I am to enter, although he cannot always
perform this security measure when there are other

unveiled women in attendance. Several times when I have visited longer than planned, Batara has popped his head into an open window to observe the scene, making certain that I am still with the living. On one amusing occasion, Batara created a commotion when his inquisitive face appeared at a window. When he could not identify me in the large gathering, he yelled out a worried cry, causing six or seven of the most conservative women to faint and others to run and hide. Although our servants are accustomed to seeing my unveiled face, and the faces of my sisters and Maha, other women do not live so freely in Saudi Arabia and their families force them to wear a veil even when household help is around. After that day I had to order Batara never again to cause such a commotion. He was forbidden from making an appearance around women not of our family!

But as I have visited this hospital more than once, and have also attended other meetings here, I knew exactly where I was going.

"No," I said firmly. "Please park my car in that space, Batara," and I gestured to an area where royal visitors have license to park at any time of the day or night. After turning the ignition off, Batara came a round to open the door to enable me to exit easily. The fabric of my billowy abaya cloak often catches on one sharp point or another, and so I am not unhappy for Batara to push any hanging fabric to the side and to hold the door open for me.

I glanced at the anxious expression on his face and chuckled to myself—not laughing, as it would wound his feelings. I am sorry that he is frustrated and anxious, but there are times when I must be alone to live my life without the protection of a man.

No one noticed me when I entered the wide doors of the hospital, as I was fully veiled, then I walked confidently and alone down the long corridor that led to the room where I was expected. As I had attended several meetings at this very hospital, I knew exactly where I needed to go. I felt as liberated as a Saudi woman can feel; it was almost as if I were on a little vacation, free from the usual chaos of life surrounded by a large household filled with servants and family members.

I saw none of my cousins when I took a moment to glance around the room. Perhaps they were all late, I thought to myself, as many members of my extended family have the view that it is important to arrive last so that every nonroyal is put in a position to wait on them. I disapprove of this attitude, but since becoming an adult I have noticed that arrogance is a disease of the royals. In fact, it strikes me that little has changed over the centuries, and royalty from all over the world believe themselves to be elevated above all others, even those members of royal families in Europe.

Suddenly there was a flurry of movement as a young Saudi woman who had likely been assigned to welcome invited guests seemed to remember that she had deserted her post. I studied her face as she made her way to me and I imagined that she was embarrassed, probably thinking that she was unlucky to have wandered off just when a member of the royal family had arrived. I could easily see that the pretty girl was alarmed—possibly frightened—that I might have been annoyed by her oversight. But I was not bothered in the slightest and, besides, she wore such a big smile that I instantly liked her.

I smiled in return, but of course she could not see my friendly face as I was still covered in the full veil, the hated attire I still wear when I venture out in public in Riyadh. Hopefully the day will come soon when the cast of disapproval on unveiled ladies no longer infects Riyadh society. To this day, there are teenage Saudi boys living in Riyadh who, taught by their fathers and the clerics, consider women to be second-class citizens and cast stones at what they consider to be an offensive sight—an unveiled female face. It is my sincere wish that the day will come when the ideas of ultraconservative Riyadh citizens will advance to meet those of the more liberal-minded residents of Jeddah, so that at least an uncovered face will not cause violence in the street.

The young lady appeared to be excited to be welcoming a member of the royal family, but she was too shy to start a conversation as she reached to help me remove my abaya. With one swift move, I discarded my black veil, then I asked her, "Do you veil your face when outside?," wondering if she was bold enough to rebel, as I had been when I was a young girl.

The woman smiled sheepishly. But before answering my question she first apologized: "I am sorry, Princess. I was called away for only a moment."

"Oh, do not worry. I am not helpless." I looked at her again. "Tell me, what do you think of the veil, the face veil?"

She was startled by my openness, but I never fail to discuss the veil when I meet young women. Nothing reveals more to me of their personality than their will to fight against any injustice against women, and certainly something as personal as the face veil,

which is not required by the Islamic faith, as all those
who are truly familiar with our holy book will know.

"I veil when in public," she said. She then
glanced around to ensure we were alone before
confessing, "But I do not like it." When she noticed my
smile of approval, she grinned impishly.

"My father would not mind if I did not cover my
face, but my mother and my brothers say that the veil
serves a double purpose, to keep bugs out of my
eyes and mouth and forbidden thoughts blocked
from entering my head."

As I turned to walk away to join the other
ladies at the meeting, I chuckled with her, saying,
"One day I hope to see all men who so love the veil
wear the veil!"

She gasped, a little scandalized by this remark,
but I could tell that she was pleased to meet a Saudi
princess who was willing to express herself so
openly.

I walked to the other women with bubbling
anticipation because I knew that this special committee
had been formed to focus solely on reaching teenage
females and encouraging them to strive for a degree
in medicine. Nothing gives me greater pleasure than
news that female students will be assisted in reaching
their educational goals. Although my government has
made education a top priority, there are still many
families who, from lack of knowledge, believe that it is
wrong to educate a girl. These are the daughters we
must assist in any way possible.

At this point I saw the woman who would one
day be my friend. I watched as a slight figure dressed
in her doctor's white coat walked in my direction. I
am a small woman, but I towered over this doctor. Her
face was devoid of any of the beauty products that so

many women use to enhance their features, yet she was attractive. While Saudi women generally prefer hair that is long, her style reminded me of the women featured in the old Hollywood movies that my son Abdullah claimed to love, when stars wore a fringed bob. Unlike most in attendance at the gathering, she wore no jewelry other than a simple watch.

We were introduced and exchanged pleasant greetings. I attempted to chat with her, but this woman was not one to make small talk. It only took me a few moments to understand that this Saudi physician was not only serious-faced and serious-minded, but she was also a woman unimpressed by royalty. I like such a mind-set because I know that none born on this earth have a say as to their earthly heritage. Allah decides all; if it were His wish, I could have been born into great poverty in another land far from Saudi Arabia. We are all as Allah desires us to be.

Soon all the expected guests had arrived, and after greetings were made and refreshments taken, including delicious punch made of pineapple juice and other wonderful fruits, we were directed to move to an adjoining area where there was an auditorium. We were to hear the personal stories of women born without privilege in our land—women who had risen to a high station in life and achieved a great deal against all odds. These speakers were going to enlighten the wealthy females of our land as to the difficulties they had faced. We hoped to come away with creative ideas to help other Saudi girls mired in similar struggles.

At this point I learned that Dr. Meena was to be our first speaker. I was anxious to hear her story. I carefully watched her small figure as she walked confidently onto the raised platform. I sensed that I would learn something very important from this woman.

After being introduced to polite applause, Dr. Meena told us the story of her life. I quickly discerned that she was the only speaker I had ever heard who made no effort to charm her audience with a smile. Yet her personal story was so engrossing, exposing what life was like, and is like, for so many ill-fated girls and women in Saudi Arabia, that I sat on the edge of my chair, captivated by her simple but powerful delivery and the story she had to tell.

"My start in life did not indicate anything good. I was born to an impoverished family in a poor hamlet in the area that is today known as Al-Kharj."

I know a lot about the region of Dr. Meena's birth. It, like most of Saudi Arabia, has been a very poor area for most of its history. But the people of the Al-Kharj are luckier than most in our land, for there are many wadis, or water springs, in the area. In fact, the region is mainly defined by a wide valley, called Wadi al-Kharj. With water, the villagers were able to at least grow grain and other plants. I recalled my father telling my brother Ali stories about the people of Kharj; they were the last of the entire Najd to succumb to his father's rule. But later the people of the area became the most loyal to our family, joining our grandfather King Abdul Aziz Al Sa'ud in his battles to subdue and unite the entire country. Since that time the people of that region have been looked upon with favor by our family, often being awarded improvements to the roads and the building of businesses and many other preferences over other areas of the country.

Dr. Meena continued her tale: "Had anyone in my small village predicted that one day the fourth and last daughter of my mother and father would go to school and love learning to the point that I yearned to be a student forever, they would have been ridiculed and possibly had stones thrown at their heads."

The vision she gave us about disbelieving and stone-throwing villagers was considered slightly comical, but, sitting in front of the very somber Dr. Meena, none had the courage to even snicker—not even the most brash of my princess cousins.

"I was the last of four daughters born to my mother." Throughout the audience of females, there was a hum of sympathy for any woman who had given birth to four daughters. I stiffened, glancing around at the women in the room expressing sympathy for the birth of a female. How angry I felt that even today women continued to support the idea that the mother of daughters is to be pitied. My mother gave birth to ten daughters. As the mother of two daughters, I consider such reactions a personal insult. But I held my tongue still, for this was not the place for a disagreement that might turn into a confrontation.

"In fact, my birth ensured my mother a hasty divorce from my furious father, who shouted the dreaded words, 'I divorce you. I divorce you. I divorce you.' My mother had three young daughters, and had just given birth to a fourth infant, and now she found herself a divorced woman. I was told that my father did not even take a moment to catch his breath; instead, he came to my mother's side and berated her, accusing her of ruining his life by birthing one daughter after another. By then his disappointment had built into a horrendous fury. He terrified my poor mother when he roughly grabbed me, the newborn infant by her side, and rushed to the door of our mud hut, slinging me by my tiny arms and shouting that he was going to bury me alive in the desert. He then shouted for my three older sisters to line up and wait for his return. He was going to throw those three in the village well. All his daughters were going to die!

"A man—my own father—was threatening to murder me and my sisters in a most cruel manner. For sure, I must have been screaming in agony at being painfully thrown about. Then a miracle straight from Allah occurred, the first of many in my life. My sisters and I were being menaced by one man, but before the murder could take place two men protected our young lives. We were saved by the words of the Prophet Muhammad. His wise words came down from the ages to be spoken by one of my uncles, who was far more intelligent than his brother, my father. My uncle had found some value in his own two daughters, although it is thought he was more kindly about females because his wife had presented him with five sons before giving birth to his two daughters. For whatever the reason, he saved four young female lives by repeating the sayings of the Prophet Muhammad, Peace Be Upon Him, whereas he has promised a great reward from God for bringing up female children nicely and with care. 'If anyone has a female child and does not bury her alive, or slight her, or prefer his children [i.e. the male ones] to her, God will bring him to Paradise.'

"As my uncle kept repeating the saying of the Prophet, he showed no aggression, but slowly reached for me, the infant in my father's hands.

"My father did not want to be known as a man who went against the words of the Prophet Muhammad. But rather than pass me to my uncle's kindly hands, my father tossed me, a helpless infant, on the dirt floor and left our home. He scowled, shouting that he was leaving to arrange our departure, saying that another man could feed five useless mouths. He never again wanted to see his divorced wife, or the four daughters to whom he had given life.

"Within hours of my birth, my poor mother, who had endured a very difficult delivery without medical care, was forcibly routed from the birthing bed by two women who had been summoned to help gather her pitiful belongings and her four daughters. Those women were preparing us to leave the only home my mother had known since the day of her marriage.

"Soon my father returned, insisting that she vacate our hut to go outside and climb into the backseat of his battered automobile with her brood of girls. She was going to be returned to her parents. My father even had the audacity to insist that her poor parents would be forced to give back her wedding dowry, which had consisted of one cheap necklace and bracelet set, a few sheep, and ten chickens. By this time, my grandparents did not have a sheep to return, for they had never recovered from supplying dowries for three daughters. They did own four scrawny chickens that sometimes gave them eggs to supplement their meager diet.

"I have been told that trails of blood tracked Mother's footsteps as she stumbled to the door, weeping, pleading with her husband to give her one more chance, promising that the fifth child would be a healthy boy. She received a slap in the face for her heartfelt appeals.

"And so a second miracle occurred within a few hours of my birth, a miracle that safeguarded my life.

As all of you know, regardless of what the Koran says about custody of children, in our country, if a man claims custody from the first day of a child's birth, no one will defy him. His demands will be met with silence.

"Thanks be to God my father did not insist upon custody of his daughters. Had he demanded guardianship, no one would have stood in his way. Had that happened, I am certain that he would have soon murdered us all, for how could our kindly uncle stand watch every hour of every day? Praise Allah that my frightened sisters and the new wailing baby, which happened to be me, were allowed to leave with our mother.

"Mother said our father cursed her for the entire trip as we were brusquely transported to the home of her aging parents. And so my poor mother found herself divorced with four girls, females whom no one wanted.

"Rather than welcome their daughter and four granddaughters, my mother's parents quarreled with their former son-in-law, telling him that he must take his family back home. They claimed not to have a bite of bread to share with their daughter and her children. But my father cursed them, too, for having a daughter who could only give birth to daughters.

"My father, like so many of that day, was an ignorant man without knowledge that it is the man whose sperm determines the sex of a child. In his unlearned mind, babies came from a woman's body, so the woman was the responsible party for all things to do with the child.

"Mother's parents watched in alarm as their former son-in-law climbed into his rickety vehicle and left their village. That's when they turned their animosity on Mother. They stood as a united front at the door of their simple home and told my mother to leave, to go to Riyadh, to find someone in the government to take her and her daughters. My unfeeling grandparents actually pushed her aside, making a shameful attempt to get back inside their home and to close and lock the door so that none of us might enter.

"But my oldest sister was very clever. She was six years old and was always smart. She has always loved the stories told by the Bedouin who visited our little village, particularly the one where they claim that once the camel's nose is in the tent, his body will soon follow. She knew that she had to get into the 'tent,' or, in this case, the hut. Understanding that the situation was dire, she pressed past the old couple and distracted our grandmother by hanging on to one of her legs. Grandmother tried to beat her to make her turn loose, but my sister later claimed that Grandmother's weak hits could not match our father's vicious punches, recalling how he often beat his wife and young daughters. So she accepted the blows and found it no trouble to hold firm. Mother took that opportune moment to gather her last bit of strength to edge past her father. I was tied in a rag wrapped around her neck, and my other two sisters were gripping the fabric of her long dress."

For the first time, a hint of a smile crossed Dr. Meena's lips. She said, "That old Bedouin saying was very wise, and I knew it was true about a camel's nose. My sister had been the nose of the camel, and we were the body, so we were all in."

A hush came over the room as Dr. Meena picked up her story.

"Mother was smart enough not to bother to debate the situation with her parents. She only knew that she had four daughters whom she loved more than her life, and that she had no shelter, other than that of her childhood home. Rather than quarrel, she pretended to collapse in a corner and there she feigned sleep. My sisters followed her example, although they were meticulous to bind their little legs and arms around Mother. Thankfully our grandparents were elderly and without strength to lift all five of us as one, so no one was going anywhere.

"Mother said she did not sleep one second of that night because her parents sat up the entire night and plotted as to how they might force us out of their home.

"And so a third miracle saved my life. The first occurred when my uncle spoke the Prophet Muhammad's words forbidding men to bury their daughters alive. The second was when my father did not claim custody of his daughters. And the third miracle transpired when my sister's quick thinking made it possible for us to have a home; although it was a home where we were not wanted.

"Those were not the last of the miracles that have brought me to this room, to speak with you as a woman who has obtained a medical degree, in a country where few women ever have the opportunity to achieve such a thing.

"I believe it was yet a fourth miracle, when my grandparents failed to make plans to murder us. Mother was very weak. Her daughters were very young. They could have set us all on fire had they been just a bit more cruel than they were. No authority would have punished them in those days for murdering five females.

"Thankfully, my grandparents were not so malicious that they made plans to murder us. They wanted us to leave, but they could not commit deadly violence."

Dr. Meena paused briefly. She looked around the room as though she were expecting someone who was not there. That's when her eyes rested on my face and I felt a massive surge of energy flow toward me. Something remarkable was happening and I was not certain what it was, but I felt no danger from the unusual energy.

The doctor resumed her talk, her eyes never leaving my face. "I believe in miracles. I am standing here as a miracle to you all. I am certain that many of you have heard your men speak about Allah's wishes as though He were in their head. I, too, have received such implications from many of our ill-informed men who assert that Allah favors males over females. But such a thing cannot be.

"On the night of my birth, Allah was there to deliver four miracles that saved five female lives, my mother and her four daughters.

"Mother said that the following morning her father left their home to visit several neighboring villages. He was in pursuit of a man, any man, who was looking to marry. But no man responded in a positive manner. Grandfather bitterly complained that he could not find any man, not even an old man with a balding head or rotten teeth, who wanted a woman with four children to take care of his needs.

"And so our lives improved in some ways, and became more difficult in others. While we were not in danger of being murdered, Mother's parents did beat us when they were frustrated by our presence. Mother's pride was terribly wounded when she became an unwelcome human addition, living in her aging parents' home, which was a small, sunbaked mud-brick dwelling with only three rooms. The bare abode, with scarcely enough space for two people, was suddenly overflowing with three adults and four little girls.

"Yet we were grateful, for we had shelter from the elements and there was some food, although never enough for four growing children."

Dr. Meena paused and gestured, waving a hand over her head.

"As your eyes tell you, I am stunted in growth. My sisters are of a similar small size. My lack of nourishment as a child explains why I must look up to all of you. None of us grew normally because we were hungry every moment of our young lives.

"I know that my mother loved her daughters with her whole heart. Many times I would feel her watching me from across the room, sad and weary to the bone, yet she desperately loved her child. My poor mother was so exhausted from her life as a slave to her parents that she had no resources left to attend to her daughters. Instead, my six-year-old sister was given full responsibility for the well-being of her younger sisters. While I felt love, life was so bleak that there was none of the joy or laughter that one normally finds in a home with four children. I cannot recall playing a game with my sisters. I cannot remember my mother singing me a bedtime song, or telling me a little story.

"As far as my grandparents, they were so bitter about our presence that they hatefully watched every bit of food as it went from our hands to our

mouths. They begrudged growing children every bite of nourishment. Those two old people, with their pure white hair and their scowling faces, had the look of people born old. I'm told that by the time I was two years old I was a child terrified of everything, but mostly of those two old people who glowered at me continually. My mother says that it broke her heart into
even smaller pieces when she felt my little hands pulling on her skirts during mealtimes. I would conceal myself in the folds of her skirts while rapidly consuming my inadequate portions of plain bread, boiled eggs, and stringy camel meat. My first memory is that of being hungry all the time.

"My darling mother suffered terribly for the first few years, feeding her hungry daughters the plainest fare. There were a few good times when food was provided by various relatives who during religious festivals would remember their poorest relations. Only then would they gather their leftover scraps in a plastic bowl and leave the charitable offerings at the worn wooden door where my eldest sister sat guard in the hope that some feeling soul would be charitable and bring us food. I have been told that we would squabble over scraps of meat in the same manner that starving dogs fight over bones.

"Daily life improved slightly after my grandmother died from a raging infection triggered by stepping on a rusty nail wedged into a wooden plank. At the death of his wife, my grandfather for the first time looked upon my mother as an asset, someone to take the place of his former slave, a woman who had waited on him for his entire adult life.

"Life remained a daily struggle, though. Education? No, not for a long time. Education for girls was never considered when my mother was a child, at least not in our rural area, although I know that city girls from affluent families often attended elementary school during those dark days. So my illiterate mother could not write her name. She could not call anyone over the phone. She could not even read our religious book, the Koran, something every believing Muslim longs to do."

Dr. Meena was still looking implicitly at me, and I felt clearly that her words were meant for me only.

"Dear princesses, you know that our religion does not call for this mental darkness for girls. This is something unfeeling men have embraced. If they keep their females ignorant, then their women have no alternative but to live the life of a slave to a man. Although my mother could not read or write, she was not stupid. She gathered information as she listened to the talk of the men who came to visit her father. She never saw the faces of those men, of course, because she had to hide herself in order to keep her honor. Prior to the men entering the hut, she cooked and arranged the food on the soiled carpet my grandfather ordered her to spread over the dirt floor. After setting the food on the carpet, she would rush to another room and sit and listen to the words of the men. That's where she overheard an interesting conversation. One of the village men was telling about how his granddaughters were attending a school specifically for girls. This was in Riyadh, which was about a three-hour trip from our small village. There was a school of sorts in the village where the boys learned to read and memorize the Koran—but it did not admit girls. During a second conversation, my mother learned about special city housing being built by the royal family. My mother was clever enough to know that nothing would change for her daughters without education. For such a thing to happen, she knew that she must move her daughters into the city.

"Already several old men in the village had come to bargain for the eldest of my sisters. Mother was in agony at the idea of any of her girls becoming a slave to a man. And so she built her courage to ask one of her brothers to go into the city of Riyadh and to apply for an apartment for my grandfather.

"At first my grandfather gave a defiant no. But about a month later, during which time my mother was continually pushing the topic, my grandfather suffered some sharp pains in his chest and began to feel unwell. He decided that he should live in a large city so as to find better medical care; in those days, small villages had few options for those in need of health care. His no became a yes; my mother's idea had merit.

"And so housing was found for my grandfather and for us, his family. Suddenly we had moved from a tiny village to a booming city, a place where opportunities could be found.

"Although she was uneducated, Mother wanted better for her girls. She never stopped thinking and planning how she might help her daughters. After we arrived in the city, my mother pushed her father to ask neighbors and others he might meet about available schooling for his granddaughters. Much to our surprise, he grumpily complied—but only after Mother promised him that if his granddaughters became educated, we would find appropriate work for traditional Muslim girls. Salaries would follow work, she implied, and our salaries would belong to him. Grandfather was greedy, so he worked the system.

"And so it came to be that Mother was fruitful in getting her three youngest daughters enrolled in school. My eldest sister claimed not to have an interest, but I believe that she was embarrassed to be nearly twelve without the ability to read or write. She knew that she would be in the beginning grades with her three sisters and other young girls, and she felt too humiliated to consider it. Sadly, she remained at home to help my mother and grandfather.

"My two older sisters did not have any passion for school, although both learned to read, write, and do their numbers. I was the child who was most obsessive when it came to education. I embraced it. I loved to learn. I never stopped reading, seeking answers to my endless questions. Although it was evident to all at school that I was the poorest child to attend classes—I wore clothes so old that there were stains and even holes in the fabric—my teachers overlooked my bleak background and took an interest in my zeal for learning.

"There are many more stories that I could share, for I spent many years working to become a qualified physician. But should we meet again I will tell you more of my story. But here I am today, a doctor.

"From my story, I am sure you understand now why I said that the villagers would have ridiculed anyone for saying that such a poor little girl would succeed in becoming a medical doctor!

"I am married now to a fine man who loves our one daughter as much as he loves his two sons. I live for my children, but I also live to help others, to heal the bodies of our Saudi children so that they may go on to learn, to help bring our country into an age where girls do not have to suffer as my mother suffered, or as I suffered, or as so many other young Saudi girls still suffer, young girls I see on a daily basis.

"I am glad to tell my story to you, to good women who are interested in helping our Saudi daughters and sisters. I have been pleased to share with you the story of my determined mother, a woman who never thought of herself but only considered what was best for her daughters.

"My mother was a great woman. She and I came together as one mind and soul to ensure that this Saudi woman who came from the dark ages fought her way into the light ages in a short twelve years.

"Carry this thought with you when you leave today. I am the daughter of a woman who could not write her name. I am now a doctor who has the training and skills to save lives. This, I believe, is the biggest miracle from God."

For a short time, the audience was silent, stunned by the story we had heard. But then I rose to my feet and began to clap my hands; soon, every woman joined me. We knew that we were witnesses to one of the most amazing stories we would ever hear: a miracle brought about by a mother's love and the education provided to a young girl who was nearly buried alive in the desert.

I only wish that Dr. Meena's father had been able to rejoice in his daughter's success. He had wanted to take an infant into the desert, where he would have scooped sand with his hands until he had created a hole large enough to hold a tiny baby, and then he would have pushed that sand over the baby so that she would have sucked sand rather than air into her lungs until she had died an agonizing death. What would he have said if he could have seen his highly educated daughter respected by so many?

Dr. Meena walked from the stage to mingle for a short while with the guests. She was instantly encircled by admiring women. She made the rounds without smiling, although I felt her personal warmth toward the world. She is a woman with big goals to accomplish and has no time to waste breaking into a smile!

I managed to speak privately with her before I departed.

This small woman was a giant in my eyes. She lightly touched my arm and said, "Oh Princess, I felt your passion for good reach my heart, even as I stood many feet away from you on that stage. That is why my eyes did not leave your face. Allah was telling me that together you and I will bring many poor Saudi girls to a place in life where they will change our Saudi world." Her eyes searched my face. "Do you agree?"

I felt a chill of premonition: by coming to this meeting and getting to know this woman, I had reached a significant turning point in my quest to change the lives of Saudi women. "Yes, Dr. Meena, yes."

I knew with certainty that Dr. Meena was a great power, a major force, and together we would revolutionize the country we loved and at the same time transform many lives, making the dreams of countless girls come true. Our goal would not require change by force; it would simply be the kind of change that comes from a change of mind. And education is the name of the road that leads to a free future for all. One woman can pass the dream on to

others until all are free. Mother to daughter . . .
sister to sister . . . friend to friend.

# Chapter Six
# Nadia: What is Freedom Worth?

From the outset, I knew that Dr. Meena was an extraordinary Saudi woman who would expand my knowledge of the land ruled by the men in my family. She would also increase my understanding of ordinary Saudi women who strove to survive the gigantic barriers set against them in the kingdom that I loved, a vast tract of desert land united by my own warlike yet famously charismatic grandfather, King Abdul Aziz Al Sa'ud.

My initial bond with Dr. Meena was so strong that before leaving the hospital that day we exchanged personal contact information, something which was rare for both of us. As a princess, I must take care about developing close connections with those who are not members of my family; Dr. Meena had developed a natural distrust of strangers during her childhood, owing to the personal hardships she had endured. But we had both felt an uncommon attachment which sealed our friendship the instant our eyes met as she presented her talk—a monologue so touching and revealing about her strength of character and determination.

I have felt instant connections with strangers on only four occasions. All were notable introductions to unique women who have altered the pattern of my life, though none have had such a profound effect on me as Dr. Meena.

We agreed to talk the following week to set up a second meeting at my palace in Riyadh. When we parted, I spontaneously leaned forward to clasp her shoulder for a heartfelt hug. Dr. Meena instinctively pulled back. I was not hurt by this reaction; I merely smiled because I intuitively felt that I should, very gently and patiently, nurture this friendship. I knew it would be an important one and that it might take time to mature. Generally I am courted by others who desire a friendship with a princess, but this was not the case with Dr. Meena. For some reason, this makes her friendship all the more valuable. I knew that she was not looking for any favors from a member of the royal family, but instead she was reaching out to me in the hope that together we might help women to fulfill their potential.

We drew apart when several other women, all admirers of this woman, rushed to her side. Despite her subdued, almost detached manner, Dr. Meena was certainly a magnet to others.

I said my farewells to my royal cousins and to others at the gathering before walking to the front entrance. The young woman I met previously met me at the door; she was patiently holding my black cloak and veil aloft in her hand. I smiled at her, but frowned at the prospect of donning the dreaded face veil. I really do not mind the abaya that drapes over my body or the scarf that covers my head. Our religion teaches that a Muslim woman should be modest in appearance, but the face veil has nothing to do with Islamic teachings. I wish I knew the man who first adopted the Ottoman Turkish practice of keeping a woman in isolation and veiling her entire body when in public. Whoever that controlling man was, he influenced the men of my land and made it a tradition to control Saudi women, restricting their movements, concealing the outline of their bodies, and cloaking their faces. Today in Saudi Arabia, as in several other Muslim states, the hated face veil is used as a weapon by the clerics and small-minded men to subjugate women and prevent them from leading free lives. With the veil, we are rendered as clumsy as those who ingest drugs or drink alcohol. We often fall when walking, as we cannot clearly see the holes and cracks in our city streets. And, most important, we are often victims of traffic accidents, for when it is dusk we cannot see speeding vehicles coming toward us. And, of course, there is no hope of any woman driving safely if she is forced to wear a black veil!

The young woman at the door began to bid me farewell, but before she did she whispered to me, "Princess, I have been thinking about what you said today, and the stories told by Dr. Meena and the other women. Together you and the doctor have opened my mind. Now I know that I must gather my courage and become unflinching against my brothers and my mother; I must bring an end to the wearing of the face veil and will. I will ask my father to persuade my mother and my brothers to agree that, once and for all, the black veil has no place over my face!"

I smiled approvingly, for here was a young woman who was on the verge of discovering the joy and power of making personal choices. I asked the young woman to keep in touch, and for the second time in one day I gave a stranger my telephone number. Encouraged by this young woman's determination, I walked away with a spring in my step—although I was aware that in awakening a strong spirit, one also awakens disharmony. There would be no peace in the family until the dreaded veil had been thrown away and the girl was treated with the same respect as that afforded to her brothers.

I retraced my steps, making my way back to my driver, the ever-loyal Batara. From behind my veil, I observed a scene I knew little about but which was a very familiar one: I watched Saudi men being trailed by one, two, three, four veiled women. Were these women all wives? Or were they sisters or daughters? One never knew for sure. There was but one certainty: the man was responsible for every decision affecting the lives of the women he ruled. Would his wife remain his wife if she gave birth to too many daughters? If his wife was divorced, would she be allowed to see her children again? Would his wife be allowed to eat meals with him, or be given the scraps after he had completed his meal? Would his wife be allowed to see a doctor if she was ill? Would his daughters be allowed to attend school? If so, would they be permitted to use their education to work and earn money? If one of his daughters earned a salary, would it be taken away by her father, or would he prevent his daughter from purchasing a few personal items for herself? Would the wife have a voice in choosing a husband for her daughters? And would the daughter be granted immunity from marrying an old man she feared and distrusted?

In reality, King Abdullah had less authority over those women, and all the female citizens of Saudi Arabia, than the husbands and fathers of Saudi women.

Such personal dictatorships rule nearly every home in the Kingdom of Saudi Arabia. Every man has the authority to act as a king, unchallenged and without question, under the roof of his home, be it a palace by the Red Sea, a modest villa in a village, or a tent pitched in the desert.

In contrast, I observed the foreign nationals walking confidently along the hospital corridor. Some employees were attired in white or blue uniforms, marking them as doctors or nurses, while others were dressed in civilian clothes, most likely working in jobs in administrative offices. None of the foreign male workers gave me a glance, but many of the female guest workers looked at me with a degree of sympathy in their eyes.

I shocked one woman, who seemed to be staring in pity but for a few moments too long, when I stopped and lightly touched her arm; I told her in English, "You think I love this veil? I hate it. One day I will have a giant veil-burning ceremony in the Saudi desert and I would like for you to be my guest."

She gasped in astonishment as I hurried away down the corridor, feeling good about my pledge to burn veils. I smiled for a long time, knowing that no one would believe the poor girl when she told them about being approached by a black-veiled Saudi woman who was declaring war against the wearing of veils.

When I reached the door leading to the parking area, I saw Batara pacing back and forth. He nodded when he saw me and escorted me back to the car. I could tell he was much relieved that I was now safely back in his care. Batara is a loyal and devoted man, and I was sorry to have caused him concern.

On the drive home, I looked back on my meeting with Dr. Meena and thought about what the future might hold. I also looked forward to meeting up with my husband, who, I knew, had attended an important family gathering earlier that day, although I had no idea what was being discussed at the meeting. I am very inquisitive by nature, so I was eager to hear all about it.

Although we have been married for many years, Kareem and I have a sharing, close relationship; there is an openness that we both enjoy and there are few secrets between us. I still find him to be a very appealing man in manner and in appearance. Other than his graying hair, he has aged very little since the first years of our marriage. He has never gained excess weight, like so many of his self-indulgent cousins, and he has kept a full head of hair, which I like. He has never been the type of man to laze around and he is certainly not boring. During weekdays Kareem keeps occupied with work, so he is intellectually quick, matching the minds of men much younger than his years. Yes, I feel lucky to have such a husband, for he is also a good father.

In contrast, so many of my female cousins claim to have grown weary of the men they married during their teenage years in arranged marriages. I have no such regrets. Although I, too, was very young when Kareem and I married, we have remained well matched.

Kareem and his cousins are the third generation of the Al Sa'ud men who have lived and ruled in a kingdom named for our family. The first generation of rulers started with our grandfather, King Abdul Aziz Al Sa'ud, who united the entire kingdom and then ruled it wisely until he died. His power passed to his sons, and so the second generation took the reins of royal power upon his passing. The second generation of power passes from brother to brother, until there are no brothers left, at which time power will pass to a son. The current ruling generation consisted of my father, Kareem's father, and our cousins' fathers, all of whom took their places in the line of rule. My six uncles, who have assumed the throne, have each been so different from the other that it is sometimes difficult to believe that all share the same father. Our second-generation kings have been King Sa'ud, King Faisal, King Khalid, King Fahd, and now King Abdullah. Next in line will be Uncle Salman, who currently serves as crown prince. All of those I know admire Crown Prince Salman and they believe that when Allah chooses the time, he will make a wise king, as has our uncle Abdullah.

But with the aging of the second generation of princes, few remain as suitable choices for the position of king. Soon the third generation of royals will step into place. When this comes to pass, I fully expect the rights of women to greatly improve, for the younger royals have a more enlightened attitude when it comes to women's freedom.

I was pulled away from my thoughts as we arrived at the gates to my palace. It had been a warm and tiring day and I was in need of a cool, soothing drink.

As soon as I walked into my home I could see Kareem was waiting impatiently for me, and without even asking me about my meeting, he surprised me with news about his meeting, where he had gathered with his royal cousins.

Discarding my veil and robes, I found a comfortable chair and reached for a glass of refreshing fruit juice. From this vantage point, I could gaze approvingly at my husband and finally relax.

It was then that Kareem—who seemed pleased and excited—began to speak: "I have very good news for you, Sultana!" I stared in anticipation: what could this good news be?

"I feel with great certainty that all the problems associated with women will soon vanish—or at least we will soon make better progress." He smiled at me with a sweetness that stirred my love for him. "Our daughter Maha will soon have nothing to complain about, Sultana."

Now I was really interested. "And why is that, my husband?"

"Today I saw the future, Sultana. Yes, I saw the future of Saudi Arabia and I was glad. Darling wife, not one voice was raised in dissent when the discussion touched on the need to bring our daughters and granddaughters into public life. In a circle of twenty-two cousins, all felt that the clerics and the radicals are holding the country back. We are ridiculed, even scorned and laughed at, by the world when stories leak out about the undisputed rights of Saudi men to imprison or kill their wives or daughters, or the insanity of the legal courts when they rule that a woman should be flogged for driving a car.

"It is unbelievable that when Assad's daughter Nashwa—a very bright and capable young woman—enters a meeting where men are present she must be secluded behind a screen so that the men she does not know will not be offended by sitting near a mere woman. Nashwa is an expert in her field, and is known to be one of the most talented in the firm, but Assad says that two or three men in the company are fools and insist that his brilliant daughter be hidden. She is allowed to speak out if she is able to overhear the words spoken, but those same men ask that she keep her voice level and not laugh or make any unnecessary noise. They say they will be excited by the sound of a woman's voice talking happily or laughing—which makes men seem like little more than animals! It is quite ridiculous and degrading to the young woman.

"When Assad heard about it from one of his managers, he ruled from that moment on that Nashwa would sit at the head of the table, at the place of most importance. He has told his daughter to speak up and to say what is on her mind. Assad is going to be rid of any man who objects to his ruling."

For once, I was speechless. I could not believe what I was hearing. For many years, I had pleaded with my husband and my brother-in-law Assad to speak up against the old ways, to use their powerful voices to help women progress in our society. In the past, Kareem and Assad had shied away from defending women, claiming that they did not relish dealing with the problems such conflicts were sure to bring.

When I finally found my voice, I did not praise my husband as he expected; instead, I reminded him, "Where have you been, husband? Have you been sitting under a rock in the sand? How many years have I pleaded for this? If you and Assad had used your princely powers before now, things would have already changed."

Generally Kareem argues with me, but today he just smiled and astonished me with a heartfelt apology. "You are right, Sultana. My brother, my cousins, and I have been wrong. We should have spoken up years ago. Instead, we allowed the stupid-minded men of religion to lead this land. We let our kings deal with the clerics and the radicals without support from the extended family. But never again will our king stand alone. Today we came together and pledged that we would make our support known to our king. Any social adjustments that are not made in the near future will be made the moment the crown passes from the old generation to the new. We will bring massive changes to the kingdom."

"Well" was all I could think of to say. "Well!"

Kareem came to sit by my side and looked at me with tremendous affection. His words when they were spoken were most welcome, although those that are rarely said. "I am glad that we wed, Sultana." He kissed one of my hands, whispering with quiet laughter: "I know the path has sometimes been turbulent, but what a fascinating life it has been." He got to his feet and gently pulled on my hand. "Come, let us go and sit with your mother's picture. I know you love visiting with her."

Later, Kareem listened carefully as I told him about my meeting with Dr. Meena. He seemed taken by her story of struggle and triumph. In reality, I did not believe that Kareem had ever before truly absorbed the magnitude of the problems faced by so many Saudi women. And for the first time since marrying my husband I saw he was a devoted partner committed to the cause I held most dear. I never discovered the reason for this, but the fact that Kareem had suddenly awakened to the importance of the cause of women was reward enough for me.

Several days later I sent a car to bring Dr. Meena to my home. I invited my sister Sara to be present during the visit, and had arranged for Amani and Maha to join us also. I wanted my girls to better understand the lives lived by women who were not part of the royal family, female citizens who did not enjoy privilege and wealth. It was one thing for them to hear from me about the plight of Saudi females, quite another to meet such women themselves.

Regrettably, Amani's female acquaintances were mainly limited to her royal cousins; as for Maha, she had lost touch with the heartbeat of Saudi women since moving abroad.

Soon it was time for our meeting. I was somewhat surprised when Dr. Meena arrived accompanied by a young woman. I recovered from my surprise without saying a word of protest, however, for I trusted Dr. Meena and knew that she would have a good reason for bringing this unexpected guest to my home.

Both women arrived without wearing a face veil, which caught me off-guard, yet made me feel happy. I like women who break the senseless rules forced upon them in my country. Dr. Meena could obviously read my mind, because she promptly explained the answer to my question.

"Forgive our uncovered faces, Princess, but we walked out of my home to enter your chauffeured car. We scandalized no one. I understand that you do not veil in front of your servants and drivers, so here we are, in plain view," she said, gesturing with her open arms.

"No need for explanations. You make me very happy, Dr. Meena," I said.

The young woman accompanying Dr. Meena was called Nadia. She was very attractive, with glossy black hair, dark brown eyes, and a light complexion that reminded me of cream. Unlike Dr. Meena, she was cheerful and I found her to be instantly engaging.

"I hope you do not mind another guest, Princess," Nadia said with a wide grin.

"Certainly not," I replied. "In fact, my sister Sara will be joining us, as well as my daughters, Maha and Amani." I glanced at the clock. "They will be here soon, but for now, please, do come and sit with me. I am anxious to know you both better."

While we waited for tea to be served, Dr. Meena told me about Nadia. "Princess, Nadia will be able to further guide us as to the girls and young women in most need of help. You see," she said as she paused to look at Nadia, "she has access to many people that neither you nor I would ever meet. Nadia is a social worker attached to the hospital where I work. Her job is to discover cases of abuse against children and young women and to help them. Unfortunately, many times she does not have the authority to remove an abused girl out of a home or to have a violent father or brother investigated by the police. But she can pinpoint the most grievous situations so that, together, you and I can step in to relieve psychologically traumatized victims. As a Saudi physician, I can enter into talks with the family. They will listen to me. You have the funds to help defray the family's expenses so that they do not feel the need to force their daughters into marriage so as to obtain dowry money. Together we can make that final push to convince the families to allow their daughters to remain single and in school."

"I see," I said. Nodding, I agreed.

Dr. Meena *was* correct. I had often read about gravely abused females in the English-language newspapers. Many Arabic-language media outlets feared the fury of the clerics, who always supported the abuser rather than the abused, and so they did not report the stories. Reporters do not ever want to bring the attention of those vindictive men to their door. Indeed, I have heard of reporters being arrested under false charges in such cases.

Every time I heard about these cases, I wondered why the girl in question did not receive help prior to being wounded, or even killed in some instances.

I leaned forward. "I am very interested in the girls who are denied an education by their backward-thinking parents. But together you and I can change their lives."

I noticed Dr. Meena and Nadia exchanging a meaningful look. Nadia looked back at me and laughed. "You are looking at one of those girls, Princess," she told me.

At that moment Maha walked into the room. I could tell that she had overslept because she appeared a bit cranky. But when she saw that our guests had arrived, she overcame her tendency to be peevish and instead conducted herself in a lovely manner by warmly welcoming Dr. Meena and Nadia.

When Maha came to my side, I was dismayed that she had chosen to wear a pair of "to the knee" loose shorts and a baggy top that was inappropriate attire for a meeting where other Saudi women would be present. Although Maha considers herself a European these days, she knows that when in Saudi Arabia, she is expected to respect our culture. She was also wearing full face makeup, something unusual for Maha, unless she is attending a formal function. There are times that Maha loves to shock those around her and I assumed this was one of those times.

If Dr. Meena or Nadia was taken aback by Maha's European fashion, they made no mention of it. For that I was glad.

Shortly after Maha's entrance, Amani and Sara arrived together, both completely veiled. Amani's full coverage, however, raised the eyebrows of my guests. While Sara threw off her lightweight veil, scarf, and cloak in an instant, the disrobing procedure was very long and arduous for my daughter.

We all sat and stared openly because the entire process seemed a show. Amani first removed two face veils— she had taken to wearing two veils in case the desert breeze caught her top veil and exposed part of her face. Her headscarf was of the thickest material, so when the scarf was removed her beautiful thick hair had been squashed in a very unattractive manner.

Amani's cloak was of the plainest and most drab fabric because she had recently read that clerics were in agreement that there should be no adornment on any of the cloaks worn by women. She had pinned the cloak in three different places to avoid any accidental opening that might reveal her long dress under her cloak. Removing those pins took a long time because one of the pins had become tangled in a thread.

I understood that the most radical clerics in Islam did not make their wives and daughters double-veil or pin-close the cloaks they wore, but I do not know this for certain. I am not friends with any clerics or with their wives.

Amani gave me a triumphant smile as she slowly and deliberately removed the heavy black gloves that reached to her elbow. I began to squirm because I hated these gloves; I desperately wanted to leap up, take those gloves into my own hands and rip them into tiny pieces. My daughters are now adults, so I have learned to restrain myself from taking such actions; I try to allow them to make their own decisions and their own mistakes.

But Amani knew how I detested her total devotion to the most ultraconservative veiling, and I believed she had taken joy in aggravating me.

Finally, Amani walked back to the entranceway and removed her heavy, black, thick-soled shoes, the most unattractive I had seen in a lifetime of looking at shoes. She deliberately posed her shoes prominently so that no one could miss their unappealing style. She did not remove her heavy black socks, which I knew reached to her knees.

I felt exhausted just watching her, but when she had finished I gave my daughter a heartfelt hug. Despite her eccentric ways, I love her with all the love I possess.

Sara introduced herself to my guests, but both Dr. Meena and Nadia were so astonished at Amani's disrobing display that they were too busy staring at me and then at my daughter in disbelief. I am certain that neither could believe that I had two daughters so outrageously contrary.

Nadia, bless her, sensed my discomfort and went back to our original discussion. She glanced at Sara, Amani, and Maha, and told them, "Dr. Meena and your mother were just discussing how I might be able to assist in helping them to find the girls most in need of help." Nadia smiled at me meaningfully. "Your mother knows that many times it is easier to pinpoint the girls who have been physically abused than girls who have been psychologically abused and are in need of help. She was just asking me about the girls who are denied an education by their backward-thinking parents. And," she smiled, "the princess just learned that she was speaking to one of those girls."

"You?" Maha asked in surprise. Nadia gave the impression of being a girl from a privileged background, perhaps the daughter of a scholar or a wealthy businessman; she came across as if she were someone who had had an easy time getting an education.

"Yes, me. I am that girl. Yet my bad start in life has helped me in my work. It is effortless for me to spot girls in need because I lived that life for so many years. I was nearly denied an education and was destined to be married at a very young age."

"Nadia is a social worker at one of our biggest hospitals," I added with satisfaction.

Maha, who has always spoken out for the rights of women, wanted to know more. She glanced at me in appreciation for having such worthy guests in our home, then asked Nadia, "Can you tell us your story?"

Sara leaned forward. "We are all ready, Nadia, to hear your story."

Nadia's conversational tone remained relaxed, even though she was about to speak of some of the most difficult times of her young life.

"My family is not wealthy, but thanks to the government we live a prosperous enough life. Father owns several huge vegetable and flower farms equipped with gigantic greenhouses, which are hugely expensive. The farms are about an hour's drive outside of Riyadh. The government assists Saudis who have the talent to be farmers to grow vegetables and flowers. My father was approved for government funding and now he is shipping flowers to the Netherlands." She looked around at us and smiled. "Can you imagine it? People are shocked when I tell them that my father supplies flowers to Europe."

I nodded and returned her smile. I knew about those farms. Kareem had told me that one or two of the major princes had felt that Saudi Arabia should find sources of income for our country besides oil. Yet oil is the best resource any country could have, and oil is what we should concentrate on developing. But those two high-ranking princes had spent millions upon millions of dollars investing profits from oil into desert farms. Without water and without proper soil, everything had to be transported to those desert areas. Every flower and every vegetable grown cost nearly five times the price the farmers received from their sales. The government was subsidizing fruit and vegetables so much it was disgraceful. But the pride of the two princes would not let them admit failure. And so government funds were used to prop up a reckless business venture that made no sense. Kareem said it would be best for the government to distribute money to the farmers and ask them to stop growing flowers and vegetables in the desert. But looking at

Nadia's proud face, I knew that at least some Saudi families who would have been very poor were doing well financially; they were pleased that they were producing something.

Nadia continued her story: "I am the last child and the only daughter. Before I was born, my mother had four sons. She received all the pleasure of her life through the lives of my four brothers. She loved me, but not as she loved my brothers. But I was lucky because my father loved me nearly as much as he loved his sons. He never considered the birth of a daughter a bad thing, or that I should not receive a proper education.

"Sadly for me, my mother and my brothers were opposed to everything positive my father wanted for me. While Father insisted that I attend school, just as my brothers had done, Mother was distressed by the idea. My brothers became frantic anytime the topic of my education was raised. They claimed that I would dishonor the entire family with new ideas. They had a horror that I might appear in public— or, for some unknown reason, even on television—without my veil. Mother and my brothers demanded that I marry young and produce children, the one thing they said every woman really wanted. They were determined that I should obey their demands without question. And I was told that if I refused to adhere to their instructions, they would lock me in my bedroom. I would be a prisoner!"

A sad expression crossed Nadia's face. "I do understand my mother's reasoning. She came from a poor family and was not educated beyond the age of ten. She can read, a little. She can write, a little. She is a traditional wife. She was married to my father when she was only fourteen years old, and having a guardian for life worked out for her. She believes that the best life for any girl is to marry young and have a man in charge.

"She depends upon my father to make all her decisions. She has only gone against him with regard to one topic, and that is me. She was determined that I marry young. She had heard from one of her brothers that education makes girls into undesirable wives and mothers, and she believed that education would divert my attention away from family life. She is fond of saying that her mind cannot stray from being a good wife and mother because she knows nothing else. And so Mother pushed until Father agreed for her to arrange a wedding. A young man was chosen for me when I was only fourteen years old and he was nineteen years old. He was the son of one of my auntie's friends, someone I had never met."

Nadia sighed, then continued.

"I wept for days, hiding in my room, protesting about the life I was going to be forced to live. But nothing was going to change my mother's mind, and my father had given up fighting with her and my brothers."

I understood that Maha was suffering; she so wanted to express her opinion, but instead she simply asked, "Are you divorced now?"

"No. Not divorced. One month before the wedding a tragedy saved me. My groom-to-be was racing his car on the highway to his village and he crossed over into another lane and collided with a big truck. He was killed instantly. I was not happy about his death, of course, but I slept the sleep of the saved. I was not going to be forced to marry a stranger and become a young mother with no hope of a free and independent life. Within a month, my mother and my brothers had started asking around for suitable husbands for me, but Father ordered them to stop their search. He thought it was a sign from Allah that I should not be married young, or married against my will. Father arranged for my schooling to continue because he said that the boy's death reminded him that females should have the means to provide for themselves should marriage not work. What if I had been married and was a mother when the young man was killed?

"Although his decision angered my mother, I was allowed to advance to higher grades in school. My grades were perfect, so Father arranged for me to attend college. I graduated with a bachelor's degree in sociology and was quickly offered a job as a social worker; now I spend my time helping girls who have no one to help them. Thanks to Allah that I have a wise father."

Apart from Amani, everyone listening to Nadia's story offered condolences for the death of the young man, and congratulations for her successes in school. And despite her disapproval, even Amani managed to look upon Nadia with kindness, saying, "The Prophet Muhammad is reported to have said, 'To seek knowledge is obligatory on every Muslim, male and female.'" Amani looked at me. "So Nadia's education is sanctioned by God Himself."

"Praise Allah for the wise words of Prophet Muhammad," Dr. Meena said, looking approvingly at Amani for the first time.

Only Allah knows the thoughts in my daughter's mind, but I hoped she was beginning to realize one thing: no one should be wed against their will.

Nadia paused to take a refreshing sip of tea before continuing her tale. Although she had her education, she still lived at home because no Saudi girl would be allowed to live independently.

Nadia soon explained the turn her life had taken: "Although I am educated, my mother and brothers show me no respect. They ridicule my work, telling me that I am spreading bad ideas throughout the kingdom. Thankfully, my three older brothers are married and have careers, so they have less time to concern themselves with my daily life. But the youngest of my brothers still lives at home, and now he has combined efforts with my mother to have me fired from my job. They want me to be helpless so that I will accept another marriage proposal. Since I cannot drive, my brother often refuses to take me to work, making me late. Already my supervisor has spoken to me about tardiness.

"My mother ignores my pleas for help because she is happy when I am unhappy. Her frustration has brought out a violent side I had never seen before. From the moment I return from a long day at work, she is yelling at me to cook the dinner and to clean the house, which she intentionally leaves unkempt for me to tidy. If my cleaning does not meet her approval, and it never does, she will slap my face. She wants my life to be so bleak that marriage will be appealing. But I am determined not to give in."

Dr. Meena spoke. "Please do allow me to speak with your supervisor, Nadia."

Nadia nodded. "If I am about to be fired, I will call on you."

Dr. Meena looked worried. "We must help each other."

I solved the problem. "Nadia, from this day on, I will send a driver and car to deliver you to work, and to take you home from work. You no longer have to depend upon your brother."

"Oh Princess, that is too much," Nadia protested.

"No, it is not enough. Our family has many vehicles and many drivers who spend a lot of time standing around waiting. You will have your own driver."

"How will I explain such a thing to my parents?" Nadia asked.

I saw her point. Since I would not want her family to know about my intervention, her mother and brothers might accuse her of having a lover. If that happened, then her life would be in danger.

"Dr. Meena," I asked, "would you like a car and driver? I will assign one of our drivers to you, and this person will be under your supervision. You can use this service for any purpose, to help yourself and to assist other young women who are stranded without a driver."

"This would be a wonderful solution, Princess. No one can complain if a Saudi female physician at the hospital uses her car and driver to transport young women to work and back home."

Nadia smiled with relief and happiness.

Maha opened her mouth wide, and I knew she was about to go on the attack regarding her opinion that all Saudi women should have the right to drive. If Maha started up, then Amani would join in with her conflicting viewpoint. I was not in the mood to hear another argument between Maha and Amani, so I changed the subject even as I pinched Maha on the leg and said, "Right. This problem is solved, and we shall solve many others. For now, let us walk in the women's garden."

And so we moved from the interior of our palace to the gardens, a restful place where we six Saudi women strolled quietly, admiring the beautiful flowers and the calming greenery. There is an aviary at the back of the garden, and it is always pleasant to watch the chirping birds as they enjoy their uncomplicated lives. They are well fed and loved, as Amani is in charge of training the employees who keep the birds happy and healthy.

It is fun for me to watch Amani's face during such times. My daughter expresses unreserved delight only when she is with her son, or with birds, or beasts. While Kareem had hoped our daughter would grow past her tender love of animals, I realized long ago that my youngest would carry this passion with her to the grave.

We sat on comfortable benches for several minutes, and that was when all of us, other than Amani, made plans to gather again in a week's time for Nadia to provide us with further information about the families she had been appointed to help by the hospital administration. Those whom she could not assist, she would pass to Dr. Meena and me. Together the three of us would help many young girls and women.

Just as Dr. Meena and Nadia said their goodbyes and walked toward the entranceway of my home, Nadia paused to dig into her handbag and pulled out folded sheets of paper. I thought she had some information to give to me, but instead she turned to Maha and Amani, who had gathered around the young woman. Nadia spoke to the girls; although I was unable to hear what she was saying, I could see that she passed the pages to Amani. She then pulled Maha's hand over Amani's, as though creating a bond between my two daughters, and said something else. I was bursting with curiosity but said nothing until the young women had left my home. I pointedly looked at my daughters and asked, "What did Nadia pass to you?"

"Mother, we do not know," Amani said with exasperation. "It is words on paper. Let us sit and read it."

"Yes, of course, daughter."

"That is a good idea," Sara agreed. My sister was excited at this development, too.

Amani, who had always been dictatorial in her manner, retained control of the papers, reading them page by page before passing them to Maha. My daughters are slow readers but, although by now I had become impatient, there was nothing to do but wait. As I have said, as the years have passed I do not deny my daughters the respect they deserve as young women—although there certainly are times when I miss having jurisdiction over them!

Eventually, Maha passed me the first page.

The pages revealed a gripping collection of Nadia's thoughts about the plight of women in Saudi Arabia. I believed that she had written the words to pass to me, if it turned out that she was not encouraged to speak. The pages read as follows:

**How unhappy is the woman who has never known freedom?**

*This is a question I have so often considered. How unhappy is the woman who has never known freedom? What can be given to such a woman to replace freedom? Is material comfort a meaningful enough arrangement?*

Some may believe that it is. After all, that is the "deal" often offered to Saudi women. Keep quiet, do not push for freedom and you will never want for shelter or food. What is not said is that in return for this passive behavior you will never taste the joy of freedom.

I have been a social worker, fully occupied with Saudi families, for the past three years. During these three years, I learned more than I ever wanted to know from the lives of the women I have encountered. I have often questioned what it is that Saudi women are guaranteed that equals a single day of freedom. I believe that nothing can compete with the wonderful feeling one gets from being free to live the life you want to lead.

After much personal experience, thought and reading, I believe that the life for females born in Saudi Arabia can best be described by the opening line in that famous book by Charles Dickens, A Tale of Two Cities. As Dickens described, it really was the best of times, yet it was the worst of times. There was wisdom, foolishness, incredulity, darkness, light, hope and despair. I believe that his words ring true for the plight of Saudi women, too.

Allow me to explain. As a social worker in a hospital, I see the best and I see the worst. The best brings promise to my heart, but the worst causes fear and anguish. It is the best of times for females in Saudi Arabia, for with every success story for a female there is a little pool of hope springing like fresh water from beneath the desert. But this spring of water is deceptive, for we all know there is little fresh water under the Saudi sands. And we know, too, that at any moment this well can become a dry bed of sand because so many Saudi men still do not want their women to be free to live with dignity. So we are happy but nervous at the idea that our little freedoms might soon disappear—they may be pulled from beneath our feet. This has happened before, and not so many years ago. A cousin older than me by 25 years has warned me that Saudi women had hope once before, during the 1970s, when political events came to pass that terrorized our government, those events being the downfall of the Shah of Iran and the uprising at Mecca in 1979. Our royal government sacrificed Saudi women to calm the Saudi clerics. For years after those events, women in Saudi Arabia were hurled back in time when it came to personal freedoms.

It is the worst of times because this hope is confusing everyone and bringing bad behavior out into the open. Saudi women are now thinking and believing that they can enjoy the freedom to study and work and have a little money of their own. Saudi men who do not want their females to have any independence, or even hope of personal liberty, are bursting with a great energy to kill all ideas that lead to freedom for women. It is as if they too feel that the tide might be turning against them and they are fearful of losing control. If they cannot erase hope from their women's minds, then they move to beat this hope from their minds—minds that have only recently started to flower and develop with new ideas and knowledge. I have talked with young women bearing the most grievous physical wounds, young women too terrified to admit that their husbands have beaten them to the point of death because they have expressed the inoffensive desire to continue their education or to work after graduating from college, or because they have hoped to postpone motherhood until they are a little older—perhaps beyond their early teenage years.

140

*In our land, this is the age of wisdom because finally we have a king, King Abdullah, who is using his power to help women. Although I am told that King Faisal was a great king for all Saudi citizens, I was not alive then to witness His Majesty's greatness; it is King Abdullah who is my personal hero. I know that he is doing more than the past two kings did together to ensure a decent and safe life for Saudi females.*

*It is the age of foolishness because there are many young men who reject any progress at all when it comes to females. These "new" religious fanatics, who are mainly young men, are very aggressive and believe it their right to roam the streets and harass any woman walking about, even a woman who is fully veiled. These young men are sitting at the feet of the older religious clerics who loudly demand that our country return to a dark time when women were not even allowed out of their homes. When they call for purdah, or isolation for women, they have a mad look in their eyes and such fervor. It is as if they have lost all reason. I have heard a clever saying that a journey of a thousand miles begins with a single step. Every woman can make that first step which will lead to freedom.*

*It is the epoch of incredulity, a period of disbelief, for we now live in an age when events are no longer totally hidden, as they were in the past. When my grandmother and mother were children, they did not hear too many horror stories, although there were whispers. But today it is different. There are written reports in newspapers and those working in hospitals have found their courage to speak. They are the ones who see, firsthand, how traumatic and dangerous life can be for some women. We are learning the evil nature of some men and what those men do to females, for no reason other than wickedness. For example, I have been talking to and trying to console a female who is a close friend to the family of a young child who was raped to death by her father, a cleric. This man was only given eight months in prison for torturing and raping his five-year-old daughter to death. The child's back had been broken during the long sessions of rape. The child's little bowel opening was destroyed by her father's male organ. The little child's bottom was held over a burning flame when the father tried to make the blood stop gushing from her shattered bottom. When this man was given only a few months for this vicious crime against his own daughter, the clerics became incensed, saying that a few months was too much, that any man could do anything to any female member of his family and no one had the right to inflict judgment or punishment against the man involved. While the father had the freedom to inflict agony and torture, the mother did not have the freedom to save her innocent child.*

*This horrible story was reported in the newspapers. But did you know this is still true—any man in Saudi Arabia can inflict violence against any female of his family without worry of true justice? What is a few months in jail for such a crime? Nothing! I fear this will never change because even the government does not want to enter disputes between a man and his family members.*

*But nothing has horrified Saudi women more than the story of this young girl, kept from her mother, beaten and tortured and raped by her father. She was a helpless child and no one could help her. Even after a public outcry, the punishment was incredibly inadequate. I heard that even the jailers sympathized with a criminal who had tortured and murdered a child. He has received no real punishment, as he was treated* as a hero the few months he was in prison. His sentence was a show to hush an angry population. While there are better times for many Saudi females and, yes, good stories to reveal, the bad stories and the horrific abuse neutralizes the joy of good things.

Although I anticipate relating many stories I have discovered during the course of my work in offering support for those involved in traumatic situations, I am ashamed because I know I do not have the full freedom to do the right thing! I must hide my actions and keep my name secret. Should my employer or my family discover that I am revealing these confidences, my life would be destroyed. My mother would take to her bed for many months and my father would question the wisdom of his decision to agree to my education. As for my brothers, they might feel it important to close my mouth, permanently. At the very least I would be shamed into living in a very small social pocket and I would live alone, almost in isolation from all that I hold dear, for the rest of my days.

But I believe that all of us must work together as one power. That is why I am reaching out with a woman I so admire, Dr. Meena, and to a princess who has the power to help some of the young women I know who have nowhere to turn, no one who cares.

If I do not have the freedom to save a single life, then living means nothing to me.

I wept. Sara wept, too. Maha's face was mottled red with anger and frustration. Amani said nothing but simply stared longingly at my mother's photograph; it was as though she wanted to crawl back in time and be in that place with Mother.

"This girl is very wise, and she is correct in what she is saying," I said. "We Saudi women are thrown crumbs of personal comfort in exchange for our freedom."

At that moment Kareem and Abdullah walked into the room, both alarmed to see the women they love in tears.

I was so upset I attacked the only two men within reach.

"Kareem! Abdullah! You two can take your crumbs and throw them into the Red Sea!" I exclaimed, before quickly leaving the room.

Kareem wanted to come after me, but Maha blocked his way, shouting, "Mother is right!" She followed in my footsteps but not before giving her brother a look of disgust.

My poor husband and son were now rigid with shock as the sweetest member of our family, my sister Sara, looked accusingly at them and exclaimed, "For shame, both of you!"

Only Amani could bear to be in the same room as the two men. I heard later that she had shared the pages written by Nadia with them both, and both Kareem and Abdullah were deeply saddened and shocked by the words they read.

Women in Saudi Arabia have experienced many moments when they felt freedom was near, but at the last minute that freedom has been swept aside by the men who rule our lives. But now the time of change had finally come. Courage is contagious, and thousands of Saudi Arabian women had finally found the wisdom and courage to toss aside their mantle of fear and demand freedom, the prerequisite for true happiness.

# Chapter Seven
# Lessons from Those We Love

Kareem has always admonished me about Maha's animosity toward the male sex, as I raised our son and two daughters in an atmosphere where I habitually questioned the customs of our own country. Each of my three children interpreted the same lesson lectured by their mother in a different way. From the time they were small children, I have never stopped advocating that every Saudi, male or female, must have state protection to live with freedom and dignity, and that no man should be held in higher esteem than a female.

My eldest child, Abdullah, fully absorbed my lesson of equality. As a result, my son clearly has a high regard for women; that is to say, he respects females in the same manner he respects males. This concern for others, whether male or female, has helped to make him into a wonderful son, a loving husband, and a wise father.

Maha, my eldest daughter, listened carefully to her mother's opinions but did not blindly accept my view that change must come to our country. Instead, she looked around her to see how females were schooled in comparison with males. Too often she saw evidence that her female friends were mistreated by their fathers and brothers. Maha came to the conclusion, as far as the government and most Saudi men were concerned, that females in her country counted for little. Since Maha is female, this did not sit well with her. As a teenager, she believed that if she focused all her energies on fighting for the rights of women she would succeed in making Saudi Arabia a favorable living space for females. But the people of my country are not prepared for a girl like Maha, so failure was inevitable. She was saddened to learn of the lost lives of her girlfriends, who were forced to stop their schooling, or were married against their will—girls who suffered in so many ways due to what she considered to be antiquated and unfair practices. Finally, after meeting with disappointment after disappointment, a dejected Maha threw aside the female prison garb of Saudi Arabian traditions and fled to live freely in Europe.

Amani, my third child, appears to have been nurtured by the most conservative clerics rather than her free-thinking mother. She calls for every female to live under the strict rule of a male. She claims to enjoy bestowing on her husband the crown of dictator. While Amani's husband is a most benevolent dictator, and living under his rule is not so difficult, I have often asked my daughter if she would yearn for freedom if her husband were a man who took joy from beating her, or keeping her from her family, or taking a second or third wife, or demanding divorce with full custody of her son, little Khalid. Although Kareem and I would shield our daughter from such a fate, other young women in the kingdom have no such protection. But nothing I say penetrates the thickness of Amani's "anti–freedom for women" view.

As I mentioned earlier, my son is a man who believes that all women should be treated as equal to men. His devotion to his wife Zain and daughter Little Sultana has proven his worth when it comes to female freedom.

In fact, an afternoon tea with my daughter-in-law Zain would bring positive change to our entire family through a circular route when we were inadvertently led to a Saudi woman named Laila.

When Maha and I entered Zain's home, she met us at the door, exclaiming joy at our arrival.

But before telling you about Laila and her impact upon our entire family, I would first like to introduce Zain, as she has so endeared herself to our family. My daughter-in-law is a very unusual Saudi royal woman and now a very important member of our small family. She is pretty, kindly, and unique in a most surprising way—she has been blessed by God with a magnificent singing voice. We were taken aback the first time we heard Zain break into song because we had never heard such an extraordinary voice in our lives.

I will never forget that day. Kareem and I had unexpectedly traveled to Jeddah for something which I no longer recall and while there had decided to visit our newly married son. On our arrival Abdullah explained that Zain had not yet prepared herself for the day, so Kareem and he were sitting with me in the sunroom, facing the blue waters of the Red Sea, when all of a sudden an extremely strong and beautiful voice burst from within the closed doors of the wing where the palace bedrooms were located.

A puzzled Kareem asked his son, "Who is that singing?" Abdullah blushed and said, "I would rather not say, Father."

My heart missed a beat, for I feared that my son had foolishly taken a concubine into his home, something many of the young princes do after they marry the woman of their dreams, little knowing that the only woman who really matters will be so wounded that the marriage will suffer.

"You must tell us, Abdullah," I urged.

"Abdullah," Kareem said in a firm voice, "you must identify this strange woman in your home."

Abdullah stared at his father with what I believed was an amused expression, as one side of his lip curled in a smile. For a moment, I thought marriage might have turned my dutiful son into a rude man. Finally, he spoke. "I will ask if I have permission to tell you," he said, then walked away, his freshly washed and ironed long white *thobe* rustling with each step.

Kareem and I exchanged looks of astonishment. What was going on with our son? Who was this strange woman who had taken up residence in our son's palace? Where was Zain?

Although the minutes felt like hours, Abdullah soon returned with his embarrassed bride. Always prepared for Saudi men, even my own son, to behave in unbecoming ways, I truly dreaded that my son was about to tell me something I did not wish to hear.

Abdullah's serious face broke into a smile when he saw our alarm. "Mother, Father, I would like you to acknowledge the owner of the most beautiful voice in the world, your daughter-in-law."

I took a deep breath and rose to my feet, hugging my son and his wife, while exclaiming, "Where did you learn to sing, Zain?"

"I have never received lessons," Zain explained. "One day when I was a little girl I started singing and over the years my voice has grown stronger." The dear girl was embarrassed and modest. "I only sing when I believe I am alone." She glanced up at Abdullah.

"And I sing for my husband, of course."

Abdullah smiled proudly and I could easily see that my worries had been for nothing. My son and his wife were showing me that they had the greatest of affection for each other. "Then you are one of the rare people who are born with a phenomenal voice."

My husband was overly excited. This is because Kareem is a fan of opera music. He later told me that he truly believed his daughter-in-law could easily win a leading role at the Teatro alla Scala, the famous opera house in Milan, one of the principal opera houses not just in Italy but also the world. Of course, no Saudi family would ever allow one of its daughters to participate in such a public role, but it is nice to think about the day when such a thing will be possible for Saudi females.

Since that day we have made requests for Zain to entertain us, but she is shy about doing so, although there are times when Abdullah will put on background music and encourage Zain to entertain the family. Her unique talent is unknown to the world, as she reveals her pleasing voice only to our family. Even her brothers are unaware of her exquisite talent, as

Zain says she lived as a shadow to her six brothers in her youth; the family was too busy pursuing boyish diversions to notice the sister's voice.

Zain appears unimpressed by her ability; she says that her husband and children hold most of her heart and singing is nothing more than a pleasant pastime. Thankfully, she makes sincere efforts to be an important part of our family life in a way that has created tremendous love from our side. Physically, she is tall and slender with very pale skin and dark eyes that glow with kindness. She has a bright smile and has endeared herself to us from the beginning of her marriage to Abdullah. I know that my son is very pleased with his wife and therefore his family is equally pleased.

Although Zain was raised in a family more conservative than our own, she appears to feel no bitterness that her parents made it known that her life was felt to be less important than that of her brothers. She remembers many melancholy moments while growing up feeling undervalued, but, unlike most females thus mistreated, she holds no animus toward her family, or our culture and country. Thanks be to God that Zain was educated through high school and she has some interest in the world outside her own life, for my son would become bored with an uneducated wife concerned only with her hair, jewelry, fashions, and furnishings. Zain is very different from most of our royal cousins, as she is unified with her husband in caring about the plight of others.

Sadly, due to the way women in Saudi Arabia are viewed by men, most females have little opportunity to participate in public life—even those women who are keenly interested in bettering our situation.

As far as the royal women are concerned, none have worries when it comes to the necessities of life. I have discovered that most of my royal cousins care only for the valuable possessions that their tremendous wealth can provide. I recognize that life is empty and dull when one thinks only of oneself and I am so very relieved that this selfish attitude does not apply to Maha, Amani, Sara, Little Sultana, Zain, or me.

Zain's marriage to my son came about as a stroke of terrific luck. Although we had heard of Zain's family, we knew nothing personal about Zain until my sister Sara attended the wedding of one of Zain's aunties, whose husband had divorced her to marry a beautiful singer from Egypt. That exciting singer was the talk of the wedding, Sara said, and she felt so sorry for the abandoned wife, who was marrying yet another royal cousin well known for his tremendous love for any woman he could snare. Sara's soft heart felt so bad for the females of the family that she spent extra time chatting with all the women of that branch. While most of the women were nice enough, once Sara had had an opportunity to enjoy a brief conversation with Zain, she was impressed with her appearance and her quiet dignity. Sara returned from the wedding, reporting directly to me that she had met an exceptional young woman. She held my shoulder and stared into my eyes, telling me, "Sultana, I know with my whole heart that your son will have an attraction for the pretty Zain."

Abdullah was at a turning point in his life and he had mentioned that he would like to meet someone special and settle into domestic life with a wife and children. Since males and females still do not mingle socially in Saudi Arabia, there is no easy way for those of a marriageable age to come into contact with very many members of the opposite sex. After Abdullah made his wishes known to me, I began to carefully observe royal female cousins of a certain age whenever I attended social functions. I had not met with success, as I am a mother who wants only the best for her son. No woman I met was educated enough, or nice enough, or beautiful enough, for my only son. Of course, Amani had four or five extremely religious friends who she claimed were perfect for Abdullah, but none of us could trust Amani's recommendations. Abdullah was not of the mind to marry someone who would be harping at him to pray every moment of the day; he has an easy, caring disposition, and is a believer and a genuinely good man.

After Sara's recommendation, she and I invited Zain's mother to Sara's home for a visit. This arrangement is not unusual in the royal family, for all females tend to love matchmaking.

Zain's mother was initially reserved; in my country, mothers of eligible daughters generally behave in this manner in order to indicate that their daughter has so many suitors that their social calendar is booked for weeks. Knowing this, I did not fret when it took a week for Zain's mother to accept our invitation.

The week passed quickly, and I was struck by admiration and delight rather rapidly after meeting Zain. Although I had no in-depth knowledge of her character, I agreed with Sara that Zain was beautiful but, most important, she was *interesting*. I know from my experiences in life that an interesting personality is one of the most important ingredients when it comes to forming a lasting marriage. Beauty alone does not hold attention for very long, as there must be a peg of unique personality traits from which to hang a marriage.

The family approved the idea of my showing a picture of Zain to my son. At first Abdullah pulled back, for he was nervous about such a commitment, but after studying her image for many long moments, he brought a big smile to my face when he said, "Mother, I see something *interesting* in her face that has touched me and created a desire to meet this woman."

With his words, I knew that my son was approaching marriage with the correct attitude, to find a wife who would interest him in the years after the initial physical attraction had calmed.

Both families then decided that it was appropriate for Abdullah and Zain to enjoy a supervised meeting at Sara's home.

The meeting surpassed my son's expectations. Although I chatted amiably with Zain's female relatives, I kept a sharp eye on my son. Zain was shy and Abdullah was confident, which is not that unusual in most cultures of the world. The words they quietly exchanged with each other I have never known, but after the social meeting ended Abdullah asked to speak with Kareem and me together, and said, "Please, this is the right woman for me. Do arrange the details, so that we can marry."

And so we did. We were pleased that neither Zain nor her mother feigned disinterest. So many mothers and daughters carry on with this charade, thinking that if they pretend to be less keen they will receive an increase in the dowry offer, although in this case

both families are of the royal family and Zain's family
was not in need of money. The truth was that Zain
was attracted to Abdullah, just as my son was
attracted to her.

And so a happy day came to pass when my son
married his cousin, Zain Al Sa'ud, in an unpretentious
but meaningful wedding ceremony held in a modern
hotel in Jeddah. As with most Saudi weddings, women
came together at the hotel ballroom, while men
celebrated under magnificent white party tents set up a
few miles outside Jeddah on the way to Mecca, our
holy city.

The event was perfect and, although I wept,
they were tears of joy and not sadness. The words are
trite, but they are meaningful, for I knew that I was
not losing my son—I was gaining a daughter.

And so Kareem and I increased our family
numbers with the lovely Zain, an important family
member who would soon provide us with greatly
anticipated grandchildren. I am so thankful that I
have always experienced a friendly relationship with
my son's wife. I know that she is a wonderful wife to
Abdullah as well as a devoted mother to her children.
If I were given the opportunity to select from all the
princesses of Saudi Arabia, I could not find a more
lovely friend and wife for my son.

But not all Saudi women are as fortunate as
Zain. The number of Saudi girls who never marry is
increasing. My own daughter, Maha, is one of these
women.

And so it came to be that it was through Zain and Little Sultana that Maha met Laila, a young Saudi woman whose personality appeared very similar to my own daughter's. As we were exchanging proper greetings with Zain, Little Sultana merrily skipped into the room, her long hair bouncing. I instantly noticed that it had been arranged in an unusual style of coiled curls held in place by tiny animal-shaped diamonds. I was exclaiming over her hairstyle when Maha stooped to examine Little Sultana's new hairdo. She questioned Zain: "Who styled Little Sultana's hair? It's very elegant."

"Mother led me to this new hairdresser. Her name is Laila."

"Is she Lebanese?" Maha asked. Her question was sensible, as it has been our experience that Lebanese women are the best hairdressers and makeup artists, as there are a number who have set up shop in Saudi Arabia hoping to make their fortune should some Saudi princess discover their talents and employ them as personal coiffeurs, perhaps to live in a palace and accompany a princess who travels all over the world to visit and stay in her various palaces.

When I was a young girl, hair salons and beauty parlors were prohibited by the Saudi religious police, who maintained that it was against Islam for a woman to enhance her beauty and that women should be happy with the way God made them. In those days it was not unusual to spot groups of unruly *mutawas* creating chaos by storming establishments for women. Often those mean-eyed men would detain all the women in the shop, customers who desired a beauty treatment and workers who were earning money to support their families by bringing joy to women who wanted nothing more than to have their hair styled, their eyebrows plucked, and their nails polished.

But we are blessed that ideas are changing in Saudi Arabia, and nowadays it is not uncommon for women to spend an afternoon at a beauty salon.

Little Sultana unexpectedly responded to the question Maha had addressed to her mother, Zain: "No, Auntie Maha. Laila is one of us."

I smiled proudly at my adorable granddaughter, knowing what she meant. "Really? She is Saudi?"

"Yes, a Saudi girl."

"Well, well, the world is changing," I announced happily, for it was most unusual for a Saudi girl to work serving others. While Saudi girls often seek careers and routinely work as teachers, doctors, and dentists (specializing in women and children), few families will allow a daughter to take on a job where she must serve others, by becoming, for example, a nurse, hairdresser, or housekeeper.

However, in the past year, new jobs had opened up in shops for women, such as the lingerie shops, and in high-end beauty establishments, although this was the first time I had heard of a Saudi hairdresser.

Zain looked approvingly at her daughter. "Sultana is right. This Saudi girl is one of us, and she has a big following in the royal family. Laila is quite inventive with her comb." Zain made a cute expression with her wide eyes and perky lips, then continued. "She even made Auntie Medina's thin locks seem full. I could not see one speck of scalp under her latest hairstyle."

"No! Really?" Maha retorted.

Females in the royal family familiar with Medina felt bad for her as, since childhood, our cousin has been afflicted with "lightweight," thinning hair that scarcely masks her wrinkled scalp. Not having ample hair is a big problem for any woman, but more so in our Arab society. Although when we are in public our hair is concealed under a headscarf, in private this is not the case. At female gatherings most display their locks proudly, as there is much attention given to a woman's hair. Hair is worn long and in a variety of elaborate styles, so as to receive compliments and attention.

But poor Medina is always reluctant to remove her headscarf, for obvious reasons. People can be cruel in my culture, and it was not unusual for the younger children to stare, point, and laugh at the nearly bald Medina, even when their mothers were twisting their ears, pinching their arms, or threatening some other such violence.

Medina had consulted a variety of doctors in the Arab world and in Europe, but none could solve the problem. One British physician claimed that she was born with an autoimmune disorder and that she must accept her fate. A patronizing Egyptian physician said the condition was triggered by the stress of living the life of a Saudi woman. A group of physicians brought into the kingdom from Syria for special consultation debated whether or not she was unconsciously pulling on her hair.

We admired Medina because her determination to solve her hair problem has never flagged. Lately, we had heard that she had hired three female hair therapists to rub her scalp for four hours each day with heated coconut oil to increase circulation to her scalp and also to plump up her hair follicles with coconut nutrients.

"Does this Laila have a special trick to help ladies with seriously thinning hair?" Maha inquired.

Little Sultana bounced from one foot to the other, bursting to speak. When Zain nodded and smiled, my granddaughter laughed and retorted, "Yes, Miss Laila said it was simple, and all one had to do is remember CCBB."

Mystified, I asked, "CCBB? What does that mean, darling?"

"Yes. Tell us the secret of the lettering, Little Sultana," Maha said with a grin.

Little Sultana glanced at her mother with a bewildered expression. "Mummy?"

Zain laughed aloud. "You precious girl, you can remember." Zain then reminded her, "Cool . . ."

"I know, I know." Little Sultana announced the words clearly: "Cool Cut and Brush the Boar!"

"What?" Maha laughed.

Zain told us. "It's a simple way for those with thinning hair to encourage growth and stop thinning. Laila says that one with thinning hair must remember the words *cool, cut, brush,* and *boar,* meaning cool your hair, don't heat it. Cut your hair and don't try to wear it long. And finally, brush against your natural part with a boar bristle brush."

"How clever," Maha murmured. "This Laila sounds very intelligent."

"She is that," Zain replied. "She is a Saudi girl who has lived a life with many knotty problems, like so many Saudi females. But she has fought oppression and followed her dream of owning her business and living as freely as a woman can live in this country. Laila is a winner."

I looked at Maha and saw her eyes shining with curiosity. Weeks later I recalled Maha's words as the four of us wandered down the hallway and into the sitting area. "Zain, I would like to go with you and Little Sultana to your next appointment with this Laila."

Over the next few weeks, Maha surprised us when she postponed her return trip to Europe several times. One day when she believed that I would be away in Jeddah with her father, she sent one of our drivers to bring the hairdresser Laila to our home, as she had invited the girl to spend several days at our palace.

Maha was unaware that I had not left the palace to accompany Kareem to Jeddah but instead was in my bedroom apartments suffering from a stomach bug I had contracted.

The sounds of women's lively voices and loud laughter drifted to my hearing, and for a moment I believed I was in a mirage of happy women, as I was not expecting visitors and thought for sure everything was a result of my imagination. When I overheard Maha's distinct voice, I realized that she was most likely chatting and laughing with some of our housemaids, as my daughter has always enjoyed discovering the lives of those living with and working for us. Wishing that my daughter was a girl who was not quite so boisterous, I turned over to lie on my stomach and covered my head with a pillow.

A few hours later, after hearing a second voice unfamiliar to me, my curiosity drove me to get out of bed and freshen myself and make an appearance to see who was visiting with my child.

Voices remained forceful until I tapped on the door of Maha's private sitting room, and then all became silent. Maha surely must have crept to the door, for I had heard nothing of her footsteps before she cracked open the door and peered in surprise at my eyes staring at her.

Knowing her mother well, and mindful that I would not go away until the mystery guest was known, Maha reluctantly opened the door. "Mother, I thought you were in Jeddah with Father."

"No, I have a tummy bug, darling. I did not feel like travel." I attempted to peek around my daughter's large frame to identify her company, but she is a robust girl at least six inches taller than her mother and heavier by twenty kilos. In our family, Kareem, Abdullah, and Maha are large and strong, while Amani is more like me physically, small and light.

I stepped into the room to see a vibrant young woman with a huge smile sitting sipping from a cup.

I stood at a distance, but welcomed her with a smile, saying, "Please excuse me for not greeting you properly, but I would not wish to share this tummy bug with anyone."

"You are most kind, Princess," the young woman responded, as she stood and lowered her head in acknowledgment.

"Mother, I would like you to meet my friend, Laila, the talented hairdresser who looks after Zain's and Little Sultana's hair."

"*Assalam alaykum* [Hello and peace be upon you]. So, you are the Laila who has so pleased my daughter-in-law, and my granddaughter." I chuckled as I recalled the story told us by Zain. "And the amazingly talented hairdresser who has made my cousin Medina's life so much more agreeable. We have fretted with Medina over her lack of hair since she was a child."

Laila smiled. "You are most kind to say so, Princess."

Maha insisted that we leave her apartments and go into our family sitting room, where she ordered light snacks, tea, and soft drinks from the palace kitchen. I sat at a distance from the girls, not wishing to spread my germs, but I selected a good seat so that I could see both clearly.

"Laila," I said, "I would enjoy knowing your story. I hear that you are an unusual girl who has overcome the obstructions of Saudi Arabia, the system that works against women trying to fulfill their dreams." I glanced at my daughter. "Maha might have told you that I lend support to females who have a strong desire to break out of the ordinary Saudi mold."

"No, she did not mention that," Laila replied.

Maha raised her eyebrows and shot me a pleading look. I knew that my daughter wished for me to vanish back into my bedroom and leave her to enjoy her company in peace, but I have always been a mother who takes a strong interest in the friends of her children and I have accepted that I will never curb this curiosity. So I leaned back into my chair and became comfortable, as I sipped hot green tea in the hope that it would settle my stomach.

"You seem so young, Laila. May I ask your age?"

"Yes, Princess. I was twenty-three years old nearly a year ago."

"Are you in college?"

Maha protested, "Mother, please. You know that Laila owns her own shop and is working. How could she be in college?"

"Oh, sorry. You are right, daughter."

"Do not worry, Maha. I am happy to tell your mother about my life," Laila assured my daughter, who was growing impatient. Knowing Maha, I knew that she would soon grab her friend by the hand to flee from me.

"You are right, daughter." I glanced at our guest. "Sorry, Laila, but I heard enough about you from Zain to arouse my interest." I laughed. "I so love it when Saudi girls are able to escape from the clutches of men, who try to prevent women from following their dreams."

"It was a man who helped me to realize my dream, Princess."

I was not as surprised as some would think, as over the past few years a number of educated Saudi men have begun secretly helping their daughters to achieve education and then to find employment. To my disappointment, Saudi mothers and sisters are too often the main culprits when it comes to discouraging their daughters from achieving an education and realizing their ambitions. The women of Saudi Arabia who are interested only in marriage and motherhood are fast becoming the biggest obstacles to females who are aching to escape such bondage. It is as though some Saudi women fear female success and achievement almost as much as most Saudi males. If they are satisfied living under the strict guardianship of a man and are content to greet each day without education and work, they fail to understand that, for others, this life is little more than a prison sentence, something to be endured. In other words, it is no life at all.

I understood this discouraging phenomenon better than most, as my daughter Amani would have chained her sister Maha to the old ways had she the power to do so, while my son Abdullah, who is an enlightened young man, fights for his sister's right to make her own choices.

Although I would like nothing better than for my Maha to share my feelings on marriage and children, I learned years ago that this was never going to happen. In the past, there were moments when I experienced great distress that this was so, but since my daughter is now an adult and lives in Europe I do not dwell on this situation. Kareem, I am sorry to say, has never accepted Maha's lifestyle, but at least he does not create strain in the family, as my husband has a marvelous capacity for burying his head in the sand and pretending that it is nothing unusual that our daughter refuses any discussion regarding marriage and family.

Although I embrace the possibility of change, suddenly Saudi life seems rather topsy-turvy to me. With the hint of change coming for females, some men are becoming our friends and supporters, while the women who should be helping us are opposing us.

I pushed for more information, much to the dismay of Maha.

"You have so impressed members of my family, Laila, that I would be honored to hear your story. Will you share it with me, please?"

Maha feigned a deep sigh and nestled into the thick cushions of the sofa. "All right, Mother. Laila, just tell her what she wants to know, otherwise we will be here all day while Mother picks and probes."

Laila looked in surprise at my daughter's impertinence. Saudi children do not usually speak in such an insolent manner to their parents. I smiled at Maha, then Laila. "Do not worry, I have an unusual relationship with my children, Laila. I want to know exactly what they are thinking, even when they are irritated with their long-suffering mother."

Laila looked at Maha. Her expressive eyes told me that she did not approve of Maha's rude conduct with her mother. Perhaps this girl would be good for my daughter, I thought, and would remind her of her good fortune in having a mother who loved her beyond reason.

"I'm really an ordinary girl, Princess," Laila declared. "Most of my friends in school are like me, with most of them wanting a say in their future rather than walking the stale path of sacrificing everything in life to serve a man and to bear his children."

I nodded, aware that education has a way of freeing girls from the belief that only a man and his wishes are important.

"Like most Saudi girls, after graduation from high school, my parents, both my father and my mother, yearned for me to accept a marriage to a man I did not know. They had several men in mind from my father's village, all too old for a girl of seventeen, and I did not want such a marriage. I fought against marriage. Just as they were about to force the situation, my mother relented to my pleas, but my father became more firm. He is a man who believes that women should be bonded to a man and to a house filled with little children. Otherwise, he says, a woman will cause disgrace to the family.

"I spent most of my days in bed with depression so severe that my mother became concerned that I might take my own life. Although she wanted me to marry and to produce grandchildren, her fear for my well-being overcame her desire to force her daughter to marry. But she was helpless, unable to overpower my father's wishes."

Laila paused for a long time, blinking back tears. Maha patted her hand in a soothing manner and looked angrily at me, as though I were responsible for the traditions and laws governing women's lives in Saudi Arabia.

My daughter spoke through gritted teeth, "Sometimes I hate my own country."

"It is all right, Maha," Laila said. "I am sorry, but I become emotional remembering those difficult times when I was so close to everything I did not want. I was terrified that I was going to be forced to submit to a strange man who would take me away from my parents and compel me to give in to his every wish. Then, to my complete surprise, my oldest brother came to my rescue. Lucky for me, he works at Saudi Aramco in Dhahran."

I smiled and nodded, reflecting for a moment on Aramco, which is the Saudi company that owns the world's largest oil fields, the Ghawar Field and the Shaybah Field. It is currently the most valuable company in the world, according to financial experts, with a value as high as $10 trillion. The company traces its origins to the 1920s, when the United States government was seeking sources of oil from the Middle East. The Standard Oil Company of California struck oil on Bahrain in early 1932, and that event brought them to the mainland of Arabia the following year, when our government granted the Americans a concession to explore oil in our newly formed country. After four long years of failure, oil was found in Dhahran, at a well named Dammam No. 7, since it was the seventh site drilled.

The Americans built their own little gated city in Dhahran approximately eighty years ago, a city formed for the single purpose of administrating the Saudi oil business. It is an important place, where men and women are not kept separate from one another. Most modern-minded people in the world find it unbelievable that even in 2014, in most of Saudi Arabia, women are believed to be so lustful that they are kept separate from the men in all walks of public and even private life, but that is not the case in Dhahran Aramco. The little community was a good lesson for Saudi men, in my opinion.

I had lapsed into such deep thoughts that Laila had ceased to speak. The dear girl was respecting my silence. "Go on," I encouraged her, then asked, "Does your brother live in the Aramco compound?"

"Yes, he does, Princess. It was there that he was exposed to a more modern view of life, with men and women working beside each other. My brother saw firsthand that women could be a productive part of society and that they do not spend their time and energy attempting to seduce every man they see, as so many of our men stupidly believe.

"The attitude shown toward women at the company changed my brother and transformed my future. After his experience with the Americans, he did not accept an arranged marriage but in fact, fell in love with a Saudi girl who was working at the company. She is an unusual Saudi woman in that she is strong-willed and commands respect. She does not accept abuse from anyone. His wife bore him a daughter and a son, and to our amazement his favorite of the two children is his daughter. Working in a company where women are respected, and married to a woman he loved, my brother had slowly awakened from the 'Saudi sleep' so common to men of our country, where they do not even notice the unhappiness enveloping the women around them.

"And it came to pass that I was spared a miserable life. When my brother learned of the ongoing struggle between my father and me, he came to our home and showed an interest in my thoughts and feelings. The biggest shock of my life was when my brother asked what would make me happy, what ambitions did I hold? I was not sure how to respond, but then he remembered that for my entire life I was known throughout the extended family as the girl with a natural talent for arranging elaborate and beautiful hairstyles. I was the one who had always fashioned the hair of my cousins on their wedding days. I was delighted to tell him that my greatest joy was working with women to enhance their looks. In particular, I took great pleasure in creating beautiful hairstyles, for that is where my true talent lay.

"I could see that he was thinking deeply of everything I had said. He seemed genuinely concerned for me and my future happiness, and he asked that I give him some time to seek out a solution. After speaking with me, he talked for a long time with our mother and told her that it was her duty to keep her daughters safe and that I should not be married against my will.

"A boulder of strength passed from him to my mother, as his words fortified my mother's will to speak back to her husband, my father. My brother obviously met with my father and gave him a similar message; Father became angry and distant, but he also ceased all talk of marriage. Most important, my brother gained guardianship over me when he asked my father to transfer guardianship to him. So nothing has given me more freedom than to have a sympathetic guardian, who is my brother.

"A month later my brother came for a second visit. Never shall I forget that day. He looked into my sad face and whispered, 'Do not worry, sister. I will run with you and together we will catch your dream.'

"My brother had returned with a well-researched plan. He had met with various people to find out the legal steps he must take to open a small business. He recognized that my natural talents drew me into the circle of those who establish and work in the female beauty business. He was glad that the clerics had become less aggressive against such establishments in recent years, although he said that one young cleric in training had told him that women should be happy with the way God had made them. He disagreed with the idea that women should be allowed to style their hair and wear makeup as such a thing meant that they were going against God!

"My brother tried to soothe that cleric but had little luck in doing so. My brother believes that such thinkers have a difficult time pulling their thoughts out of the gutter.

"My brother was happy to learn that Saudi Arabia's Technical and Vocational Training Corp (TVTC) had announced that they would soon issue business licenses to women to open and operate beauty salons. Since the Kingdom of Saudi Arabia has many unemployed women looking for work, this is a method to help those women find jobs. And so he found a small outlet in a strip of buildings designated for business and he purchased one.

"Once this was accomplished, my brother invited me to dinner to celebrate. That is when he presented me with the business license, which stated that he was the owner of a beauty salon. He assured me that it was in name only, that the beauty salon was mine to organize. He gave me the start-up funds and left the business to me. Since he was appointed as my guardian, my brother signed papers giving me the authority to open up a bank account at one of the women's banks in the city. So I am now allowed to handle the money I earn."

I was happy to hear this news, as I have heard numerous complaints from young women who are given permission to work but never allowed to collect a salary. Most fathers in Saudi Arabia demand that their daughters' salaries be given to them. So many girls never see a single riyal they earn, which is a great crime, but so long as every Saudi girl is required to be ruled by a male guardian nothing can be done.

Laila sighed loudly. "Now, three years later, the business is thriving and I am so happy that I am the first person in our home to rise from my bed and many days even prepare breakfast for all in our home before my brother drives me to my business.

"There is such joy in my heart, Princess. When I gaze at my six-chair salon, with its walls covered in colorful photographs of beautiful women with luxurious long, dark hair, I can barely believe that I am the one who has made this possible. Most pleasant for me is the realization that the four divorced Saudi women who work in this salon are supporting their little children with their earnings. This fact adds sweet cream on the cake of life.

"So I am a Saudi woman who respects and admires her brother. Had he not stepped forward to help me, I would be without a single riyal to my name. I would be helpless to advance my dreams or to facilitate other women with work so they might provide the basics of life. I would most likely be in a loveless marriage to a man who would think it his business to follow my every move. Going to market, I would be forced to follow his footsteps, all the while stumbling along covered by a full veil. I would be his slave, cooking his food and cleaning his house, and delivering a baby every year. I would be miserable because I am not yet ready to be married. Although I know I will marry one day, now at least I can taste freedom and have some time to organize a business. I can buy my own clothes and even purchase gifts for my family members.

"Operating this business is a full education, in my opinion, because Saudi Arabia is filled with people from all over the world who come into our country to work. The women from these foreign lands long to visit a place where they can have their hair styled and their fingernails painted. While my employees and I work our magic to make them even more beautiful than they are, these women tell us many things about their home countries."

Laila glanced at Maha. "I am discovering that there are many scandalous things that occur in these foreign lands, unusual situations between men and women that create a lot of gasping and giggling in my little shop. I am learning that there is a big world I know nothing of, but, as time passes and I save funds for travel, I would like to leave Saudi Arabia and explore other lands and other cultures. Who knows, I might one day become mischievous just like those girls from other cultures so different from my own, something that I would have never considered until I became free to think my own thoughts. Without operating my own business, I would have never known that girls, too, can have fun and enjoy freedom.

"And, that, Princess, is my story."

"And what a wonderful story it is, Laila," I replied. "Now you can plan your future without fear of any man. I pray to Allah that every female born in our country may achieve her personal dreams." I glanced at my daughter, who was gazing at Laila with an intense expression I had never before seen. "Maha?" I interrupted.

"Oh, Mother, sorry. I was thinking how unfair it is that any woman should have to endure fear and trauma such as Laila did, only because she prefers to postpone marriage while she pursues a career."

"Yes, you are right, daughter."

"Mother, I believe that you should rest until your stomach has calmed. Shall I walk you to your quarters?"

My oldest daughter has always been blunt, and I took the hint that she desired privacy to discuss these points with her friend, so I excused myself and returned to my private quarters to rest. For several hours, I reclined in bed and attempted to read *Memoirs from the Women's Prison*, a thought-provoking book written by Egyptian physician, feminist, and author Nawal El Saadawi, a highly respected woman once imprisoned in Egypt's notorious Qanatir Women's Prison. Nawal is one of my heroes. But even her book could not keep my mind from dwelling on Maha and how my daughter had exchanged expressions of affection with Laila.

What was going on with my daughter?

I was to discover the answer soon enough.

Several weeks later, Kareem returned home in a rare rage. I was sitting at my dressing table, applying kohl to my eyelids and eyelashes. Kohl is an ancient cosmetic for the eyes, used by many Middle Eastern and African women. Kareem so startled me that I spread kohl over my forehead rather than on my eyelids.

"Kareem, husband, what is going on?"

"Sultana, did you know what Maha is planning?"

"No. What is our daughter planning?" I asked, although I felt a dread working through my chest and stomach.

"Maha is taking her hairdresser with her back to Europe."

I sat without speaking, remembering those affectionate glances and wondering if they were a result of forbidden thoughts or were perhaps nothing more than two young women enjoying a normal friendship. But never would I have expressed my concerns to my husband.

"Sultana? Did you know about this?"

I answered truthfully, "No, Kareem. No. You are telling me this information. I knew nothing about such a trip before this very minute."

"Our daughter is crossing a line, Sultana. She can do as she pleases when in Europe, but I expect different conduct when she is in Saudi Arabia."

"A line? I do not believe that Maha has crossed this line you are speaking of."

"She is taking a Saudi woman out of the kingdom."

"Surely the woman's guardian has given her permission. Does she not have the right to visit Europe? In fact, when I met the young woman she expressed a sincere interest in traveling, something she has never before done."

I asked Kareem, "How did you discover particulars of this trip?"

"Amani called me."

"Amani?" I was more than surprised. Maha was not known to divulge her secrets to her younger sister.

"Amani said she had accidentally stumbled across some airline tickets made out to Maha and her hairdresser."

I recalled that Amani had visited our home a few days earlier and had asked if Maha was in her quarters. Maha was away at the time, and I had thought nothing of Amani's curiosity about her sister until I later walked into Maha's rooms and found Amani searching through one of the wooden storage chests that hold many of Maha's private papers. Amani had said she was looking for some photographs to show her husband, but now I knew that Amani had been spying on her sister.

"I am sure there is a good explanation, Kareem. As I mentioned, I met this hairdresser Laila and she is a lovely woman. She works hard at her craft and is highly respected. She and Maha became friends and nothing more. You know how Amani thinks, husband. She sees wrongdoing when there is no wrongdoing. Please, let us wait and speak to Maha."

At that moment Amani rushed through the door, her abaya and veil floating behind her; she was moving so fast her Islamic garments were falling off her body.

"Mother," Amani screeched, "did you know that Maha has taken a lover?"

To my despair, Maha arrived at that exact moment and overheard her sister's accusing words. Maha grabbed her sister by her long hair and yanked her across the room. Amani screamed loudly and Kareem and I had to move fast to separate our daughters.

My anger was directed at Amani, while Kareem was upset with Maha.

"Apologize to your sister," I ordered Amani. "You cannot make such reckless accusations!"

"Daughter, you will disgrace us all," Kareem said in a cold voice to Maha.

As Allah is my witness, that was the moment Abdullah, Zain, and Little Sultana called out from the hallway. They could hear the commotion and were very alarmed.

"Do not enter this room," I shouted to my son, as I pulled on Amani's ear, which produced a scream from my daughter. Of course, my demand and our shouts created such anxiety that Abdullah did not obey but instead pushed through the door and hurried into my rooms, perhaps thinking that intruders were in our home and I was trying to warn him to run away with his family. We had agreed in the past that it would be best for someone to sound the alarm should we ever be in danger of a kidnapping.

My son was shocked when he saw his father, mother, and two sisters in a twisted bundle, each one holding on to another.

"Mother, what is going on?"

My heart plunged in distress when I saw Zain and Little Sultana clutching each other, mother and daughter in a state of fear. When Kareem, Maha, and

Amani also realized that Little Sultana was a witness to our family scene, we instantly pulled away from one another. Everyone was mortified at being thus caught and looked to me to offer an explanation. For once in my life, I could think of nothing that would absolve the embarrassing moment.

Little Sultana shamed us all when she spoke the truth of the incident in her tiny voice: "You were fighting. I saw you." Little Sultana looked from her father to her mother, then to Kareem and finally to me. "You were fighting."

We all fell to our knees, wanting desperately to win back the trust of the most precious little girl in our world. Even Amani was in tears, realizing that she was the one who had created the shameful episode.

Our hearts broke when the darling child looked at us in disappointment; she clutched her mother's fingers and pulled her from the room, all the while shaking her little head while muttering to herself, "They were fighting."

All was explained to Abdullah once his wife and child had returned to their palace. My son felt so strongly about the incident that he returned to our palace within a few hours to meet with Maha. The two met in her private quarters and talked for several hours, so we knew nothing of their conversation.

After his visit, Abdullah came to his distraught parents to express his feelings. My son was rightfully angry that his wife and child had been a witness to our family brawl. Abdullah was flushed with anger as he spoke harsh words about the incident.

"This is all Amani's fault. My sister believes she has the right to tell everyone how to live. I no longer have patience with my younger sister. She needs to mind her own business unless someone is physically harming her, her children, or a member of her family. Please give Amani a message from me, for I do not want to see her anytime soon. On the next occasion she feels the urge to spread a rumor, tell her that she will have to deal with her older brother."

Abdullah had a hard look on his face as he stared at his father, one I had never before seen; he knew the events of that evening had in some way resulted from Kareem's easy acceptance of Amani's unsubstantiated gossip about her sister.

Kareem moved toward his son, who held up his hands to keep his father from showing the affection I knew Kareem wanted to express. Abdullah was not harsh, but he was firm.

"Father, I respect and love you, but I must say these words. You owe your daughter Maha an apology. Once you look into the matter, you will discover that Maha is not in a relationship with the hairdresser. They are friends, only. But if they were in a relationship, you must remember that your daughter is an honest woman who has never hidden her feelings. She does not lie, about anything. She has harmed no one, and she should not be harmed by anyone in this family. Maha does nothing but try to help others to live a life of freedom. That is something you love in Mother. Please find the same love for Maha's work."

My son walked to me and I shuddered, thinking that my son might have critical words for me, too. But instead he gazed at me with a lovely smile and leaned down to give me a tender hug. My son knew that I was a mother who would never turn away from any of my children, no matter their personal choices in life. He also understood that there were valid reasons I did not speak openly with Maha, or anyone in the family. In our culture, a woman who prefers women to men is considered a great sinner who should be severely punished. If such information leaked from our household to the wrong person, who then might involve the clerics, it would be dangerous for Maha to return home for visits.

Our disappointed son departed, leaving his parents so despondent that neither of us found it easy to speak coherently.

In a day's time, we pushed our emotions aside to sit and talk about our children, coming to some important decisions. We agreed that we needed serious meetings with both of our girls. First, we talked with Maha, who easily confessed that she was attracted to Laila but that Laila did not share her feelings. Although Laila had chosen to postpone marriage, her excuse had nothing to do with any physical attraction for another woman because she did not have those feelings. She wanted nothing more than a friendship with Maha.

Maha is a young woman who respects those who are honest and good, and she was happy with an innocent friendship with Laila. She thought it a nice gesture to fulfill Laila's dream to see something of the world, and thus she had invited her new friend to visit her in Europe. Laila's brother, who was her guardian, had signed the travel papers so that Laila could visit

Europe for a month. Laila's assistant, a hardworking girl from Egypt, was going to assume responsibility for the shop while Laila was on a rare holiday.

My husband apologized to Maha, and the two came together closer than ever before because there were no hidden thoughts or ideas. Although Kareem was not pleased to know for certain Maha's feelings about men and women, he said that never again would he disrespect his daughter.

As for Amani, I told Kareem that he should be the one to discuss this business with our youngest, for she is a girl who has always listened to her father and ignored her mother. That meeting did not go so well, according to Kareem, as Amani was petulant, claiming that Maha's business was her business and, besides, she did not believe her sister's words that the relationship was nothing more than a friendship. Even Kareem was exasperated with Amani and said he left her without his usual affectionate farewell.

Another dilemma was what we must do to lessen the sadness of Little Sultana, who had received a major shock upon witnessing a physical fight between family members.

Abdullah smoothed our path, as he advised us that he had sat with his sad daughter and spoken about human imperfections, how sometimes people become overly excited and behave in unbecoming ways.

Little Sultana was not eager to see us for a week or so, but finally she reconciled in her mind that those she loved best were less than they should be, but she would love them still. We were eagerly awaiting her visit, all of us dressed as though we were going to a fine party, when our little sweetheart walked into the room with a bouquet of flowers. She paused, looking at each of us as though she had never met us before, then finally hurried to Maha and offered her the flowers, speaking the words that were in her heart. "Auntie Maha, Father tells me that you feel differently about things from many others. Please never change because I love you just as you are."

Kareem's eyes grew large with emotion, and he swept Little Sultana and Maha together in his strong arms. I rarely see my husband weep, but on this occasion big tears rolled down his cheeks.

Kareem and I both sat in surprise when we saw Amani approach her sister. She began to sob, too, clinging to her sister and begging for forgiveness. Amani was in a different mood from the one she had been in when her father had left her a few days earlier. Perhaps she had been thinking about the destructive actions that had brought the fury of those she loved upon her head.

Maha was aloof but said nothing harsh; she even stroked her sister on the shoulder. A weeping Amani made the rounds of all family members, her eyes overflowing with tears as she asked each of us, "Please give me another chance. I will be less critical. I will. Please do forgive me."

Of course Kareem and I forgave our youngest child and assured her that all would be forgotten, though I thought to myself that only time would tell when it came to Amani, the most difficult of my three children. I noticed that Maha and Abdullah exchanged a look of suspicion, no doubt wondering how long Amani's contrite behavior might last.

Maha later confided that although she had never allowed any of our opinions to alter her feelings or behavior, she was much relieved that everything was in the open and that everyone appeared much more at peace with her uniqueness.

For sure, we were all regretful that any of us had ever wished Maha to be someone she is not. We do love her just as she is, a young woman filled with passion to right the wrongs of our world. It took the wisdom of those we love, Abdullah, Maha, and Little Sultana, to bring us to this place of total acceptance and love.

Allah is good.

# Chapter Eight
# Guided by the Ones We Help

Although it has been a dream of mine that all my children might join hands with their mother in my life's occupation of struggling to achieve education and freedom on behalf of girls and women, never could I have imagined that Amani would become involved. But something important had happened with my youngest, and she was soon to prove that recent events had improved her outlook on all others.

While my keenest interest revolves around the importance of education, my daughter has never shown an interest in causes other than animal rights and religious philosophies. Most disheartening for me, she has actually spoken against high educational levels for females; she follows the teachings of clerics who often discount the importance of education for girls and women in my country.

I have discovered, however, that sometimes dreams do come true, and Amani was soon to make her mother very happy.

After the meeting at my palace with Dr. Meena, the female physician who had so impressed me when I had first met her at a conference at a Riyadh hospital, and the young social worker, Nadia, I patiently waited for one or both to make direct contact with me either by telephone or in person, as they had an open invitation to visit me in my home. Now that Dr. Meena had access to a car and had a personal driver, I knew that there were no transportation obstacles for the doctor, or for Nadia, who was now being transported back and forth to her work, making her brother's acts of revenge by intentionally making her late for work negligible.

The three of us had concurred that Nadia would continue her hospital social work as usual and would remain alert to situations where Saudi females were victims of abuse, and would make these cases known to Dr. Meena and me, so that we might take the appropriate action to save the girl from circumstances that might result in injury or death. Several weeks had passed from the day of our meeting, so I resolved that if I did not hear from Dr. Meena soon, I would contact the good doctor to ask if there was any movement from Nadia. Knowing that there were females in dire need, I was eager to get started with our work assisting them.

So much had been happening within the family that I was far behind schedule in my work, as I have a number of educational projects for girls that occupy much of my time. So when I received information from one of my employees in Palestine regarding an ongoing educational project I had initiated years ago, I decided that I would devote the rest of the week to the work at hand. As I was studying the report I had received, Amani dropped in to our home in Riyadh—though it was clear that this was not a casual visit.

My daughter sauntered into my office without knocking. It is a habit she has carried forward from childhood, but one that has never troubled me. My children know that they are the most significant part of my life, and I generally stop whatever I am doing when they express an interest in talking with me.

"*Sabah alkhair, Ummi*," Amani said with a sweet smile.

"*Sabah alnur, Ebnah* [daughter]," I responded. I stood to greet Amani, first kissing her on her right cheek and then the left, then back once more to the right cheek, as is customary in Saudi Arabia.

After my greeting, I looked behind Amani to see where her son might be. "Where is Khalid?" I asked. It was rare to see Amani without her young son either clasped in her arms or trailing in her footsteps. My daughter is a devoted mother whose son loves her intensely.

"Oh, Mummy, my mother-in-law has been complaining that she does not see her grandson nearly enough, so I sent Khalid with Jo-Anne so they might have a nice visit. Today was a good day for Khalid to visit, as I have some work I must do."

"That is good, daughter. Little Khalid makes all his grandparents very happy." I was also pleased that Khalid's English nanny was with him because I worried about my son-in-law's mother. She had not shown any mothering skills when managing a toddler on her own. She was the third wife to her husband and had given birth when she was older than most first-time mothers. She had stopped producing children after the birth of her one son, a very kind Saudi royal cousin who had later married Amani. We all knew that she rarely took care of her son. She had taken advantage of her wealth to employ four or five nursemaids so that she did not have to bother with her child. She even hired a wet nurse when her son was first born so that she could avoid nursing her infant. When asked, she startled us all by claiming that a nursing baby was known to cause cancer of the breast due to the tugging on a woman's teat.

Most Arab women adore children and like being surrounded by those little innocents, but Amani's mother-in-law had avoided children at every opportunity. Why she wanted to see little Khalid for a long visit was a mystery, as I had heard from good sources that small children adversely affected her nerves. Sara told me that she had been in attendance once when Amani's mother-in-law had become hysterical at some of the royal children being disorderly and noisy during play. Should little Khalid spill his juice or tug at her earrings or hair, the woman's anxiety was bound to build—and I knew from personal experience that my grandson was fascinated by jewelry and long hair. Thankfully, Khalid's nanny Jo-Anne was a skilled professional and was highly competent. She would know exactly when to take Khalid out of his grandmother's arms to put him down for a nap so as to give his paternal grandmother an opportunity to relax.

I did not inquire about the work Amani mentioned, as generally her work involved meeting with some of her religious friends who made detailed lists of social behavior they considered taboo. The lists would find themselves in the hands of all their relatives, so we would know how to better behave as good Muslims.

Amani glanced at the large pile of papers on my desk. "What are you doing, Mummy?"

She surprised me on this day. I had never known her to inquire about my projects. I was quick to respond. "I am working on one of my most special projects, darling."

"And what is that?"

I selected one of the many papers piled on my desk. "See this list? These names represent Palestinian girls who are going to be pulled from school unless their parents can find money to finance their education. I am reading over the information before giving my approval to have funds sent to these families."

Amani pulled up a chair and sat beside me. "Palestinian girls?"

"Yes, darling. This is one of my pet projects, something I have been doing for years. I support several hundred needy Palestinian families so that their children might remain in school."

"Really?"

I gazed at my daughter in dismay. Many times in the past Kareem and I had discussed the particulars of moving funds into Palestine for the Palestinian families and girls I supported. Those conversations had transpired while my children were in attendance. Maha and Abdullah had conveyed curiosity and had even become personally involved. While Maha assisted me by compiling information about the girls and their families, Abdullah had occasionally traveled to Lebanon or to Paris, where the funds were passed from my son into a courier's hands, who would go on to Palestine to distribute money to the various destitute families. We were compelled to be very careful about how we delivered funds; Israeli security is very strict when it comes to the amount of foreign currency being sent into the country to assist the Palestinians, even if the cause is nonviolent, such as education.

"Yes, Amani. Your father and I have been supporting many families who have daughters in Palestine for many years. We also help families in Egypt and Yemen. This is a duty for Muslims who have ample money. We must share our wealth and help others."

I saw that Amani was listening carefully, so I continued speaking.

"You might not know, but your Auntie Sara sends art books and art supplies to schools all over the Muslim world. She has given many full scholarships to girls and boys who have shown an interest in art and architecture. Some of those students are studying in Europe at this moment.

"Your father is interested in adequate health care for all, and he has donated substantial funds to help build small hospitals in communities that have no health facilities. We are a family who wants to share the wonderful wealth we have been given. We have more than we need, so we share."

"Why did I not know this, Mummy?"

Although I yearned to take my daughter back in time to remind her of the many conversations she must have overheard, I held my tongue because my youngest child has always been sensitive when reminded of her often selective memory. Perhaps if I moved slowly, Amani might finally join me in embracing the crucial cause of education for all. Certainly no one was more passionate about a cause once her mind was fully engaged with it than my Amani.

"I am sorry, Amani. For some reason, I thought you knew about my interest in the area and my concern for all children who suffer, no matter their nationality. Although poverty is widespread in many countries in our neighborhood, Palestinian families have suffered more than most when it comes to normal life. So many families are destitute because jobs are difficult to find, and with the turmoil that affects all who live in that region it is often the case that no one in the family can find work. Many families struggle to meet expenses for food and shelter. Education often has to take second place to the basic necessities."

"Please do tell me more."

"Of course. I feel that I am helping those who take good advantage of assistance, which makes me feel very positive. There is a long history in Palestine regarding education, with many parents holding education in high regard; it is something that is truly valued. Despite the political upheavals and chaos that exist within Palestinian communities, school enrollment in Palestine is quite high by any standards. You might be surprised to know that, unlike many young people across the globe, a survey found that Palestinian girls say that their first priority is to become educated. It is my goal to help provide education for such girls. And the only thing I ask of each recipient is that they help another girl with education after they graduate and are employed in a good position.

"Yet it is very difficult, Amani. You will probably have a hard time imagining this because your life has been so easy in comparison. From the moment of your birth, you have wanted for nothing. You have been greatly loved by both parents. You have had more food and clothes than needed. You had

188

the privacy of your own rooms. You were allowed any pets you wanted in a country that frowns upon such a love for animals. You were encouraged to seek an education.

"But, darling, had you been born a Palestinian girl, life would have been much more challenging. While I am sure that most girls in Palestine are loved by their parents, perhaps they go to bed hungry at night. They witness the tension shown by parents worrying about finding the money to buy food. They most likely live in a tiny house with many other people, perhaps sleeping in one room with four or five siblings. They want to go to school but perhaps there is no transportation to take them there. Perhaps they do not have the funds to buy a uniform or books. Perhaps their father can no longer walk or ride to work because there are security fences separating his home from his work. So many unique problems face children in that area.

"Since Palestinians have always embraced education, the main obstacle for most to continue their education is poverty. Families are large, while employment is insecure. Many cannot afford to pay fees to keep their children in school. Perhaps a girl has several brothers. If so, and the family is forced to choose between educating their son or their daughter, as I have always found in our Muslim culture, the son will be chosen."

Amani's dark eyes flashed with an intensity of feeling; it was the same look she gives when she is upset about an animal in distress. My heart jumped with hope. I so wanted all my children to embrace my conviction that education for all is a great first step in solving so many gender problems in our world. Although there are many educated fools, I have found that educated men tend to support education for females, understanding that an educated woman is an asset to any society. If females receive education, they will be able to support themselves should their husbands prove to be less than capable of providing for them and the family. Educated women also fight for their daughters to be educated.

"And so, Amani, your mother is doing everything in her power to help girls stay in school so as to achieve a method of financially supporting themselves and their families. With education comes empowerment, Amani. The road that is education is the one that leads out of poverty for all. This I believe to be true."

Amani nodded, but said nothing.

"Anyhow, daughter, in order to discover the girls in most dire need of assistance, I have quietly employed twenty Palestinian educators who closely observe the students at their schools so as to recognize studious girls who begin to show signs of stress or whose attendance ratings drop. When such signs appear, these educators speak with the girls and visit their families to discover the problem. Many times the families are so poor that they feel they must encourage their daughters to marry young so that family maintenance diminishes with fewer mouths to feed.

"So this is how it works: I receive documents every year listing the names and explanations of the girls' situations. I read about the individual cases. Normally, I finance the families of these girls so that money will not be a valid reason to pull the daughters out of school. Only rarely have I refused a request: the times I have had to say no have involved fraud. Only two of the people I employed to assist in leading me to girls who needed help were dishonest. Those two

were placing false names and case histories on the
annual list, so that they might pocket the money for
nonexistent students."

Amani reached to me for a heartfelt hug—a
"mummy hug."

"Mummy, I have been mistaken. I know now
that education is important."

Amani gazed at me silently. I know my
daughter well and can sense when she is experiencing
a mental debate. She was deciding whether or not to
divulge additional information. I wanted to tell her
to speak, to move her concerns from her mind into her
mother's mind, but I did not. Over years of dealing
with two very independent daughters, I have come
to know through experience when to push and when
to be patient.

On this occasion I knew I should be patient.

Finally Amani smiled and confessed her
thoughts. "Mummy, after what happened with
Maha, I have been thinking a lot about my behavior. I
do not want to be a person that everyone dreads. So I
am praying to Allah to help me restrain my actions, or
at least to be less aggressive when I express my
thoughts. I have been so sad that you and Abdullah
and my father, and yes, Maha, appear to be avoiding
me. Please know that I will be a kinder person,
Mummy."

I fought the urge to speak, to reach out for my
daughter; instead, I held back because I believed that
she needed to tell me everything.

"Mummy, I have also had a change of heart
about the importance of education. I know that you
have been talking to me for years, but after meeting
Nadia and Dr. Meena I felt strongly that they could
guide me to better things.

"I have met Nadia twice at her hospital offices. Remember the note she passed to me? Well, I read it more than once, and each time I felt touched by her sincerity. I experienced a strong pull to go to her so that I could understand her job requirements, and to see for myself some of the girls she meets in her official capacity as a social worker."

Amani looked at me expectantly, so I finally responded. "That's wonderful, Amani," I said. "You are making your mother very happy, darling, to do these things."

"I am making myself happy, Mummy," Amani replied. "Although I believe that our faith teaches us that a man should be the head of the household, there is no harm in a woman receiving an education." She paused meaningfully. "And, in many instances, I admit, education can save a woman from a lifetime of abuse."

My daughter was moving emotionally in the right direction, but spiritually and intellectually she was treading carefully. I felt a great gladness that my daughter was at least overcoming the false teachings of some of our clerics, who so eagerly twist the verses in our holy book so that females will remain under the pain of bondage to males. I knew that once Amani became more involved in meeting with and helping other women she would see for herself how many men of religion trick those who trust their every word. All I desired for my daughter was for her to develop a sound and balanced character so that she might better know whom to trust and also to become more capable when facing the good and the bad of life.

And so, for the rest of that day and part of the next, Amani pored over the Palestinian documents with me. My daughter became ardently engaged in the lives of the young girls we read about and whose futures would greatly improve because of the sums our family provided for their education.

Amani was especially enamored of two young women who had known only poverty and bad luck for most of their childhoods. One girl in the report was named Tala. She was in dire need of assistance to complete her education. Without our help, her future would be as bleak as her past. The poor child had lost her mother to disease when she was only six years old. As the lone daughter of the house, she had been made responsible for doing the housework and cooking the meals for her father and three brothers. Like all the girls requesting help, Tala was required to write a one-page letter telling us a little about her life. She described the difficulties of preparing meals while standing atop a rickety stool, as she was too short to reach the hot plate burner set atop the kitchen table. The family lived in the West Bank, so her father insisted upon dishes from that region, such as *kofta bi tahini*, which is meatballs cooked in sauce and served with rice. He also liked kofta cooked in tomato sauce and served with potatoes. Her mother had grown up in Gaza, so Tala's brothers were accustomed to dishes common to that region of Palestine, such as lentil stew and various eggplant dishes.

Amani's eyes grew red as she fought back her tears, despairing at the thought of a six-year-old, motherless girl being given the responsibility to cook meals for five people. She seemed to be little more than a slave in her own home, worn out and broken like a little old woman. Since her mother's death, Tala had never received a new dress or a new pair of shoes, as she had worn her cousin's old clothes.

The second girl who had caught Amani's attention was called Hiba. She was the oldest of five daughters and her family was poorer than most, since her father had suffered severe physical injuries at work, driving heavy equipment. He would never work again. The family was, therefore, at the mercy of charity organizations or relatives who had very little to share. None of the daughters was going to remain in school because of their extreme poverty. The children were hungry most of the time because they were only eating two tiny meals a day. Some days there was no food at all.

My daughter's heart burned in agony. She wanted to travel to Palestine to deliver the funds to make sure Tala and Hiba received what we were sending, but I assured her that we would speak to the girls when the time was right. There had been a number of occasions when I had made a special effort to cross-check that the funds I had sent had arrived as they should and that the appropriate families were benefiting. Of course I would never reveal my true identity when speaking with the recipients, as I wanted them to feel comfortable to speak freely; I have found that identifying myself as a princess causes people to get so paralyzed by nerves that our conversations do not go smoothly.

Amani felt the power of the joy derived from helping those desperate girls. There is no joy so profound. I knew in that moment that my daughter had experienced the essence of true joy that results from giving freely to help others. Amani would never be the same again, I knew.

How fortunate we felt to be in a position to help so many young girls and women.

Almost overnight Amani became my close confidante, replacing the argumentative daughter who since her teenage years had caused much grief and worry within her family. Working thus with Amani, never have I been so confident that all three of my children would follow me in service to others. For true happiness comes from investing your energy in a cause bigger than yourself.

The following week Dr. Meena and Nadia met with Amani and me at my home in Riyadh. Maha had returned to Europe the previous week with her friend Laila, who was overjoyed to be traveling out of Saudi Arabia for the first time in her life.

Amani and Nadia embraced and began conversing as though they had known each other for a lifetime rather than a few months. Dr. Meena nodded in approval, although she did not seem surprised by the camaraderie between Nadia and Amani. Knowing that the doctor was Nadia's mentor, I assumed that Nadia confided in the doctor all elements of her life, including her new friendship with my daughter.

"Tell me, what has happened with Fatima?" Amani leaned forward with interest while she inquired of Nadia.

I sat silently, truly pleased that Amani was so easily and confidently taking charge. Although I am not old, and thanks be to God I feel young and healthy, with a lot of energy, I know a time will come when I am unable to work so hard. I have always wanted my children to train in the work that I do so that they will be able to meet the challenge of fighting for women's rights, as I do now. After all, my time on earth will one day end and someone must take my place. If I have learned anything in my short lifetime, it is that there will always be plenty of men working to keep women under their rule. So long as this is so, we women must remain strong to continue the battle for justice.

"Her story grows more tragic by the day, Amani," Nadia replied.

"Tell me about this Fatima," I said. Never have I been uninterested in hearing about a woman who needs help.

"Oh, I saw Fatima when I was in Nadia's offices," Amani said. "I did not speak with her, but I saw her waiting to speak with Nadia." Amani looked at me with sad eyes. "This poor girl is only twenty years old, younger than me, but her life has been so brutal that she looks as though she has lived for forty or fifty years."

"Tell me," I repeated to Nadia. I knew that such premature aging was an indication of countless troubles.

"Yes, Princess," Nadia said. "She has suffered much the same as many other Saudi women, and more than most. I will tell you her full story."

"Yes, you must, Nadia. I know that we can help her," Amani said with a great passion in her voice.

"Fatima came to my attention when she was admitted into the hospital with severe depression. This was a big problem because she is the mother of twin daughters and had no one to help her care for the children. She was admitted only because one of the secretaries in the outpatient clinic saw her sitting, looking disheveled, with two crying children who appeared to be soiled and hungry. The secretary discovered that the woman had nowhere to go, and that her husband had divorced her. She had no way of supporting herself or her daughters. Someone had hailed a taxi and paid her fare to send her to the hospital. Although she did not have any paperwork for admittance, someone in the clinic took mercy on her and led her to the admitting area.

"On the orders of the secretary in charge, someone in the clinic went to the hospital cafeteria and purchased three meals. All three gobbled the food. They appeared to be starving. The secretary took charge, speaking with her boss, a doctor from England, who agreed that Fatima should indeed be admitted as an inpatient. At least she would receive rest and food while she was put under observation. And she could keep her two daughters, age three, with her.

"When she refused to speak, social services were notified about her case and so I went to her room to assess the situation. Although she seemed frozen from fear and continued to refuse to utter a word, I could tell that she was relieved to meet with a Saudi girl. All who had met with her previously were foreigners, including the secretary, who was from the Philippines, the doctor from England, and a variety of other hospital assistants from around the globe."

Dr. Meena expounded on the point of nationals working at Saudi institutions: "As you know, Princess, the hospital has employees from all over the world, representing many countries, from America, Canada, Europe, Asia, Africa, and the Middle East. In the past there were very few Saudi employees, but we are gathering in numbers. But there are no Saudi nurses and not so many Saudi doctors, so when Saudi citizens are admitted often they never see another Saudi."

I nodded, knowing that this was the situation in most hospitals and medical clinics in the kingdom. However, the statistics were improving, as there were more Saudis being trained in health-related fields with each passing year.

"May I continue, Princess?"

I was becoming more anxious by the minute to hear this story, and to work on a solution, as it was clear that Amani was eager to do something grand for this particular woman. "Of course," I replied. "Please do tell me this story."

"Fatima was in the hospital for a week before she began to respond to my questions. Thankfully, the nurses on that floor were attuned to her situation and they took turns entertaining her twin daughters. After a week of food, rest, and kindness, Fatima began to come out of what I call a locked-in syndrome. This affects so many abused women, who appear stunned to find themselves in a helpless situation. That's when she told me her story."

Nadia lifted her briefcase from beside her and opened it to retrieve a few papers. "Princess, I wrote Fatima's story as she revealed it to me. I think it is much more compelling that I read her words rather than tell you from my point of view. Is that fine with you?"

"Of course. I agree. I think it is best to hear Fatima's story from her own telling."

Nadia smiled at Amani, and my daughter encouraged her new friend by gesturing with her hand to resume the story.

Nadia cleared her throat and slowly read what she had written:

"You are talking to the most unhappy woman who has ever lived. When I was a tiny girl, my mother told me that I was the greatest disappointment in her life. She wanted a son, but Allah gave her a daughter. She was desperate because she was the third wife of my father and he was miserable with all his wives because, with my birth, he was the father of five daughters and no sons. Three years after my birth, however, my mother gave birth to a boy, which elevated her status in the household. My father showed great appreciation for that son, and my mother became so enamored of her boy that she hated me for every moment I took of her life, for every bit of food I took into my mouth. As I grew older, my mother saved all slaps and shouts for me, while she spoiled my brother, who became a little tyrant.

"My father became so affectionate toward my mother that she had given him two more sons by the time I was eight years old. My life was a hell. No one loved me. My mother and father laughed when my brothers insulted me or kicked me. When I was ten years old, my mother told me that I would soon be married to an old widower in the neighborhood because he liked little girls better than grown women. He was known to be very abusive, and there was talk that he had killed his last two wives with his hands, as both young girls had shown signs of being beaten by their husband. When I wept and protested, my mother lifted me in her arms and held me before the one mirror in our home; she told me to look at my reflection in the mirror, that I was so ugly that I was lucky that anyone wanted me for a wife, even an old man. I had not known that I was so ugly until then, but my mother gestured in the mirror at my big nose and small eyes, then yanked on my teeth, telling me that they were too big for my mouth. That is *why my teeth stuck outside my lips, she said, and I could not fully close my lips over those big and ugly teeth.*

*"Thankfully, the old man died before our marriage could take place, but my mother kept looking for a replacement groom. My brothers laughed at me and said I would have to be killed, ground up and fed to the goats and the camels because no one would marry me and there was no point wasting good food on an ugly girl who would be a burden forever. It was said that I was pointed out to over twenty potential grooms and all had turned me down.*

*"But when I was fourteen years old a man with a disfigured body agreed to marry me. At first I was glad because I could not imagine how life could be more miserable. But I was wrong. The man who married me was uglier than me, and his physical ugliness had created a very angry personality.*

*"The horror of married life came early, on the night of my wedding. My mother had told me that I should prepare myself for a lot of pain because there would be blood when the marriage was consummated. I could not imagine why this was necessary. My mother refused to tell me what would happen, but she did say that the marriage bed was painful and humiliating and that there must be blood from my body or else. If there was no blood, then I would be in serious trouble, divorced on the spot and returned to my family home, where my brothers and fathers would take me to the desert and bury me alive to reclaim the family honor.*

*"I was so terrified, but there was nowhere to turn. I thought about the pain and the blood for days. Some young girl told me that my new husband would cut his finger and then he would cut my finger and he would rub his bloody finger on my bloody finger and the*

marriage would be considered honorable. After that all I would have to do was clean his house, wash his clothes, cook his meals, and basically obey his orders. That did not sound so bad, as I had been doing that in our family home from the time I could stand.

"So on the night of my wedding I received a brutal shock. I fought my husband when he tried to force me to take off my clothes, but he was a strong man despite his disfigured body. His problems were with his bowed legs and strangely shaped feet; the upper part of his body was strong enough to kill a large animal. His arms were huge, nearly as thick as my body. But the biggest shock was yet to come. No one had warned me that men have a secret weapon, so when he took off his clothes and I saw that big thing of his I started screaming. That's when he threw me on the hard floor and forced his weapon inside my body. Suddenly I understood the pain and blood my mother had warned me about. There was plenty of blood because he kept stabbing me with that weapon. At least I did not dishonor the family and end up buried alive in the sand.

"For three or four days, he had a good time stabbing me with his weapon. I really thought I was going to die. Anytime I pleaded with him to stop, he would start doing it again. He became angry at my cries and started beating me. He beat me so severely that my lips burst open and my nose was broken.

"After that assault, I felt nothing but fear and dread for my husband. There was no affection between us the way I had seen affection grow between my mother and father after she had given him three sons.

"My troubles increased when I gave birth to twin daughters nine months after my wedding night. I gave birth at home alone because he said it was a woman's duty, that it was natural, and any woman who needed *help was not worthy of living. And so I tended to myself at the birth, although I did not know what was happening after I had given birth to one daughter and still there was childbirth pain. When I gave birth to the second daughter, I knew that I would be in trouble because my husband was a violent and ignorant man. His friends and family were equally stupid and my family would never have come to my aid, so I was helpless and alone with two infant girls who needed a lot of care because both were smaller than most newborns.*

*"Indeed my husband was so angry at finding himself the father of double girls—double trouble, he called them—that he beat me so savagely that he broke my arm and some of my ribs, as well as breaking my nose a second time. I really needed medical care, but he refused to take me to the hospital. He expected me to cook him a meal after beating me unconscious.*

*"Some weeks later I looked in the mirror and saw that I was even more ugly than before because my nose was so big and misshapen; no woman could be more ugly than me.*

*"Although he continued to stab me with his weapon, I was glad that the attacks occurred less frequently than before. He even took a second wife a year after the babies were born. The second wife was a young girl who had been orphaned when her parents were killed in a car accident and her uncle did not want to accept responsibility for a female child since he had two daughters already. Once that young girl came into our home, he enjoyed stabbing her more than he stabbed me, so I had some relief, although I felt bad for that girl, who was no more than eight or nine years old. She cried pitifully for her mother night and day. I tried to comfort her as best I could, but she was so terrified and heartbroken that I could do little to help her.*

"Later I gave birth to another girl, but she was dead at birth. That's when my husband divorced me and threw me out of the house. My parents sent word that I was not welcome to bring my daughters to their home, so I just sat with my daughters a few houses down from my former husband's house. A few people brought us food, but after a week of sleeping on the dirt the elders in the village talked about the pity of it all. My former husband did not like being talked about, so he came to Riyadh and met with some government people, who directed him to a special house for abandoned women and children. Thanks be to Allah that he did not want custody of our daughters because I love my girls more than I love my life and without them I would have no reason to live.

"But I do not know what to do. No man will marry a physically ugly woman with two daughters. Perhaps a great beauty with daughters might find a husband, but I will never have such luck. I hope the government will let me live in the place I have been living, although I am not happy living there, as there is nothing to do but look at the walls, eat meager food, and watch my daughters as they cry from boredom. There are no children their age and there are no toys or books for my little girls to play with. I do not have the money for such luxuries. It is another prison for us all.

"I am the unhappiest woman in the world, but I have two girls who need me. I do not wish to be sad and sit and stare at nothing, but this sadness has grown inside me like a cancer and I am helpless to be happy and to find the energy to smile."

"And, Princess, that is the story of Fatima," Nadia said. "I feel she is a special case who needs our attention."

"We must help her," Amani said as she wiped a tear from her eye. "And her two innocent daughters."

Dr. Meena shuddered and looked at me with enormous sadness. Remembering her own story, I knew that she could understand better than most the harsh reality of Fatima's life.

I reassured everyone. "Of course we will help her. Nadia, you must speak further with Fatima. After she becomes involved in the decisions that will affect her life forever, then we can decide what steps are to be taken."

"Perhaps she would like to be educated?" Amani offered. "She is still young. Perhaps she could have a private tutor to teach her at the same time her daughters are instructed?"

"That is a possibility," Dr. Meena replied. "Rarely is it too late to educate. I know of a forty-year-old woman who has just recently received her college degree."

"These are all good suggestions," I said. "However, if possible, I believe that Fatima should guide us. I discovered something very important about helping others some years ago. A certain magic occurs when the one abused is given the opportunity to make a personal choice without anyone dictating to them. For Fatima's entire life, she has had no choice in anything to do with her life, whether or not she would be educated, the chores she was ordered to perform, the food she ate, or the man she married. If she is given the opportunity to think, to explore, to feel a passion for something, then she will most likely succeed. If we tell her what we think is best for her, then personal satisfaction or accomplishment is less likely."

Amani stared at me with new respect. "You are so right, Mother. We must be guided by the ones we help."

"Your daughter is right, Princess," Dr. Meena concurred.

Nadia smiled broadly. "I am eager to put your idea into practice, Princess. I have always decided for those who needed me, but now I see that I should encourage their participation and I should follow their needs and wishes."

All approved the plan that Nadia would speak with Fatima, and if she agreed, the four of us would meet with the woman who called herself the unhappiest in the world. Something good would be determined for Fatima's future once she decided what it was she wanted for the rest of her life.

I silently thanked Allah that I was blessed with ample money to assist Fatima and her daughters along whichever path she wanted to follow.

After our meeting ended and all left my home, I sat and stared, drawn to thoughts of my own life from the time I was a young girl until the present day. Despite my wealth, my attentive husband, and my precious children and grandchildren, rarely have I felt good about myself or taken time to consider what I have accomplished. Truly, I have always felt myself to be the little girl my mother fretted over, and the naughty daughter my father fumed about, but in truth I suddenly realized that there is much more to Princess Sultana than my mother and father could ever have imagined. My strength of mind and the passion that so worried and disturbed them were nothing more than an early indication of the determination I would put to positive use as a woman.

For all the years of my life, I have lived to serve, to fight for the betterment of life for women, and I have indeed changed lives for the better.

Suddenly, I felt a great satisfaction in the work I was doing, realizing that it is so significant that I could never have chosen a more worthy path. My work is not only important but life-altering.

And I am glad. My only regret is that my dear mother is not here to see her daughter triumph over the evil that strikes so many innocent girls and women. I know that my mother would be proud of her little Sultana.

# Chapter Nine
# Princess Aisha

Even in this year of 2014, when events are slowly moving in a positive direction for Saudi women, daily life still remains uneasy for most girls and women in my country. This is because there are many Saudi men who appear to take great joy in warring against women! No doubt they feel threatened. These uncompromising men are poised like angry tigers, ready to condemn and decree punishment for every female thought or action. Regrettably, even some Saudi females are shamefully guilty of denouncing a Saudi woman who dares to seek a better life through education and freedom.

I derive no comfort from the knowledge that Saudi women are not alone when it comes to the misery of inequality. Tragically, it has come to my attention that many of the three billion or so female occupants of our planet suffer under the lash of repression, ignorance, and violence.

According to the United Nations, there are 193 countries in the world. I have traveled to 49 of these countries and have studied the conditions of daily life for citizens in many others. As a woman who has devoted my life to freedom for females, I am always most curious about the treatment of women in every country I visit or read about. I have lived through many personal struggles in the land of my birth, so it is shocking for me to discover that some governments and cultures are even more repressive against women than those of Saudi Arabia. In particular in this category are Afghanistan and Pakistan.

Although I know some highly educated and emancipated women from Pakistan, these women are from the country's wealthy class. The poor women in Pakistani villages might as well live on another planet, as their lives are so different. I have no firsthand knowledge of the treatment of women in Afghanistan, though from the news reports and books that I have read it is evident that nearly every Afghan woman is shackled by the men of her family.

Gender experts agree with my personal assessment of Afghanistan and Pakistan, and it was with a heavy heart that I recently read the UN's list of the ten worst countries for women, ranked in this order and for these reasons:

1. Afghanistan: This violence-laced country holds the notorious title of being the worst country on earth for females. The UN findings are that the typical Afghan girl will live a very short life, to an average age of forty-five. More than half of all brides in Afghanistan marry before they are sixteen. The majority of Afghan women (87 percent) admit that they are regularly beaten by their husbands. Afghanistan is the only country in the world where more women than men commit suicide. These helpless women feel

so hopeless that they set themselves aflame to escape their brutish lives.

2. Democratic Republic of Congo: Rape and war go together, and girls and women routinely suffer this indignity in the Congo. The UN team investigating the conflict in the eastern DRC reports that the rapes of girls and women are so ruthless and methodical that they are unparalleled. I have read horrifying reports that say armed gangs not only rape women but also force the sons of those women at gunpoint to rape their own mothers. Such a revolting and brutal experience is undeniably beyond imagination.

3. Iraq: Iraq used to be a rare haven for women in our Muslim world, with Saddam Hussein's government ensuring basic rights for women. But after Saddam came other evil men who appear nearly as corrupt as Saddam, men who only support their own religious faction, of which there are several in Iraq. Now the sectarian violence in the country often targets girls and women. Iraq's female literacy rate was once the highest in the Arab world, and is now the lowest.

4. Nepal: Parents routinely sell their young daughters to sex traffickers, who then market the children to brothels where they are brutally raped every day of their young lives. Those fortunate enough to escape this cruel destiny face early marriage, which often leads to early death in childbirth.

5. Sudan: The fate of females, both young and old, in Western Sudan is a horror show, with abduction, rape, and forced displacement a common occurrence in a woman's life.

6. Guatemala: Poverty is widespread and deep in the country. Domestic violence, rape, and a

terrifying rate of HIV/AIDS infection have affected the lives of many impoverished females.

7. Mali: Few females escape the torture of genital mutilation. Girls are routinely forced into early marriages. One in ten females dies in pregnancy or childbirth.

8. Pakistan: Honor killings in Pakistan are widespread. High-ranking men in villages often rule that Pakistani women will be gang-raped as punishment for men's crimes. Religious extremists routinely target and murder female lawyers and politicians.

9. Saudi Arabia: The UN reports that under our Saudi Arabian guardianship rule women are treated as children for their entire lives. I can say from experience that this is true. Unable to drive or to mix in public with men, Saudi women are confined to a life of strict segregation. Male-upon-female abuse is still common in Saudi Arabia. There are numerous cases where wives are beaten and raped by their husbands. If divorce occurs, fathers often take full custody of their children, although there are guidelines for custody in our Islamic faith. Should a man ignore these, no one will step in to help the mother and children. In some of the most appalling cases, girls are raped by their fathers. When such crimes occur, our religious clerics side with the rapist, saying that he can do whatever he pleases with the women of his family.

10. Somalia: A long-lasting and vicious civil war has broken down what is left of civilized society. Females, both young and old, are exposed to attack and rape by armed gangs.

How can these appalling statistics exist when there are so many people across the planet calling for equality, basic human rights, and dignity for all women? The UN report represents a black mark against the entire world, both the men and the women who do not take to the streets in their millions to stop this genocide against females.

Despite the fact that there are eight countries considered worse than Saudi Arabia, when it comes to women's rights, few will disagree that life for females in Saudi Arabia remains difficult and complicated.

The restrictions against Saudi women are great and small, but sometimes it is the small restrictions that are the most irritating and confining. Most women cannot imagine what it is like to worry about every little thing in their day-to-day life. For example, a Saudi girl must be careful not to enter a conversation with a man not of her family. Should she be so reckless, she might be accused of being a prostitute. If such an accusation is made, she could find herself in a jail cell waiting to be flogged. Saudi girls living in conservative cities or villages must still cover their faces or they can expect stones to fly in their direction. Since Saudi women cannot drive, many must take public transport, as there is often no male available to take them to school or to work or to a doctor's appointment. Saudi girls must be very cautious when taking public transport, as some taxi drivers falsely believe that an unaccompanied girl is looking for a man to show her some fun. Perhaps that man will make an inappropriate pass and, if so, she will be ruined forever should anyone discover his impropriety, regardless of her innocence.

These restrictions mean that my sadness at seeing Maha off on her return to Europe is also mixed with a sense of relief. My daughter is a brash girl who lives freely in Europe and sees no reason for change when she is in Saudi Arabia. Thus, Kareem and I are always nervous during her visits. Although her father and I could protect her from most self-inflicted troubles, we do not wish to embroil our family in any scandal, as individual scandals involve everyone related by blood in our culture. Should Maha become marked as a girl others might consider shameful, her brother Abdullah and her sister Amani would be smeared with the same embarrassment, no matter their lack of involvement in whatever activity Maha might have indulged in, such as driving or some other pursuit considered taboo by our culture. My son and youngest daughter have chosen to remain in their country of birth and to make good lives for themselves here. They must be protected.

But Maha is not the only young princess bold enough to push against Saudi female discrimination. There are others. One princess in particular comes to my mind.

One of Maha's favorite cousins is Princess Aisha, a daughter of a ranking prince who once served as governor of a Saudi province. This cousin is an unusually private man; we know very little about his true feelings on any subject. For this reason only, I will not name him in this story, although he lives a public life, serving in various government positions.

Maha and Aisha met at primary school and their friendship survived into adulthood only because the girls reconnected in Europe when Princess Aisha attended a well-known boarding school in Switzerland. Aisha has spent many holidays with Maha in Europe, and I know that they share similar feelings about Saudi Arabia and the lack of freedom for women, Maha having confided in me some of their conversations.

After her boarding school days, Aisha enrolled at a number of European universities and, at last count, has obtained three university degrees. Princess Aisha has been attending school longer than any of us can remember, though we realize she is using continuing education as an excuse to escape repressive Saudi Arabia. We often joke that Aisha is bound to receive several Ph.D. certificates and possibly an M.D. prior to her life's end.

Princess Aisha is tall and slim, has light-brown hair and dark-brown eyes that flash with the eagerness of life. Her movements are exaggerated, as this princess talks with her hands and displays lively facial expressions. She is not an outrageous girl like my Maha, but she has a decidedly feisty spirit. Her personality creates a lot of problems in her immediate family because she is the most forward-thinking of all the children in her unusually large family. My cousin has married four women, and each of those women has children. But Aisha is the youngest daughter in the entire family, and her mother is the youngest wife, a lovely woman from Morocco.

Aisha's six older half-sisters share the same mother, who was my cousin's first wife. Mothers generally have the most influence on daughters in my country, as fathers rarely take an interest in their female children. Their main focus is generally their sons; they allow their wives to tend to the daughters, unless there is some big event that claims their attention.

Aisha's older sisters are all married and all claim not to understand the need for any Saudi woman to have the freedom to drive or to marry the man of her choice or to spend most of her time out of the country, as their younger sister does. They appear happy with Saudi society as it is today and has always been.

I know both mothers personally, and the mother of Aisha's six half-sisters is one of the most conservative of all the Saudi royal women. When television was first introduced into Saudi homes, it was she who insisted upon wearing a veil when watching because there were "real men in the box," she claimed. She truly believed that the presenters could see her as easily as she could see them. It is said that she still has this habit, although the family does not want it known.

On the day of her marriage, this royal cousin had announced that no man would ever again see her without her veil, even her brothers. We were all quite relieved that she never gave birth to a son, as we assume the poor child would never have been allowed to see his mother's face, which would have been a traumatic situation.

This royal cousin instilled many of her beliefs and values in her six daughters, all of whom assert that they should be ruled by a man, and that no woman should ever question any male—particularly one in authority. Aisha's mother, on the other hand, born and raised in Morocco, is a more modern woman, who enjoys a fairly free life with her husband; she feels that her daughter should pursue her dreams. She is very proud of Aisha, with her multiple degrees, and believes she has given birth to a rare genius, which she announces at every female gathering, much to the amusement of all who know that Aisha is a very bright girl but is far from what any intellectual authority would declare a genius.

When Maha was visiting the kingdom the year prior to her last visit, Aisha happened to be in the kingdom, too. Although they only saw each other twice, Maha said those two visits were exciting because Aisha was engaged in a big fight with her six half-sisters. Accusations were flying, according to my daughter. Maha always relishes upheavals, although I cannot explain why.

Despite Maha's amusement, the family episode was serious. The family quarrel had occurred because someone had placed various sexual items in Aisha's luggage, all forbidden in our extremely traditional Saudi culture, and most especially in the hands of a single female. Sexy magazines, skimpy lingerie, and even a box of condoms had been strategically hidden in various inner pockets and slipped between regular clothing in Aisha's baggage. Whoever was the culprit clearly wanted Aisha to have difficulties with customs officials or with her father. Since Aisha is of the royal family, her luggage was not inspected at the airport, so she did not know if the prohibited items were planted before she left Europe or after she returned home.

Since Aisha still attends school in Europe, perhaps one of her friends thought it a funny joke to do such a thing, not knowing enough about Saudi culture and the harm that might come to an unmarried Saudi caught with such articles. Should the light of suspicion have shone on Aisha, indicating that she was romantically involved with a male, her reputation would have been seriously damaged; in fact, it could have cost Aisha her freedom—or her life. Only those who have visited Saudi Arabia, and are aware of the restrictions placed on females, can appreciate the seriousness of such circumstances.

When unpacking her bags, Aisha had been startled to find the items in her luggage. She was so alarmed that she quickly closed her suitcases, thinking that she would find a way to discard the items later without anyone finding them.

But that was not the end of the story.

Within a few days of Aisha's return, two of Aisha's devious half-sisters had searched her room in the hope of finding something compromising. Their search had been successful. Poor Aisha was suddenly in big trouble.

Maha, who knows Aisha well, swore to Aisha's innocence. Maha says that in all the times she and Aisha have visited each other in Europe, she has never known of Aisha dating anyone, and she was certainly not guilty of being in a sexual relationship.

Aisha is too intelligent to jeopardize her freedom and future well-being. She is keenly aware that one day her father will insist upon her marriage, although he appears to have forgotten how the years have passed, as Aisha is in her late twenties, already old for a Saudi bride. Aisha had told Maha more than once that she would go to the marriage bed as a virgin, even if she was a woman of forty when she finally married. To do otherwise in Saudi Arabia is a great risk. Even older brides are expected to be virgins, unless they are women who have been widowed or divorced and are marrying for a second or third time.

We know firsthand of one specific occasion when a thirty-year-old princess bride who did not show blood on her marriage bed was taken home to be unceremoniously dumped on her family's front door in disgrace. Little did it matter that she was a girl who had always been into playing sports with her brothers, who were kind enough to let her participate in games of soccer and even ride their bikes when no one was looking—in the past, girls were forbidden to ride bicycles or any other similar mode of transportation. The physician she visited after her wedding said that it was certain the youthful sporting activities had caused her hymen to rupture when s h e w a s a child, rather than its being the result of an illicit sexual relationship; the tearful girl swore that she had never ever been alone with a man not of her family. She was indeed a virtuous girl who was shunned by society from that time, and later married as a second wife to a man below her status.

According to Maha, Aisha is the same kind of guiltless girl. She is chaste and does none of the things our men like to claim all women do when they are unsupervised.

Maha just happened to be with Aisha on the day her sisters found the shocking and prohibited items. My daughter described the unpleasant scene, saying that when she and Aisha walked into the family palace Aisha's six sisters were waiting on her with tongues wagging with false accusations. To Maha's disbelief, one of the six was enthusiastically waving a *Playboy* magazine, which was opened at the centerfold page showing a nude playmate.

Those sisters were thrilled to have discovered the offensive items. All had hated Aisha since the day she was born to the fourth wife of their father. Aisha was a beauty even as a baby, and her half-sisters had been critical of her from that day to the present, detesting her beauty, intelligence, and ability to escape the life they so claimed to love. All who know those six women doubt that they love their lives, filled with empty luxury, as they constantly profess, but they have said it so many times that to express doubt about it now would be awkward for any of them.

Those irate daughters even called their mother to come out of her quarters to see what they had found so that she could witness the depravity of her husband's youngest daughter by a rival wife. That royal cousin had never in her life seen a picture of a nude woman, so when one of her daughters pointed it out, while another flashed a couple of the unsuitable and skimpy nightclothes they believed Aisha had purchased, the old woman fainted. And so she lay on the floor throughout the melodramatic scene.

The quarrel escalated, with Aisha claiming her innocence while the six half-sibling sisters roused themselves into a state of fury, accusing her of working as a prostitute in Europe rather than going to school, which of course was a ridiculous claim but one so many in our culture easily charge against any woman who lives freely.

Maha said the dispute spiraled out of control, though it became hysterically funny as the old princess kept waking from her stupor to look up and point at the nude playmate before fainting yet again.

My daughter is often very mischievous and unforgiving when she deals with those who condemn her friends or demonstrate that they are hypercritical about the way some people choose to live their lives. I do not agree with my daughter on everything, but Maha is Maha and she does as she pleases. To no one's surprise, since that dramatic day she has never received an invitation to visit that home, but Maha says it was worth being banned for the entertainment alone, as she had never laughed so freely for so long!

Princess Aisha was allowed to return to Europe only because the prince and the father of all the girls was out of the country and her foes were unable to voice their complaints directly to the man who was

Aisha's guardian. Although innocent, Aisha was understandably relieved to escape the kingdom, but confessed to Maha that she felt the shadow of doom trailing her steps even as she entered her apartment and attended school in Europe.

Her malicious half-sisters finally achieved their goal. A month after Aisha returned to Europe, her bank account was closed and she was left without any funds. Her father ordered her to come back to Riyadh. She had no alternative but to return to the kingdom. Once in Riyadh, she was interrogated by her indignant father, who did not mention the specific items found in her luggage, although he pointedly asked her, "My daughter, are you pure?"

When Alisha promised on the Holy Koran that she was as chaste as a newborn baby, he wasted no words, telling her, "This is good to know, because your marriage has been arranged. Your mother will advise you on the details."

Aisha told Maha, "There was no time to appeal to escape marriage to a stranger because my father jumped to his feet and fled my presence before I had time to move my tongue to speak."

And so Aisha was married to a young man not of the royal family but from a good family, well known to the royals, as they share close business dealings and are highly respected.

For one of the few times when such a hasty marriage occurs, there was a happy ending. It was discovered that Aisha had been truthful about her purity, as she had never lost her virginity, even after many years of living freely in Europe. Aisha's mother smugly showed the bloodstained marriage sheet to her sister-wives, and to her husband, who was relieved and pleased.

Most surprising, Aisha found love with her partner and led a happy life, as her husband's job took him to Asia. Living away from Saudi Arabia suits Aisha and her husband.

Aisha gushed to Maha that she feels she won a big prize when she married her husband, as the two of them have much in common and enjoy a friendship and romantic love. She recently frustrated her six half-sisters when she profusely thanked them for pulling her back into the circle of Saudi life, where she married the man of her dreams.

Even in Saudi Arabia there are times when those of our sex are blessed with a good man and a happy marriage. No woman deserves it more than Aisha, who for years was searching for something—something that would bring love and happiness into her life. That something was a special man who was living in Saudi Arabia and waiting for fate to bring them together.

Ten days after Dr. Meena and Nadia met with Amani and me at my palace in Riyadh, they returned for a visit with Fatima, the unhappiest woman in the world, whom we had discussed at our previous meeting. She arrived with her two precious twin girls, young toddlers of three years. Once I knew that the daughters were to be in attendance, I invited Little Sultana to visit me, briefly explaining to my granddaughter that two small girls who were living a sad life would be visiting and they might enjoy meeting a little princess who could present them with some nice gifts and enjoy a little tea party while the women met and discussed serious matters.

Little Sultana was thrilled to be part of something important. Abdullah confided that his child had spent many hours going through her toys, sorting them into suitable gifts for the toddlers. Abdullah had tears in his eyes when he told me that Little Sultana insisted on bringing her favorite toys that appeared as new. He said that he had insisted that she did not bring her favorite doll, Jasmine, and saw a flicker of relief on her face—Little Sultana admitted that Jasmine felt unwell and perhaps it was best to keep her tucked up in bed at home. Not unnaturally, there was, it seems, a limit to Little Sultana's generosity!

Little Sultana looked like a dream, wearing her simple pink dress, with her long hair in a braid. She sat very patiently with me, waiting for our company to arrive. She was anxious that the little girls who had lived such a wretched life might not be comfortable in a palace with a princess. She was fretting as to what she might say or do to put them at ease.

"They are little girls, darling," I reassured her. "They are five years younger than you, so you will be like a big sister. Make them feel welcome and play a few games. They will be excited, I know."

Little Sultana nodded with a seriousness that broke my heart. My granddaughter is the most tender, loving child I have ever known. Her sensitivity for the feelings of others is splendid and brings the softness of my mother to mind. She too was a most sensitive and caring person.

Just then Amani arrived, along with our guests. My eyes sought the face of the woman I did not know, the mother of the two little girls. I recalled that Fatima was only twenty years old, several years younger than

Amani. The horrific abuse she had endured from the days of her childhood had prematurely aged her, as she appeared to be a woman of forty or more. I had prepared myself to see a woman with a very unattractive face, as even Fatima had described herself as such. Although she was no beauty, I found her to be a gentle-faced woman with a very pleasant demeanor. Her nose was large and disfigured, but I knew that came as a result of the beatings she had endured from her husband. I instantly decided that if Fatima was responsive to my suggestions, I would pay for surgery to repair her damaged nose and any other injury resulting from her years of physical mistreatment.

How sad that her evil family had convinced this woman that she was repulsive in appearance, which was not the case. But she believed it to be so, which was not a surprise, as I have long been aware that ugly in the mind is the same as ugly in the mirror.

Little Sultana carefully approached the frightened twins, who were understandably shy, unsure of what to do or where to go. My granddaughter spoke slowly and kindly to the girls, who appeared to take to Little Sultana instantly. My granddaughter politely asked if they might be excused to go to the adjoining sitting room to enjoy a tea party.

The twins joyfully scampered alongside Little Sultana and I knew that all would be well with those three children. Besides, I know children adapt very quickly to strange or unusual situations. They are happy to play in an opulent palace or a humble tent; it makes little difference to a child.

Nadia, as was her way, put everyone at ease. Dr. Meena observed and Amani drank her tea.

Although Fatima was quiet, I could tell she was a careful spectator of all in her view. As a woman who had habitually suffered from the negative aspects of human nature, I was not surprised that she held herself back as though she expected the unexpected, perhaps for one of us to fly into a rage for no reason, because that was her previous and only experience with family members and her ex-husband.

Suddenly, Nadia became very serious. She began to update us with the dire news that the hospital administrators were recommending that Fatima live permanently in the home for abandoned women but that the girls be placed in a newly established orphanage set up by one of the royal princesses.

Fatima appeared startled and promptly began weeping. "No, no, I must be with my girls. They only have their mother. My girls will be terrified without their mother. For their entire lives, they have only had me and we must not be parted!"

I was stunned by the information, believing that the hospital would provide appropriate guidance so that Fatima and her children would remain together in a safe place, although I had plans to help her in other ways.

"Nadia," I said, "surely there is a better solution. A mother should not be separated from her children." After seeing the shy toddlers that were now with my granddaughter, I knew that they would suffer terribly without their mother. I was not going to allow such a thing to happen.

Nadia replied, "You are right, Princess. This is not the best resolution. But the home for abandoned women is nearly fully booked with women who have nowhere to go and the administrators there believe that the girls would be happier with other children."

"This is nonsense. Children belong with their mother," I replied.

After studying my face for many long moments, Fatima spoke in a broken voice: "Princess, why am I here? What is a poor woman like me doing in the palace of a princess?"

"Fatima," I reassured her, "I may be a princess, but I am a woman first. And do not let this palace fool you. As a child, I suffered many troubles, for I too lived the life of a girl whose father appeared to love his sons and not his daughters. My life is very happy now, but I know the pain of rejection."

Fatima stared at me with a doubtful expression, probably questioning whether I could be trusted. I comforted her a second time.

"Fatima, I will not allow anyone to take your daughters."

I continued to stare at the poor woman in danger of being forced to live in a home for abandoned women, alone and lonely, while her babies were taken to live in fear elsewhere, far from their mother. Fatima sat back in her chair. She was a woman as frightened as a cornered animal, staring first at me, then at Dr. Meena, who had been quiet until now.

"Princess, I was hoping that you would do something to keep this wrong decision from going forward. Neither Nadia nor I can go against the wishes of the administrators of the hospital or the women's home, as all are Saudi men who deem all women mere pawns to move here and there at their whim, without concern for what's best for the woman or her children."

A distressed Amani spoke for the first time: "What will we do, Mummy?"

"I am thinking, daughter," I replied in a worried tone. While I was not going to allow this unfortunate woman to be parted from her children, solving the problem would take time. My thoughts were scattered: I was remembering my own bleak childhood and thinking, once again, that only women were working to solve the issues faced by another woman.

I was beginning to feel very lonely in the fight against cruelty and discrimination toward women. The battle had been long and hard, as I was one of the first females in the royal family to push against these crimes. While some females favored my protests, few of my gender stepped up to protect our own. Now men were making careless and unfeeling decisions about two young children, removing them from their mother. We urgently needed the men of Saudi Arabia to confront the men in charge and to object on our behalf. Thus far this had only been a dream. Although many Saudi men disagreed with the religious clerics' harsh rulings against females and were against the cultural traditions that kept women in bondage, those dissenting men remained silent in the face of the cruelest punishments meted out to girls and women. Many times I had wondered why Saudi men failed to help their Saudi women. Whether it was girls who were being killed for minor offenses or being married as children, I had never heard of any man who had rushed to protect an innocent girl or woman.

I can only surmise that our men are too frightened to confront the establishment and the clerics or, even more shamefully, they remain silent because they derive great pleasure from the advantages of their dominant status. But I knew that the time had come to insist that our men join this battle.

While I sat quietly, my mind was busy, thinking of what I might do. "When are these administrators planning to separate Fatima from her daughters?" I asked.

Nadia looked at Fatima with concern.

"I must know how much time we have," I said.

"In two days," Nadia said in a low voice.

"No!" Fatima cried in anguish. "No!"

Dr. Meena quickly moved to Fatima's side. "Do not worry. The princess is going to help us."

Amani moved to stand beside Fatima, stroking her hand. I knew at that moment that, whether he liked it or not, my husband Kareem was going to have to help solve the dreadful dilemma we were facing. He was a good man, and a man with some influence in the kingdom.

"Please wait, I am going to telephone my husband," I said, as I hurriedly left the room.

Fate was on my side when I heard my husband's voice at the end of the line. I quickly explained the situation and the impact it would have on poor Fatima and her daughters unless we intervened.

To my astonishment, Kareem did not fuss at me for throwing such a problem unexpectedly in his direction, as he would have done in the past. Since revealing earlier in the year that never again would he ignore the sad plight of Saudi women, he was a more patient man, never losing his temper over my responses to dire situations affecting women and children. He was now showing me that he intended to keep his promise to me and had meant the words he had spoken.

"Sweetheart," Kareem said, "you are right. We cannot stand idly by and allow a woman to lose her babies. The answer to this problem is easy. Let us take Fatima and her daughters to one of our homes, either to Cairo or to London. We have done this in the past. Fatima can live with our servants in another country and can keep her children by her side."

"Are you quite sure, husband?"

"Sultana, you would never again be happy if we did not do something. The truth is that she should not be separated from her children. If we leave this decision to government officials, the result will be tragic. Let us not give them a chance to destroy this woman's life. Tell your Dr. Meena and Nadia to advise the officials that Fatima has been rescued. The administrators and officials will be relieved to have a problematic woman and her girls off their hands. They will not question anyone. Should they create a problem, I will call them."

"You are right, husband. I will not let her return to that place."

"Go and handle it like you always do, Sultana. If there is a second problem or any new development, call me back."

"Are you sure we should take her abroad? Could she not live with us here, in our palace, or in Jeddah?"

"We can discuss the particulars with the woman, but with such a family as you have described, they would soon be coming to us and attempting to take her back—bartering for her and taking advantage of our good intentions. Her family would only use her. They would harm her again, given the chance."

"You are right, husband. I had not thought of that possibility." For sure, the last thing I wanted in our lives was for Fatima's evil family and ex-husband to demand money. Those people deserved nothing good. I said goodbye, feeling the most positive I had felt in years, for I had been rescuing women alone for most of my life and now my husband was my full partner, truly interested in playing a role in helping females to gain freedom.

I returned to my guests with a broad smile on my face. All looked at me in hopeful anticipation. "All is well. I have spoken with my husband. He is in full agreement that we cannot allow such a poor decision to be made."

I gazed at Fatima, who was surrounded by three women who were prepared to defend her right to keep her little children, and those women were Dr. Meena, Nadia, and my own precious daughter. I felt so very pleased.

"Fatima, would you like to work for my husband and me? If so, I will arrange to place you in a position where you will be safe and your children will be with you. You will receive lodging and all necessities, a salary, and your children will be provided with a good education. You will have nothing to fear."

"Princess, Princess, I do not know what to say."

"Say yes, Fatima." Amani laughed. "Just say yes."

"Yes, of course. I would be honored, Princess. I would be honored."

My heart was beating rapidly with pure happiness that my husband and I were going to save this woman and her children. I was mentally counting off all the good things I might do for Fatima, a woman who had known nothing but neglect and abuse her entire life. For sure, she would never be abused in our home.

While Nadia and Amani were hugging and exclaiming their joy with Fatima, Dr. Meena wore a very serious expression. She sauntered over to me and asked to speak with me privately. We walked into another room and the good doctor looked at me with sincere concern.

"Princess, I believed that we would solve the problems of individual women in another manner. I do not think that you will be able to take every woman who finds herself in difficult or dangerous circumstances to live in your home."

I smiled at Dr. Meena, who was too serious for her own good.

"Doctor," I told her, "you are correct, of course, that I will not be able to personally move all the Saudi girls and women with problems into my palace. We will find other solutions for other women. But this case is unique. There are twin girls involved, and the difficulties are more complicated than usual. If they are taken from their mother, the girls might be separated, which would be terrifying for these young girls. I promise you that we will find different answers for other cases. But for now, let us celebrate that I will have the opportunity to change Fatima's life and the lives of her daughters in the most extraordinary way."

Dr. Meena smiled for the first time since I had met her. "You are right, Princess. Fatima's case is unlike all others."

She grasped my arm and entangled her hand in mine, as though we had been friends from childhood. With a very cheerful expression, she led me back to Fatima, saying, "Now, you must call and tell me all the lovely surprises I know you have in store for this woman. She has won the Princess Sultana lottery, and for that I am as happy as she is going to be."

Little Sultana jumped up with glee when she learned that the two girls were going to have a safe home with their mummy and that she would see them from time to time.

My most rewarding moment came when Fatima gathered her twin daughters in her arms and wept with a happiness I have never seen in my life. As I stared at Fatima, who looked lovely to my eyes, despite the damage that had been done to her face, I saw a woman who was living a moment of perfect happiness.

To my mind, there is no more rewarding and beautiful sight.

# Chapter Ten
# Solving Fatima's Problem —
# and Then Came Noor

To observe the physical and emotional healing of a woman who has known only neglect and exploitation from the moment of her birth proved to be one of the greatest joys of my life. Fatima entered my palace in need of medical attention; she was so emotionally shattered that she was frightened of all Saudis. I sensed that she was afraid of me and my family, although our only desire was to ensure her well-being, save her from further harm, and bring gladness into her life. After twenty years of abuse, Fatima's emotions had been damaged. Joy for life had never been triggered in her as a young girl, so her only emotions were fear and terror. All other sensations appeared flat; they were unable to spike into hope or joy. In her entire life, nothing pleasant had ever happened, though she derived much gratification from loving her twin daughters. Even then, her enormous devotion to her toddler girls was undermined by worry about what might happen to them in Saudi Arabia: as poor girls from a family such as hers, they would surely have followed her path to grief and sorrow.

But there are times when we humans must walk, filled with anguish, through a dark alley to find joy on the other side. Thankfully, that is what happened to Fatima. While she had been forced to leave her home and suffer mightily, her troubles had led her and her daughters to my palace door; there, she would find many opportunities for herself and her children.

Before Dr. Meena and Nadia left that day, I thought to ask Fatima to provide information to them about her former husband and the young girl he had married, who was certainly undergoing endless torture similar to that which Fatima had endured. If possible, I thought we might save that young girl too, although Dr. Meena appeared uneasy about my plan, quietly reminding me that we had ample numbers of girls and women to save without going into villages and raiding homes.

Dr. Meena had won my respect from our very first meeting, as I knew she would always speak honestly when she disagreed with my plans. I assured her that I would do nothing to bring attention from the government or the religious authorities, but I reminded her that a young girl was being raped and beaten by a brute of a man. I know how such men react if they are offered a sum of money, so I was thinking that I might persuade my husband to send one of his assistants to save the girl and any children she might have. Although still unconvinced, she did agree that Nadia could use her position in social services to find the girl, if possible.

After Dr. Meena and Nadia departed, with plans for us to meet again in a few weeks, Fatima became very nervous, for I was a stranger to this woman. I told Amani to ring for Selma, one of our chefs from Egypt, and Haneen, a highly prized nanny from Jordan who lives in my home and helps when my little prince grandsons come over for extended visits. I knew both of these women could help to soothe Fatima, as she was frightened and did not know what to expect from this new experience. I knew that she needed to be surrounded by those who might easily communicate with her.

When Little Sultana had met Fatima's twin girls, she had behaved like a little mother to them. Once the excitement had eased, she was thrilled to discover that the girls would remain for a time in her grandmother's home. When the time came for her to leave with her father, who had arrived to pick her up, she calmly convinced my son that her work would not be finished until the twins had eaten their dinner and were bathed and ready for bed. My son glanced at me with a twinkle in his eye and said, "Mother, I see that my life will end as it began, living in a palace with a female who will forever be saving those in need."

"There are worse things, my son," I said with a smile.

And so Abdullah telephoned Zain, and my daughter-in-law was fine with the idea of Little Sultana spending the night at our home.

Although Fatima had fallen into a life she could never before have imagined, I was very worried about her state of mind, as she was becoming more nervous by the minute. I quickly realized that the presence of Dr. Meena and Nadia had calmed her, and I wished I had asked them to remain awhile longer. Clearly, too much was happening too quickly for the young mother.

I saw that Fatima's left eye was twitching and her hands were trembling. Her voice cracked when she responded to questions. One moment she appeared to be excited and the next she showed signs of terror. I am certain that she had never been inside the walls of a palace; I watched her eyes grow huge in wonder as she scrutinized our enormous rooms and the luxurious furnishings and decorations. I really was afraid that she was going to swoon.

Once she was introduced to Selma and Haneen, Fatima became even more distressed. She looked at me, then turned her back, speaking to Haneen in a secretive whisper.

Haneen appeared puzzled for a moment, then smiled and kindly stroked Fatima's shoulder, answering loud enough for me to hear,

"Of course we are not slaves in this palace, Fatima. We work for the princess and her family. I love my job and I am free to leave anytime I choose."

Poor Fatima! She was afraid we might imprison her. I wanted to rush and reassure her, but I did not. The sooner Fatima was comfortable in her own room, the quicker she would calm down. We have many unused rooms in our Riyadh palace, and Fatima and her daughters were given a generous-sized apartment to call their own.

Selma and Haneen were told that they should forget their normal duties for a few days and instead help Fatima and her girls to get settled. Both appeared content with their new circumstances, as they are accustomed to my ways; they have told me in the past that their work is never dull, for they never know for certain what they might be doing each day. I know that Selma enjoys her duties as a chef, so I told her to be in charge of preparing whatever food

Fatima and her girls might enjoy, then to join Haneen in making our guests feel comfortable.

Amani busied herself determining Fatima's and the girls' measurements because they were in need of new clothes. All three were wearing very plain garb, and my daughter had noticed that there were rips and holes in the fabric, while the soles of their sandals were nearly worn through. We keep a variety of new garments and footwear in a large closet in the area near the servants' quarters in case those who work for us do not have the funds to buy the necessary attire, particularly when they first come to work at the palace. I also maintain a collection of children's clothes, shoes, hair bows, and other accessories, as there are times when I hear of some child in need and I always rush to help when children are involved.

Haneen and Little Sultana took Fatima's daughters into the large bathroom, which created a lot of excited exclamations from the toddlers. They particularly liked the small rubber camels and sheep waiting for them. Their little hands played with the little toy animals in the warm bath water. A scented perfume was emptied into the water that produced a lot of bubbles, which created even more excitement.

Such childlike joy brought great happiness to Little Sultana, as well as all the adults observing those innocent girls, who had probably never had such a bath or new toys in the three years of their lives. I noticed that Little Sultana's pretty frock was already soaked before I left the area, but I did not care. My granddaughter was cheerfully immersed in aiding others, and I had never felt more certain that she was going to make charity for humanity her life's work, and that is my wish.

I left Fatima in Selma's competent hands and thanked Amani for taking charge of gathering the necessary toiletries and clothing for our guest and her daughters. Amani had the guise of a compassionate woman on a mission when I left her to retire to my bedroom so that I might rest for a few hours before Kareem arrived home from a long day at his office. My husband rarely complains about my charity work unless I exhaust myself to a weary condition, leaving me physically incapable of relaxing with him after a day of work and catching up with family matters. I knew that he'd had several important meetings that day and he enjoyed sharing information with me. He would also want to know something more of Fatima and her girls, so that we could discuss several options with her and make a final decision about her permanent residence.

Returning to my quarters, I relaxed with a soothing bath and, after dressing in a comfortable kimono-type gown Abdullah had purchased for me when he was in Japan, I brushed out my long hair. After that drawn-out task, I lay across my bed, thinking I would not sleep but only rest my eyes.

Several hours later I awoke to little kisses across my forehead and on my cheeks and then my lips. Kareem was home and was in a wonderful mood because his day had been unusually successful. He had also spent quality time with Abdullah in the morning. Our son is my husband's best friend, and my son feels the same about his father.

I was even happier to see my husband because for the first time in our lives I knew that he had finally realized the importance of the work I was doing, that every woman saved bettered the world we lived in. I had been preaching for years that every female lost harmed us all, and now finally my husband appeared to understand.

Kareem and I enjoyed coffee together and then he encouraged me to call for Amani and Little Sultana to spend time with him while I checked on Fatima and her girls.

A few moments later Little Sultana ran into our quarters to share her excitement about our visitors. I was glad to see that Amani had dressed Little Sultana in dry clothes, although my granddaughter was wearing an outfit that was mismatched and too small. Obviously Amani had pulled something from the servants' quarters, but Little Sultana was as happy as I had ever seen her.

Little Sultana tugged on my hand, telling me, "Jaddatee, Afaf and Abir did not know that the round ice cream ball was to be eaten! They thought the ice cream balls were toys. They threw them at Auntie Amani. See her dress? It is dirty now."

"Oh, I see," I said, as I examined Amani's dress. The bodice was soiled with strawberry and chocolate stains. Amani is always immaculate—she could not bear wearing stained clothes even as a child—but now she shrugged indifferently, dismissing the spots with a smile.

As I was leaving the room, I heard Little Sultana excitedly telling her grandfather that she was helping to save two little girls and that she wanted those girls with the same face and hair to leave our home to live in her father and mother's palace.

Little Sultana was quite taken with the twins. I had not asked their names but was pleased that Fatima had named her girls Afaf, meaning chaste or pure, and Abir, meaning serious and beautiful.

When I walked into the quarters occupied by Fatima and her girls, Haneen met me with a finger poised across her lips. "The twins finally fell asleep," she whispered. "They were exhausted after long baths and a full dinner."

"Did Fatima eat, too?"

"A little. She seems very shaky, Princess. I believe that she needs to see a doctor."

"Of course. Fatima and her two daughters will all receive a thorough medical examination tomorrow."

"She is very nervous still."

"Who can blame her? Fatima has led a most dreadful life. She has never been able to trust family members. The sight of all these strangers trying to help her must be very intimidating. I hope that you reassured her that she will not be a slave."

"Oh, I did, Princess," Haneen said with a big smile. "She asked me a lot of questions. She wondered if you beat your servants and was quite relieved when I reassured her that I had never heard you raise your voice to any servant, and certainly you have never been known to beat us!"

"Oh, the poor darling. I am so sorry for the life she has led. But she has no more worries, although she is not sure of that yet."

My heart broke for Fatima. Little did she know that she would be protected for as long as I lived, and then my son and two daughters would take care of her once I was no longer of this earth. It felt wonderful to know that there was one previously abused Saudi woman who never had to live in fear again.

I walked quietly to their bedroom and peeked in. Fatima was sleeping. To feel secure, I suppose, she had placed a daughter on each side of her, and in the same bed. I couldn't blame her. Fatima had come very close to losing her daughters through unfeeling government bureaucracy.

The following day Amani arranged several medical appointments with her personal physicians. My daughter has good relations with several of the palace doctors, and so they made a special appointment for Fatima to see a female internist from Egypt and for the twins to be examined by one of the best pediatricians in Saudi Arabia, a lovely woman from England.

We were relieved to hear that Fatima was not diagnosed with any serious illness, but were not surprised to learn that she had many old injuries from the beatings she had sustained from her husband, including broken ribs, a broken hand, and a broken nose; all had healed poorly without being set properly. She would have pain in her hand forever, if the bone was not rebroken and reset. She also needed extensive dental care, her husband having broken more than ten of her teeth.

I sent word through Amani to the physicians that Fatima would soon be leaving the kingdom and I would ask them for referrals to wherever it was Fatima would be settling. I wanted to have her nose repaired, the bones in her hand reset, her teeth repaired, and anything else that was needed.

Youth, thanks be to Allah, is very resilient, and both girls were healthy other than being plagued by parasites, which is not uncommon in poor families in my country. They received the appropriate medicines and I was told not to worry about Little Sultana, as it was unlikely that she would be infected. Still, I called Zain, so that Little Sultana could be checked by the same pediatrician for those parasites.

One of the girls needed glasses, while the other had perfect vision. I had always believed identical twins were exactly the same, so this information was a revelation to me.

Over the next few weeks Fatima became psychologically calmer, as she came to realize that she was indeed safe, and Kareem and I meant what we said; she no longer had to be afraid of being made homeless, or of having her children taken. She would never again have to worry about being abandoned. She could work for us for the rest of her life, although we wanted her to rest her weary body for some months before any decisions were made about her future.

When she was in a relaxed mood, I asked her, "Fatima, would you like to think of marriage again one day?"

Fatima visibly cringed, staring at me with wide eyes and an open mouth. It was as though she feared I had lost my mind and could possibly be dangerous. She swallowed so hard I heard sounds from her throat. Finally, she responded in a weak voice, "No, Princess. No, please. I have had one ruler. I never want another man to rule me. No."

"But you are so young, Fatima. And not all men are like your ex-husband."

Poor Fatima gestured toward her face, stroking her large crooked nose with her fingers. "With this ugly face, no man will love me like your husband loves you, Princess. No, Princess, it is not possible. All I want from this life is to be free from worry that I will be beaten, or that I will be hungry, or that someone will try to take my children from me. I will be the happiest woman alive if only this can be my future."

I approached Fatima and hugged her gently. "You have my word, Fatima. If that is the life you want, you shall have it." How marvelous I felt, knowing that a woman who had once called herself the unhappiest woman in the world now had the opportunity to be the happiest woman alive. I would make sure this was Fatima's new reality.

"Thank you, Princess. Thank you. You have saved us all," she said, looking at her children with a smile so gentle and full of love that she looked as beautiful as a woman can be, to my eyes.

I encouraged Fatima to spend as much time as she needed to rest her weary body while she devoted every moment to her girls. It was rewarding to see a young mother taking such joy in playing with her children. When I hired a tutor to start lessons for the twins, Fatima asked if she might join in, as she had never been educated and she thought it a good opportunity to learn to read and to practice with numbers.

Three months after Fatima and her girls came to live in our home, we discussed all options with her but asked her to make the decision as to where she wanted to live. She thought about her situation for some weeks before she came to us with an answer, asking that if possible she would like to stay in Saudi Arabia as she was so familiar with our country and was afraid of going to England or Egypt or another strange land.

By this time, my family had grown very fond of Fatima and her two precious girls. After several family discussions, we invited Fatima to live in our small palace in Taif, so that we could keep a check on her well-being as well as that of her girls, whom we all wanted to see well educated. Amani mentioned that both girls were showing signs of high intelligence despite their youth and she believed we should prepare them for a high level of education. Perhaps, like Dr. Meena, they too may achieve high academic status one day.

And why not? Dr. Meena had accomplished that great goal without the backing of a princess sponsor. With our support, the twins can pursue their dreams, whatever they might be.

And so I am pleased to report that a young woman named Fatima is helping us as we help her, for she is one of the most loyal and diligent employees it has been our pleasure to hire. She is so efficient that she is now the supervisor of our home in Taif. She has good relations with all our servants there, as well as members of our family. Fatima makes a good salary and saves much of her money, as her room and board are free. Her daughters can attend any school they like, as Amani has assumed financial support for the twins.

Little Sultana now enjoys Taif more than any other of our holiday homes because she claims to be responsible for the happiness of Afaf and Abir, both of whom love Little Sultana as an older sister, rather than as the granddaughter of their mother's employer.

Such interactions are good for my children and grandchildren, for we were given the gift of wealth without earning it. It is our good fortune that Allah placed us within this family. Since we are undeserving of the wealth we have been given, we must make certain that we share and that we treat others with the same dignity and respect we enjoy. Such courteous relations with those who work for us help to keep my children and grandchildren grounded. After all, as Muslims we are taught that we are no better than any man or woman, and that no man or woman is any better than us.

It is good to follow such teachings, and better yet to believe they are true. And I do.

A few days after we had settled Fatima and her girls, I received an unexpected telephone call from Dr. Meena. She asked me to come to her offices at the hospital so that I might meet yet another Saudi woman who was in her outpatient clinic.

"Is this poor woman in need of immediate help?" I questioned, as I was in the middle of a very busy morning.

Dr. Meena paused for a long time. "Princess, I believe that you should meet her in person and decide for yourself. Please, can you spare only one hour of your day to come to me?"

Knowing Dr. Meena is not a woman who would push unless I was needed, I agreed that I would organize my day so that I could leave the palace and go to the hospital as soon as possible.

I postponed the projects I had scheduled and a few hours later I returned to the hospital where Dr. Meena works. Once more I found myself walking through the long corridor, scrutinizing the mysterious figures draped in black abayas and veils going about their business. One woman was walking slowly ahead of me, her cracked feet inside her plastic sandals slapping on the hard tile floors. Another woman, a Bedouin, was wearing a face veil with a small opening through which I could see the unremitting stare of her black eyes.

Like me, nearly everyone around me was wholly swathed in black. I sincerely hoped most were happy women who felt as I did, that I was a woman with a full life and I intended to wear the veil only until the tradition for veiling in Riyadh and other conservative cities had ended.

Soon I spotted Nadia. She had on her abaya and headscarf but was without her veil. Such a sight made me happy—Nadia was rebelling against the custom of veiling. She was moving quickly in my direction, noticeably impatient for my arrival. My mind was set to see Dr. Meena, but I greeted Nadia pleasantly before asking, "Has this poor woman taken a turn for the worse?"

Nadia gave me a broad smile, one I felt was inappropriate under such emergency circumstances. But I shut my lips tight and offered no criticism.

"No, Princess. The woman is fine, for now." Nadia's next words rang out strangely. "Although her family might be in danger."

"What?" This errand was becoming a mystery for me. What was Nadia speaking about?

"Please, Princess, come with me to the outpatient clinic, where Dr. Meena is waiting with the woman. Her name is Noor."

I followed Nadia's lead, although the affair was becoming more intriguing by the moment. I was growing increasingly keen to hear this story. A few minutes later, as we approached the hospital's outpatient clinics, all of which are stationed in a straight line off the main corridor, I heard a strong female voice raging in anger.

"That is Noor, Princess," Nadia told me.

"Oh?" I remarked. I could not understand exactly what was being said, but I assumed that the poor woman, having endured abuse, and now finding herself in the company of others who were there to protect her, had found the courage to defend herself against her husband.

Nadia escorted me into Dr. Meena's small office before saying a hurried farewell. The adjacent door, which led into an examination room, was open. As I stood by the door, I was not prepared for what I saw. A robust Bedouin man, wearing a soiled white *thobe* and a disheveled *shemagh* (the traditional red-and-white checked headdress worn by Saudi men), was slumped in a chair with his head hanging to his chest, looking as though he had suddenly died. Was he a heart attack victim? I inhaled sharply when I saw streaks of blood running down his neck and onto his arm. This man had been in a fight, most likely while attacking a helpless woman!

He could not see my face, but I could see his. It was pockmarked with large scars, indicating a serious case of untreated teenage acne. When he came out of his apathy to glance up at me, I saw that the whites of his eyes were red. He looked weary, yet he found the energy to smile roguishly, whispering, "Are you the princess?"

Well, I was not going to honor his question! He was obviously one of those men proud of abusing the women in his family. I scowled at him, but, due to my face covering, he was spared my look of anger.

Dr. Meena's hearing is apparently exceptional, for she called out, "Please, do come inside."

By this time, my inquisitiveness had grown to a high peak. I did as Dr. Meena asked. She was standing beside a female patient whose wrinkles filled her face.

In Saudi Arabia, such characteristics cannot really be used to peg a woman's age, for many of our women age early. I guessed that she was most likely fifty years or older. She was dressed in a red cotton dress with brightly colored embroidery designs on the bodice. A black headscarf was draped around her neck.

The woman had a bitter expression as she sat on the examining table with her bare feet dangling. Her rough brown hands were clasped across her chest; she seemed to be nursing a badly bruised and scratched arm. My eyes dropped to her bare feet, which were in dire need of attention, as the skin was rough, with patches of thick dry skin; her toenails were broken and split. Her general build was that of a slim, wiry woman with little flesh on her bones.

I was looking at a Bedouin woman. She was surely the wife of the beast sitting outside the doorway. My first thoughts were that I had been called to help save this woman, who had probably been punched, or worse, by her husband, although I could see no visible signs of abuse. Her ruddy complexion showed no evidence of bruises or scars. As my eyes examined her entire body, I did see dried blood on her hands, most likely defensive wounds, I thought.

"Princess, thank you for coming."

"Dr. Meena, yes, of course."

Dr. Meena nodded her head toward the woman. "This woman's name is Noor. Her husband, Mohammed, waits for her in the other room."

I looked at the woman named Noor and lifted my veil from the bottom and smiled. She did not return my smile, poor thing. No doubt she was recovering from the most recent physical assault.

"What is the problem, Doctor?" I asked, my anger building inside me.

Noor rudely interrupted and, pointing with her finger at the open door, which is a terribly offensive gesture for any Saudi to make, spoke loudly: "The problem is that lazy man. The time has come for a divorce."

There was no response from her husband, Mohammed.

Noor was panting in anger as she screeched, "Are you asleep, you donkey?"

Dr. Meena intervened. "Noor, please, we are here to solve problems. Do not create new ones."

Noor's gaze fixed on Dr. Meena. "But he *is* a donkey!" she said.

I overheard low laughter and a male voice saying, "I will never divorce you, Noor, never. You will be my wife until the day you die."

With a dismissive wave of her brown hands, she shouted an order: "I demand a divorce!"

I was becoming disoriented with the scene unfolding before me, holding my hand to my forehead and wondering what on earth was happening. And why I had been called.

A younger version of Noor stepped into the room. She nodded and smiled but did not speak. She shifted closer to her mother. Noor appeared not to notice her daughter.

Dr. Meena moved to the open doorway and said a few quiet words to Noor's husband before pulling the door shut.

With privacy ensured, I completely removed my veil.

"What has he done to this poor woman?" I inquired.

"Princess, please, sit for a moment," Dr. Meena said, gesturing to a small table and two chairs. "I will sit with you. And, please, do forgive me for interrupting your day for an unusual situation." I shrugged but did not speak, glancing back at the sour-faced Noor, who was suddenly struggling to get off the examining table.

"Please, Noor. Sit still. Give us a moment."

Noor begrudgingly ceased her struggles and reluctantly resumed her previous position, sitting motionless.

Dr. Meena ceased speaking in Arabic, communicating with me in English so that our words might remain confidential.

"Princess, please excuse me for telling another woman's story, but Noor is very agitated. Her daughter is very passionate as well. Both women are so emotional that, once started, they cannot stop talking."

"Please, Doctor, do tell."

"Princess, as we have discussed, our goal is to help Saudi girls and women escape abusive relationships. We also use our energy to save young girls from marriage and, very importantly, to keep them in school. This big task can be very depressing for all, as there are so many tragic stories attached to Saudi women. Even though we relish our victories, with young women such as Nadia or Fatima and her daughters, we all know that our small fingers plunged into the tiny holes in the barrier of human misery cannot stop the dam from overflowing and that there are many thousands of young girls and women who it is impossible to save."

Dr. Meena pursed her lips and looked away, choosing her words very carefully. "Princess, although we both know that it is girls and women who most need us, what should be our commitment to helping a woman who brought abuse upon her own head and who has possibly become a danger to others?"

"What are you saying, Dr. Meena?" I asked, as bewildered as I have ever been in my life.

"I am sorry to confuse you, Princess," Dr. Meena replied. "I called you here today to help solve a most unusual problem. I believe that together we can stop a murder."

"A murder?"

Dr. Meena glanced at Noor, then back at me.

"Who," I asked, "is in danger of being murdered? This Bedouin woman?"

"Perhaps," Dr. Meena replied. "Or, perhaps her husband will be the victim."

I found such a scenario difficult to believe. Noor's Bedouin husband was a massive man who appeared quite muscular, while wiry Noor was a small woman.

Dr. Meena gave me a strong and steady gaze. "This is so. We have two abusers and two abused in this relationship. I really do not know who to help, or who to protect. Noor is not a very pleasant woman, but she is very hardworking and has ruined her health supporting a lazy husband and their four children. Mohammed is a man who manipulates, and he is guilty of psychological and physical abuse."

My eyes widened in astonishment.

Dr. Meena observed Noor and her daughter for a brief period before continuing her very bizarre tale. "Princess, allow me to tell you Noor's story."

I lightly nodded my head.

"Noor is a true desert traveler, a Bedouin girl. I believe that she has been formed by her genetic inheritance and by a harsh environment. In her youth, the family was nomadic, spending only the hottest part of the year in the oases and moving out into the plateau for grass for the animals in the latest part of winter and the early part of spring. She was one of four daughters of nine children. She says that when she reached her tenth summer, her father observed that she was stronger, swifter, and more cunning than her five brothers.

"Due to her diverse capabilities, and on her father's orders, Noor was never given women's Bedouin work, which, as you know, would have consisted of tent raising and cooking and tending to the produce when they were in a fertile area where they might attempt to grow some millet, alfalfa, or wheat. Noor did men's work from an early age, when she was put in charge of the prized camels. Her brothers were told to tend to the goats and the sheep.

"Noor's extensive abilities were a surprise to the entire family, and to her tribe. She showed a special rapport with the animals and instinctively sensed health problems even before the beasts showed signs of distress. To everyone's surprise, soon Noor was helping to medically diagnose and treat animals alongside the Bedouin village animal doctor.

"Like the other Bedouin girls and women, Noor wore the veil when the family came to Riyadh to sell some of the women's wares, but when in the village Noor refused to cover her face. She claimed it hindered her ability to repair trucks or tend to the livestock.

"Her daughter says that no man was courageous enough to confront Noor, even though she was female and young. Those who knew her from youth say that her temper frenzies must be seen to be believed. Personal witnesses told Noor's daughter that her mother reacted with such ferociousness that she was physically feared. Who knew what she might do?

"Even so, we know that Bedouin women can be very forceful, and a number of them do not wear the veil when they are in their villages or working in the fields.

"From what I have been told by her daughter, when Noor was thirteen her father began to treat her better than he treated his sons; in fact, he began to strongly favor his daughter over his sons.

"By this time, the family was seminomadic, living most of the year in a small oasis village not too far from Riyadh. The sons were the eldest of the children and by now were all married, with families of their own. All of Noor's brothers had found employment in the oil industry and had moved across the country to where their work was located.

"After the family settled in a village, Noor's mother and sisters learned a new craft, the art of making silver Bedouin jewelry. By this time, many foreigners were coming into the country to work in our schools and hospitals, and you know how the foreign women love the Bedouin jewelry. So the family's fortunes flourished in comparison to how they had once been as nomads. Noor's father used some of the family income to purchase a white Toyota truck.

"In the beginning, Noor's father did all the driving. Then he suffered a stroke shortly before he was fifty years old. Without any sons living nearby to assume the responsibility, he encouraged Noor to learn to drive. Noor taught herself and, despite her claims that she was a skilled driver from the moment her hands touched the steering wheel, her daughter revealed that during the learning period Noor accidentally ran over a

Bedouin couple and two small children. Thankfully, Noor was traveling at a very slow speed, so no one was seriously harmed. She did kill a couple of goats and a dog, however.

"You and I know, Princess, that it is not unusual for these strong-minded Bedouin women to learn to drive as children and to transport livestock and produce to the family farms in the little villages."

I nodded in agreement. I had personally seen Bedouin or farm women driving trucks and automobiles in several regions of Saudi Arabia. There were many farms in the Taif area, and it was not uncommon to see them helping their husbands or fathers by transporting goods on the country roads. Due to the remoteness of their locations, the government authorities chose to ignore their willfulness.

Dr. Meena continued her most interesting tale: "Noor was different from other village girls in so many ways. She had a special skill when it came to driving and soon became known as one of the most capable drivers in the village. Noor also had a natural flair for all things mechanical. Word soon spread throughout the tribe that no one could repair a vehicle like the young girl, Noor. Young men began to notice Noor, who was not a great beauty but attractive enough and, most important, was capable of tackling every aspect necessary for life. Those young men realized that such a woman would increase their abilities to succeed. Perhaps a poor man might become wealthy with such a gifted wife.

"Noor became so famous in her area that her father received more offers of marriage for Noor than his other three daughters combined. While this was good for the family, so much attention had created a very egotistical side to Noor's character. She soon felt herself above all women and all men. According to the tales told to Noor's daughter by Noor's own mother, she became a difficult girl. I believe that she was worn out with work and so cranky that she verbally abused everyone in the family. She was so aggressive, in fact, that no one would stand up to her. And Noor? Well, her father had led her to believe that she was the smartest and most capable person in the village.

"The family thought that a husband might be able to curb some of Noor's greatest excesses, but Noor liked her life just as it was and arrogantly rebuffed her mother's pleas to accept a marriage offer. Her father was secretly pleased because he was afraid to lose this very competent daughter who could do anything she set her mind to, including bartering for better deals for the produce, driving and repairing the truck, tending to the prized camels, and so on.

"With her brothers living elsewhere and her sisters accepting marriage proposals, Noor was her father's frequent companion. The two of them became so close that the father depended upon Noor to handle much of daily life, the same way most fathers depend upon favored sons.

"Finally, a few years before Noor's father died, his daughter reluctantly agreed to marry, but only if the one chosen for the honor signed a document consenting to live with her family, along with a lot of other unusual requests, such as acquiescing to Noor's demand that he not take a second wife or expect more than three children born of their union. All these ideas are totally foreign to any man in Saudi Arabia, and most certainly to the simple village men considered good matches for a village girl. But as eager as those men were to marry the very industrious Noor, her suitors refused to emasculate themselves publicly by agreeing to such unusual ultimatums. While they wanted Noor to work for them, to make their lives easier, they were not looking for a female to rule their homes."

Dr. Meena shrugged. "That is, all but one man. A young man named Mohammed, the man you just saw in the sitting room. Mohammed readily consented to her demanding marriage terms."

Remembering the blood I saw covering his neck, arms, and hands, I asked, "And so Mohammed did not attack Noor? She caused those injuries I saw on him?"

"It is not that simple, Princess. Noor does beat her husband, but Mohammed beats Noor, too. It's a terrible situation and someone is going to get killed."

My mind resisted what I was hearing. "How does she beat him? He is twice her size."

"Oh, Noor is very clever. She attacks him while he is sleeping, hitting him with boards and clawing him with her strong nails."

"Oh, my," I finally muttered. "What does she say are her reasons for beating him?"

Dr. Meena sighed. "Noor is desperate for a divorce, and Mohammed refuses to agree to it. He is very lazy. He married Noor for all the wrong reasons and has spent his adult life with a slave wife who does all the work. Now that Noor is old and is no longer physically able to work as she once did, Mohammed has become very mean and is becoming more violent by the day. Noor thinks if she beats him enough he will divorce her. She is very weary of being a slave to a man who will not lift a finger to help."

"So, he won't divorce her because he needs her to do all the work?" I asked.

For sure, if Mohammed wanted a divorce, it would be very simple. Any Saudi man can easily divorce his wife by telling her three times that he is divorcing her. Then he must notify the authorities of his divorce. Divorce for a man in Saudi Arabia is a simple act, whereas for a woman it is a much more difficult task. Society is generally against a woman seeking a divorce and the clerics often refuse to grant her request, telling her to go home and make her husband happy. Obviously, this had happened to poor Noor. She was not allowed to leave the man who had used her for his entire life. She was being forced to remain with him.

I glanced toward Noor. When I looked at her more closely, I found that she appeared quite frail. She was certainly too old to work a farm. No wonder she was so cranky.

"I really do not know what to say, Dr. Meena."

"I understand, Princess. But I am worried because the violence is increasing. Noor is no longer so healthy, she cannot be the unique 'wonder woman' she once was. This is creating frustration because she is incapable of doing the work she used to do. Now she realizes that Mohammed has never loved her. He only wanted her to work and support him and the children."

Dr. Meena appeared to be thinking aloud. "Their marriage was unbalanced from the first day. Mohammed is a lazy creature, happy to allow his wife to run the family and the business while he sits around the campfire and shares Bedouin tales and quotes poetry."

Dr. Meena raised her eyebrows in the telling. "His daughter says that her brothers left the area because they could no longer bear to see the conflict between their parents. All the children feel sorry for their mother—and sorry for their father.

"Mohammed actually admires Noor and believes that her slavish detail to work increases his stature in the village. One of his favorite stories has to do with one of the Al Sa'ud princes who visited the area for a scheduled Majilis."

A Majilis is when male members of the Saudi royal family meet with Saudi males from specific tribes or villages so as to listen to their complaints, to accept petitions for financial assistance, or to handle land disputes. The Majilis are very informal, as the Koran teaches us that all men are equal, so at such meetings men feel free to address the prince by his first name.

"Yes, of course," I replied to Dr. Meena.

"It seems that when the prince was having coffee with the men of the village, Noor burst into the gathering, stunning the prince when she began to berate the village leaders, accusing them of kissing the prince to his face and cursing him when he turned his back. She claimed that the local medical clinic was run so poorly that the doctors there were untrained and their skills were so lacking that villagers were needlessly dying. Noor's sharp tongue did not excuse the prince; she told him that she had received substandard care for a minor problem and that she'd had to cure herself. She said that she could run the clinic better than any doctor sent by the government. She did not know when to shut her mouth and went on to tell the prince that she would think that with such wealth from the oil that the royal family could at least manage it well enough to improve simple medical services in the small villages.

"It did not benefit the situation when the prince, who, luckily for Noor, happened to be a gracious and good-natured man, appeared to respect her and even told the village elders that Noor was a woman with a good mind and they should listen to any advice she might give."

My mind was racing. I suddenly recalled Sara sharing a story about Assad, her genial husband. Assad had spent several weeks attending Majilis in more than one village near Riyadh to keep a close connection with members of a certain tribe. Assad said that during a visit to one of the villages a tough Bedouin woman had shocked everyone at the gathering when she had interrupted to make complaints about the medical facilities available and about the lack of organization on the part of the royal princes.

The incident described by Dr. Meena was nearly identical to the scene depicted by my brother-in-law. I hesitated sharing the news that the prince involved happened to be married to my sister, so I bobbed my head without speaking, although stunned at how small our world really is and how human paths cross so unexpectedly.

Dr. Meena and I gazed at each other, and then we looked at Noor. She knew that we were speaking about her. I nodded and smiled, but she did not respond.

My sympathy increased for her situation. Although Noor was strong in many ways, and stood up for herself, her life had been a great misery of backbreaking labor. She was old now and unable to maintain her usual routine. She could not escape her husband—in Saudi Arabia, a husband is a woman's guardian. She could not simply leave her village and go off on her own. Such a thing is not allowed in my country.

"What do you propose we do?" I asked.

"I wanted to ask you, Princess, if you thought your husband might send someone from the government to speak with Mohammed and encourage him to agree to a divorce. If the situation continues to escalate, I believe that Noor or Mohammed will go too far with their beatings. At the moment Noor is using boards, and Mohammed is using his fists. But at some point one of the two will use something more deadly, perhaps a sharp instrument like a dagger. Although there is a lot I do not like about either of these people, I do not want to see either of them in their shroud. If I do not do something, I believe there will be a murder and I want to prevent such a thing happening."

I hesitated. Never had any Saudi man I had ever known intervened between a man and his wife. Personal privacy regarding men and their female family members is considered sacrosanct.

"I will speak with Kareem tonight, but I am not hopeful, Doctor."

"Believe me, I understand," Dr. Meena replied.

"For the moment, what will you do?"

"I am going to admit Noor for a few days to give them both time to cool down. If your husband can think of something he might do to convince Mohammed to divorce Noor, then Noor will live with one of her children. All have agreed to offer her a bed."

I sighed and then said, "Then I will go, Doctor. Thank you for calling me. I will speak with Kareem tonight. I will call you tomorrow with his thoughts on your idea." As I prepared to leave, I gave Dr. Meena a knowing look, for I felt this woman understood me better than most and I believed that I understood her. I stood up and reattached my veil, then straightened my outer garments.

I left without saying anything to Noor or her daughter, although I felt bad for them both.

As I was about to walk from the room, I received a final shock. We all heard Mohammed call out to Noor, telling her once again that he would never divorce her. Noor appeared to snap, leaping off the examining table, flinging open the door and running at her husband. She jumped up and down, beating on Mohammed's head with her clenched fists. When I saw that her eyes were a sinister black with hate for her husband, I realized that Dr. Meena was right: Noor might be capable of murder.

Mohammed stood up and looked down at Noor with a snarl—then I believed he was capable of murdering Noor too!

Thankfully, two of Dr. Meena's assistants intervened before anyone was seriously injured. I glanced back to see Dr. Meena standing with pursed lips, shaking her head in dismay.

I quickly left the room, feeling more confused than I have felt in many years.

As I walked up the corridor to leave the hospital, my heart was heavy with unfocused feelings. I wanted to shout at someone, but I closed my lips. The air in the hospital was still and hot, and within a few steps I began to feel perspiration running down my neck and back, little streams feeling like crawling insects.

So many questions and thoughts raced through my mind. Every marriage was complicated. How far should I go in my quest to save abused women? Although Noor had been abused psychologically and was now enduring it physically, she was also guilty of abusing Mohammed.

What if I had made mistakes in the past? What if I had condemned guiltless men while conniving women cunningly reshaped the reality of their lives? The entire foundation of my life was built upon fighting against ruthless men so as to protect innocent women. Women have always been the blameless party in my mind and men the abusers.

All these thoughts were spinning in my mind as I continued walking. Doubts about my ability to evaluate abusive situations multiplied. Angry tears blurred my vision and before I could get out of the hospital to reach my car I had collided with another veiled woman, who screamed as though someone had plunged a dagger into her heart. So startled was I that I staggered. Several foreign women attempted to keep me from falling, but I slipped through their hands and crashed a second time into the same veiled woman. Both of us tumbled to the hard tile floor. Her veil and headscarf were askew, and when she raised her head the movement revealed a long smooth neck. Her abaya was to her knees, exposing very shapely, muscular brown legs that clearly belonged to a very young woman. Who was she? What was her life story? Whoever she was, she was physically very powerful, proving the point when she leapt from a prone position to standing without any effort. Was she a secret athlete? Women in Saudi Arabia are discouraged from participating in sports, so some girls clandestinely train at home so that no one in the government is aware of their sporting interests.

I was acutely embarrassed to find myself rolling around on the floor; it was one of the few times in my life I had been pleased to be wearing the veil. I was so stunned by all that was happening that it took me a few moments to push myself back onto my feet. Several people began questioning me, asking if I was all right, but I was on the verge of tears so I just brushed past them all, running up the corridor, stumbling and gasping. Thankfully, no one chased after me, and I made it to my car and my startled driver.

Never have I been so relieved to arrive home and to retire to my quarters. Later that evening I told a concerned Kareem the reason I had taken to my bed without a word and that I felt so pessimistic; I could feel a severe depression building inside me.

I dreaded even asking Kareem to intervene in a marriage, for I already knew the answer my husband would give. I finally built up the courage and described in full the day's events, describing Dr. Meena's fears about a possible murder, which in turn had prompted her request for me to ask my husband to intercede and encourage Mohammed to give his wife a divorce.

Kareem did not have to think about his answer: it was an instant no. He, like every other man in Saudi Arabia, does not believe that one man can know another man's life with his wife. The matter is private.

Kareem was also surprised that I had been called by Dr. Meena in the first place. "This is not the sort of problem that can be solved, Sultana. While the doctor should medicate them both, they must go home and work out these problems as a man and wife. You often work miracles, darling, but you cannot come between a man and a woman who live as man and wife."

"But what if one of them murders the other? I'll never forgive myself. If Mohammed is killed, then Noor will be executed. If Noor is killed, then Mohammed will continue to sit by the fireside and entertain his friends with his stories. This would not be right. How can I face Dr. Meena?"

"Sultana, you cannot shape every woman's life. If one kills the other, then it was meant to be. Their fate rests in God's hands."

I was frustrated by failure, as I always want to intervene and believe that any situation where a woman is being abused is my business, even if that woman is abusing her husband too.

When tears formed in my eyes, Kareem told me, "Do not think of trying to make me feel guilty, Sultana. This time it will not get you the results you are seeking."

"It is not a ploy, Kareem. I am simply depressed. I prefer problems that are clearly black or white. When problems are clouded with ambiguities, I do not know what to do. This episode has led me to question so many decisions I have made in the past. I now fear that I have made endless mistakes in my life's work. Mistakes, mistakes, mistakes . . . one mistake after another."

My husband was the perfect foil for the traumatizing day I'd had. First he looked at me solemnly before kissing my hands and expressing his love for me. Then he left our quarters for a few moments to go to the kitchen and bring back a glass of my favorite fresh pineapple juice. My husband passed me the drink before sitting on the edge of my bed.

When he finally spoke, he said, "Sultana, do you trust me, darling?"

I nodded my head, speaking in a low voice, "Yes, I trust you."

"Good. Then listen to me. Sultana, I have lived each day with you for many years now. Darling"—he then inclined toward me to stroke my face and look into my eyes. "Darling, I know you better than you know yourself."

I moved my head slightly.

"Sultana," he said with complete seriousness, "you, Sultana, are the only person I have ever known who has never made a single mistake."

I was so startled by my husband's words that I choked on the juice and coughed for a long time before I could catch my breath.

I stared at Kareem. I watched as the beginnings of a small smile formed his lips into a curve and, knowing that my husband was making a joke, suddenly my sorrow turned to joy and I could not restrain my laughter. He laughed with me. We laughed loudly like children, laughing until I felt that our combined laughter had eradicated the poisons that had been building in my mind and heart. Kareem made me realize in that moment that we all make mistakes, and mostly we all try to do the very best that we can in this life.

From that moment, I once again forged ahead in my quest to help females, although I have my eyes open for any situation where a male is being mistreated and, if so, I will step in. Anytime I have doubts as to my actions, my husband smiles, telling me, "But you are a perfect woman who has never made a mistake, so push ahead, darling."

There are times when our children are in our presence when these exchanges occur, and they trade glances that appear to convey that they think their parents are slightly crazy.

Some people have an aversion to merriment, I suppose.

That is when Kareem and I laugh most freely, because my husband's words never fail to remind me that I am only human and I will make mistakes in life. Despite this, I must remember to take the greatest joy from my victories.

As far as Noor and Mohammed are concerned, a good solution was found without help from Kareem or me, much to my relief. Dr. Meena felt, certainly in the short term, that medication might help to soothe the situation and she proposed medicating both with drugs that fight anxiety. This proved to be an excellent solution, which had a miraculous effect. The last Dr. Meena heard from Noor's daughter, the couple had ceased physical fighting, although on occasion they were known to practice their verbal skills on each other when involved in a dispute. As a result of this more placid approach to life, the couple found themselves more able to discuss and work out their differences without resorting to physical violence; they have also negotiated a more equal share of their workload. Common sense and justice for both parties prevails!

The episode was a good lesson for me, and for Dr. Meena, as we now often remind each other that we must use our time, energy, skills, and money to solve the most serious problems of abuse against women in Saudi Arabia.

# Chapter Eleven
# Faria and Shada

## Faria and FGM

Not long after I had helped Noor, my assistance was needed again, this time with a young woman named Faria, who had undergone a traumatic ordeal and was desperate to escape from her situation. Faria is a member of one of the most conservative tribes in the kingdom, which I cannot name for fear of reprisals against Faria's family. It is they who would be in danger, although they played no role in Faria's flight to freedom; in fact, they would most likely punish Faria, given the opportunity, as her desire to leave her life behind is an affront to the women of the tribe. There is an interesting history to Faria's story, too, as the men of her family and tribe strongly dislike and disrespect my own family, the Al Sa'ud rulers. Faria would surely be put to death for reaching out to what these men consider the most despised family in the kingdom.

My father's family, the Al Sa'ud clan, are descended from the Anazah tribe, which is one of the largest and most ancient tribes in the region. However, unlike many tribes, who determined long ago to maintain the purity of their clan, the Al Sa'ud has fraternized with many tribes since the early 1930s, when my grandfather, King Abdul Aziz, early in his rule plotted to cement political alliances by marrying a daughter of every tribe in the area. There were a few tribes who refused a union with my family— tribal ties go deep in Saudi Arabia, with many men loyal to their tribe first and to the country second, hence there are tribes in Saudi Arabia today who feel no allegiance to their Al Sa'ud rulers; they would be pleased if our family was overthrown and new rulers installed and, if at all possible, for the rulers to hail from their own tribe.

My grandfather's idea was brilliant, however, for marriage and children generally develop courteous feelings between even the most oppositional tribes. The years have proven his genius in this matter, for the success and wealth of many tribes in Saudi Arabia are intimately connected to those of their rulers. Most of the Al Sa'ud disagreements have occurred with the tribes who rejected that early bond with my grandfather.

The men of Faria's tribe have, in fact, never blended with other tribes through marriage and consider themselves to be the purest of any of the regional tribes. As they do not feel any kinship with other tribes, they believe they have the right, or even the obligation, to flout government bans or laws with which they disagree. Genital mutilation of females is one of the bans they ignore.

My grandfather banned the most extreme forms of male circumcision during his early rule, as well as all female circumcision, better known these days as female genital mutilation (FGM). Faria's tribe still inflicts this ghastly ritual upon its females.

While there are twenty-nine countries listed by the World Health Organization (WHO) where FGM is common, there are other areas where the practice exists but affects such a small number of individuals that the countries in question do not register on such lists. I have read many reports written by Westerners who say that FGM no longer occurs in Saudi Arabia, but this is not true. While the practice has been outlawed and the number of women affected is admittedly small— only two Saudi Arabian tribes and various immigrant populations settling in our land still maintain the custom— each case of FGM is a personal tragedy that demands our attention.

As I have said, there are two specific tribes in my land whose girls are in danger of FGM. This fact is unknown to most of the world, but who can intrude on decisions centered around Saudi Arabian women by their men? No one has the capability to enforce laws concerning females upon a defiant tribe, not even the men who rule Saudi Arabia. Why? The reason is simple. First, and most important, relationships between men and women in Saudi Arabia are deemed restricted and privileged. Second, the happiness of a woman's life is never considered. In fact, female life is not particularly important at all. The men of my family would never go to war against any tribe just to ensure protection of women. Issues to do with family decisions regarding females are considered exclusive to the family, even in the eyes of our central government. So many harmful things continue to happen to women because governments across the planet are not concerned with the safety and well-being of their women.

For those who do not know, the WHO describes FGM as a procedure that intentionally alters or causes injury to the female genital organs for nonmedical reasons. The WHO goes on to report that:

- The procedure has no health benefits for girls and women.
- Procedures can cause severe bleeding and problems urinating, and later cysts, infections, and infertility, as well as complications in childbirth and increased risk of newborn death.
- More than 125 million girls and women alive today have been cut in the twenty-nine countries in Africa and the Middle East where FGM is concentrated.
- FGM is mostly carried out on young girls sometime between infancy and the age of fifteen.
- FGM is a violation of the human rights of girls and women.


While many uninformed people believe that FGM means only a little cutting, this is not true. In most cases, FGM involves partial or total removal of the external female genitalia, creating serious injury or even death in young girls and women. The practice is barbaric and has no persuasive basis in any religion, although many girls who undergo the brutal procedure are of the Muslim faith.

Often it is the mothers who insist upon their daughters' being mutilated, for an assortment of reasons. Many mothers who were cut as children believe that what was good enough for them is also best for their daughters. Wishing for their daughters to remain chaste, they wrongly believe that genital cutting limits sexual behavior. Other women in the tribe make mothers feel disloyal to their culture if they choose not to have their daughters cut.

Babies as young as two weeks and girls as old as sixteen are mutilated. Most do not receive any anesthesia. Shockingly, their genitals are cut away by an untrained woman or man using dirty scissors or blunt razors. The instruments used to perform the procedures are used on multiple victims without any sterilization.

This is what happened to Faria. The young woman came to Nadia's attention after she was admitted to the hospital with hemorrhaging and infection. Faria had been brought there by her family only when she was near death; their fear had spurred them on to seek medical attention. Her infection was so widespread and serious by this time that the hospital team predicted that she would not survive the night. However, Faria surpassed the doctors' expectations. Each evening they would announce that Faria would not live out the night, only to find her still with the living when they returned on their rounds the following morning. Faria defeated the odds and clung to precious life.

Her will to live soon fueled the interest of the Western physicians and nurses, who began to devote many extra hours to her care. After a week of extensive medical attention, Faria woke up in the hospital ICU, surprised to find that she was still alive.

One of the British physicians in charge of Faria's care was familiar with our country's history. Although he knew that immigrants from other nations, including women from Indonesia and Egypt, for example, were often admitted to hospitals for necessary medical care resulting from recurring health issues caused by FGM, he rarely saw Saudi girls or women who had been circumcised. Faria was one of the first. Aware that the practice had been forbidden many years earlier, he was worried about other young girls in the area. Due to his concern, he notified Nadia and mentioned that an intervention by social services might be appropriate.

Nadia later said that her ears pricked in interest, for she had never worked on an FGM case, although she had heard a number of stories about women admitted as a result of long-term effects from childhood cutting; so many women suffer horribly for their entire lives after being victims of FGM.

There are constant infections due to the abnormal flow of urine. Most victims of FGM develop scars that cover their vagina, making sex extremely painful. There are substantial problems during pregnancy and childbirth. Women who have scarring have long labors, tissue tearing, and heavy bleeding. All of these problems cause stress for the mother and the baby. Added to the physical problems are psychological and emotional ones, as the procedure is generally performed on very young girls who have no idea why they are being restrained and violently and painfully cut.

Knowing that the subject is taboo in Saudi Arabia, Nadia picked her time carefully, going to visit Faria in her hospital room when Faria was alone. When Nadia first spoke to me, she related, "It was difficult to get Faria to talk, but once she started she described in great detail what had happened to her. I dared not interrupt."

Faria had tearfully told Nadia the tale of her cutting.

"I was stupid. I should have fought them. I should have run away into the desert. My fate alone in the desert would have been less traumatic than what I have endured while under the protection of my parents.

"I had heard about the cuttings, the wonderful time of becoming a woman, so I reluctantly accepted that I must undergo it. Once, when I expressed doubt, my mother angrily said that if I refused I would become a freak. She claimed that my female parts, my clitoris, would continue to grow until it became huge, the size of a male penis. I would be ridiculed. I would be considered unclean. No man would agree to marry me. My mother and younger sisters would be scorned.

"The idea of having a clitoris as big as a penis convinced me and I accepted that I must do anything I could to avoid such a fate. As the time approached to be cut, I even got a little excited. A big party had been planned for the girls who were going to undergo the procedure. Our parents were purchasing special gifts for the grand occasion. Some of the girls scheduled to be cut at the same time were my friends. We were going to be honored, brought into the society of women, or so we were told.

"We were also told a fairy tale. We were promised never-ending happiness. After the successful cutting and healing, we would become engaged. We would marry a handsome man within the year and be happy wives and mothers. What woman does not want marriage and children?

"The party went well enough, although I began to feel nervous when several of my friends who were going to be cut began to tremble and sob. Those girls were more informed, as they had older sisters who had warned them about the pain and the blood. Those girls were terrified, as they knew something of what to expect.

"I was the oldest girl in my family, so there was no one to warn me. Although my mother had undergone the cutting when she was a young girl, it had been many years earlier and her memory had slipped. She appeared to have forgotten the horror of it. My mother was not the type to talk about intimate subjects anyhow. While I was under the impression that the procedure might hurt slightly, I was assured by my mother that the cutting and the pain would be quick, like a sharp pinch on my arm. Mother claimed that the rewards would be well worth any discomfort. My mother lied.

"When the time came, the six of us were led from the party hall into an adjoining room by women we did not know well. Two other women were waiting for us. There were six mats placed side-by-side on the floor and we were each told to take off our undergarments and lie down. We did as instructed without question.

"I took my place on a mat located in the middle, wanting to know what was coming, as I assumed the women would begin with a girl from either side first. I became more frightened by the minute because I could smell fear, the fear of my girlfriends, the ones who had been forewarned by their sisters.

"I was told to raise my dress over my head, leaving my bottom bare. I was also told to lift and spread my legs. I did as ordered, although my heart was fluttering in fear; all I wanted to do was jump from that mat and run away. But there was a woman sitting beside me, her hands on my shoulders, ready to discourage me from fleeing.

"The two women who had been waiting for us were the hired cutters of our genitals. So they were ready, poised with big scissors in their hands. The business of cutting started almost immediately. High-pitched screams blended with moans from both sides of me. When the hysterical screaming failed to cease, I decided that it was time to leave. I sat up. The woman who had accompanied me into the room grabbed my shoulders and pushed me back down on the mat. I had not noticed until that moment that all the women assigned to the teenage girls were very large women, strong women, who were chosen to subdue young girls.

"And then my time came. First I felt hands between my legs, and strong fingers grabbing a small part of my genitals. That part of my body was painfully pulled and stretched, then I felt the metal of the scissors. That's when I felt excruciating pain. Imagine, if you can, being operated on without anesthesia. My flesh was being cut away without the benefit of any numbing agent to deaden the pain. I began to scream. I could not stop. The agony intensified when those probing fingers grabbed other loose skin at my private area. All my skin down there was slashed away until I was smooth. I felt that I was being cut to pieces! Someone began sewing me up with a big needle and thread. That, too, was terribly painful and by this time I was on the verge of passing out.

"The stitching did not stop the bleeding. No matter what they did, warm blood gushed from my body. I felt the liquid pooling under my body. Someone began to call for gauze, which was pushed and packed inside my body. I have a memory of being taken to a small room where they put the babies and girls who suffered the most severe side effects, such as uncontrolled hemorrhage. I vaguely recall overhearing the deafening shrieks of babies and

young girls. I am sure that my screams mingled with
their screams.

"I truly believed that I was dying, but the pain
was so acute that I welcomed death as a release. I lost
awareness shortly after being taken into that room, and
when I regained consciousness I was in a different
place being treated by very soft-spoken nurses and
doctors. I was still delirious with pain, but I overheard
bits and pieces of conversations. I understood that I
had nearly died from blood loss. I listened to two
nurses whispering that I no longer looked like a girl, as
everything God gives to women in their private parts
had been sliced from my body.

"My mother had promised me dreams of
womanhood and marriage and children, but instead
she had paid to have me made into a cripple without
the crucial body parts to live the life of a contented
wife and mother."

Nadia's tears had interrupted Faria's story at
this point. I was fighting back my tears, too. Nadia
was naive regarding the genital mutilation of females,
but I was aware of many aspects of this barbaric
ritual, as several of my older sisters had undergone the
procedure in the days shortly after the practice was
banned, when news of that ban had not yet reached
the ears of every mother in the kingdom.

My mother and father were born into different
tribes. My father's family lived in the Najd region,
where they never practiced the primitive tradition of
cutting female genitals. However, that was not the case
in my mother's tribe. In the old days, my mother's tribe
still followed the tradition of ritual cutting, though
this stopped completely during the 1950s. Tragically, my
sisters who were born prior to 1955 were subjected to

the nightmare of genital mutilation; the younger daughters, including Sara and me, were spared.

My older sister had once told me the particulars of her own genital cutting. I was completely horrified, but delighted that my grandfather had seen fit to ban the practice during the early part of his reign after he had personally witnessed the graphic circumcision of a young boy whose skin was flayed from his penis to his knees. He was told then that some tribes followed the tradition of a similar cutting of their females. My wise grandfather instantly banned both gruesome practices, although some tribes chose to ignore his ruling, thus young girls like Faria are forced to suffer the unendurable even today.

Nadia was very distressed and emotional as she recounted Faria's story, and I patted her hands, offering what little comfort I could. Remembering my own nightmares after first learning about female mutilation, I understood her emotion. But getting back to the important task at hand, I asked, "What is going to happen to Faria, Nadia? Do you know?"

"Princess, when I advised Faria that I was from social services and that I was there to help guide her with future plans, she spoke without even thinking, saying that she must escape her family. She is bubbling with anger that her own mother pushed her into such a torture. She says if she is forced to return home she will be forced into an arranged marriage. She is now very fearful and against early marriage. Her fear stems from the fact that doctors told her that she will have to confront a host of problems following what has happened to her, with painful sexual relations being one of the most troubling.

"Her only desire now is to stop the cutting of females. She knows that she must complete her education so that she can become a legal expert, perhaps a barrister, and work tirelessly to prevent this kind of abuse from continuing."

"Is she speaking from early emotion surrounding this significant event, or do you believe she is calm through her entire mind and heart?" I asked.

Nadia paused, remembering her conversation with Faria. "Princess, I have met with Faria three times and I feel certain that she is speaking from a place of composed preparation rather than from a state of emotion."

Nadia looked into the distance, remembering what she had been told by the young victim, before looking into my eyes. "If she is indeed sure of this decision, what do you think might happen to help her achieve such a goal? If I go to her with a plan, perhaps she will reveal more of herself to me."

"You are so right, Nadia. This is all very fresh for Faria. Perhaps she will want her mother's comfort in a week's time. We will not rush her, of course. Please call my daughter Amani, so that you can arrange a private meeting between my daughter and this young woman. My daughter is now involved with all aspects of my work and she has a keen mind. Once Amani meets with Faria, she will speak with me, and then we will devise a workable solution according to Faria's settled emotions and true wishes."

Nadia was pleased, as she and Amani had connected nicely, with both young women trusting each other. I so wanted Amani to assume true responsibility and not simply follow my instructions. I felt more than pleased to give up total control of my work so that my daughter felt herself a true participant.

And so I struggled to turn my mind away from the horrors Faria had endured. I did not have long to dwell on this young woman's problems, because my husband came rushing into our home to tell me about a young Saudi woman, the daughter of one of his employees. The poor girl had been arrested for a very serious crime.

## Shada and the Anti-Witchcraft and Sorcery Squads

Although I know that there are many Saudi women in grave situations, each misfortune brought to my attention always seems to be the most urgent. But in the bizarre case of Shada I truly felt that I would be unable to save her from certain execution.

Shada is the daughter of one of Kareem's faithful employees, who works as a mechanic's assistant in our family garage, located in our expansive Riyadh estate. Although most of the royal estates in the kingdom are equipped with every facility needed to support a small city, including medical clinics, horse stables, large playgrounds, car repair shops, restaurants, and mosques, Kareem has paid special attention to our car repair facility. He organized the building of the garage after Abdullah reached an age to own and drive his own vehicle. As it happens, the building of our garage facility was not quite finished when our son Abdullah visited a local service shop in Riyadh in order to repair his vehicle. It was then that he became involved in a very unpleasant incident, which I will relate here as a short aside.

Shortly after arriving at the shop, our son was accosted by a very angry mechanic, who was physically assaulting his Saudi boss with a large steel wrench.

When Abdullah saw the wrench-wielding mechanic attacking the owner of the shop, he tried to remove the wrench from the man's hand. But the mechanic was strong and held on to his weapon. In the struggle, the wrench came down on my son's head. Although Abdullah managed to keep his footing, his head was gashed. At that time several other customers intervened and my son was saved from being more seriously battered. It is clear that the mechanic was very angry and was determined to badly injure his employer or anyone else who got in his way.

We later discovered that there was a reason for the man's anger. His Saudi employer had refused to pay his salary for over a year, and the man's wife and children were suffering in their home country, as they did not have money to buy the necessities of life. Added to that misery, the Saudi boss refused to allow any of his employees to leave their jobs and return to their home countries until they had worked for the full two years of their contracts.

It is a sad fact that in Saudi Arabia there are a number of very wealthy Saudis who grow wealthier still by hiring poor people from countries all over the world, requiring them to leave their homes and travel to the kingdom to work and earn money to support their families. The Saudi employers do not have to pay any expenses, as the poor people borrow money to pay the agents in their countries to find foreign employment. Generally, they must pay their travel expenditures to the kingdom, too. Once those people are in the country, their passports are seized by their Saudi employers. From that moment, the foreign employees are at the mercy of unscrupulous employers, who have no intention of paying their salaries. While the employers will provide the most basic shelter and enough food to feed their workers, many do not pay the monthly salaries as agreed in the contract. Once in the kingdom, an employer might claim that he is holding their salaries until the end of their contracts; meanwhile, those workers have no funds to send home to their families.

It is a shameful scandal that such wrongful things are common in my country. I even know members of the royal family who act thus with their workers, and these are people with more money than a bank full of employees can count. I do not know what to say, other than that it is wicked and unethical. How I wish there would be laws to protect such hardworking people, but in my country the poor do not have a voice. That is why the soft-hearted royals so often become the voice for the indigent and the helpless.

Of course that foreign mechanic's anger gained nothing good for him; indeed, it won him a long prison sentence. Only Allah knows what would have happened to that man's family but for my son's charitable action. Once Abdullah heard the particulars of the case and learned that the Saudi shop owner had abused his staff and kept back their salaries, he was displeased with that man and felt sympathy for his employees. My son hired a Saudi lawyer to gain permission to question the man sent to prison. Once the man's trust was won and information was forthcoming as to his family's contact information, Abdullah arranged for the family to receive twice the man's salary for the duration of his prison sentence.

Now the wrathful expatriate who once hated all Saudis, and even tried to harm Abdullah, has come to respect and love my son, a Saudi man.

Allah blessed my son with a good heart, and Abdullah has never been able to bear the exploitation of any human, and certainly not when the abuse is so injurious that a person is driven crazy and wants to fight, even knowing that his act will gain him imprisonment or even a death sentence. Such a thing is the behavior of one who is hopeless and has nowhere to turn.

Thankfully, Abdullah was not seriously harmed in that attack, but Kareem nearly lost his mind thinking about what might have happened. Kareem's voice was loud and high-pitched when he told me the story, saying, "Our son could have been killed, Sultana. It is a serious matter to be hit in the head with a wrench."

We now have our own garage and highly trained workers from Germany and the United States, who are paid well and who are very happy with this Saudi family. There are five or six Saudi men who assist these skilled mechanics.

And so now I will return to the bizarre story of poor Shada, who is the daughter of one of Kareem's Saudi mechanic assistants. Although I did not know her personally prior to the incident that threatened her life, I had seen her a few times from a distance and was told that she was a very shy girl. Since she was just a schoolgirl and did not work for our family, I had no occasion to enter into a conversation with her. I had heard more about her father, as my husband praised the man for his attention to detail and his quiet manner.

However, this all changed when Kareem came bursting through the door that day, telling me that there was an acute emergency that had to be dealt with—and one that involved Shada.

To get my mind off Faria's troubles, I had been reading an interesting report about the current happenings in India, where some men appeared to have lost their minds and believed that any woman walking down the street was available to be raped. Kareem's anxious face got my attention, however, so I sat up and listened carefully to what he had to say, laying the papers on my desk for later reading.

"What has happened?" I asked.

Kareem was nearly incoherent, but finally he told me that the daughter of one of his favorite employees was in jail, that the religious clerics were saying her crime meant that she would lose her head. Shada had been accused of being a witch.

This was very alarming, but before I recount the story Kareem told me, I feel it is important to give a little background into Shada's home life and also to explain some very disturbing developments relating to witchcraft and sorcery that increasingly dominate certain parts of Saudi society.

Shada's mother stays at home with the family. As the mother of five children, she stays busy from the moment the sun rises until she sleeps at night. Shada's father seemed occupied with work and he was saving all he could because Kareem said he was fond of saying that the years were running at him and soon he would be an old man.

Those who work for us have neat accommodations on our property and have no expenses for utilities or transportation. Kareem supplies the basics of food, such as rice, potatoes, beans, tea, coffee, and chickens. Several times a year the employees are given sheep and camels for feasts.

There is a nice large plot where they can grow vegetables in order to supplement their diets. All can choose from the clothing we provide for our employees, but if they want something special, they do spend their own funds for those extras. We have first-aid facilities at our clinic, and unless there is a major health problem all their health needs are met on the palace grounds. Two years ago Kareem had a dental clinic built and it recently opened, so now we have two dentists on staff.

With nearly all the necessities supplied, Shada's father saved most of his salary so that one day he could retire. His dream was to return to the village of his birth and build a modest home, with ample funds to support his essentials for old age.

The family felt it was the best luck to live and work for a prince for the time being. And they were doubly delighted to work for a prince who had never once cheated them out of their hard-earned money. They know that many poor citizens who work for the royals are not so fortunate.

The bizarre incident that led to Shada's arrest happened when she visited one of the newest malls in Riyadh, a mall that is teeming with people from every walk of life, from the most affluent Saudis to the poorest expatriate workers from various developing countries. These people from different socioeconomic classes brush near to each other while promenading past exclusive shop windows displaying the most costly clothes and jewelry, although they rarely have occasion to mingle or to enter into discussion with one another.

Shada had never been in any mall—she is not a girl who has money to go shopping, so there was no reason for her to take a stroll into a world of dreams.

Apparently, on this occasion, Shada's parents had allowed her to go to the mall with another family they knew. As I have said, this was her first visit to the mall, and it was her naivety that led to the crisis.

I have been told that Shada was so taken in by the sights she saw that she could not stop staring at everyone and everything. This is a bad habit in Saudi Arabia, where people guard their privacy with great resolve and most particularly the privacy of females.

When Shada entered a lingerie shop and saw what she said was the most beautiful woman in the world—a young Saudi woman who had slipped out of her veil while in the privacy of the shop—Shada walked close to the woman and gawked open-mouthed at the woman's face. She also ogled her cloak and went so far as to bend down to examine the woman's expensive designer heels.

The Saudi woman became very offended, even distraught, and, covering herself quickly, ran from the shop to locate her parents, who were having a coffee nearby. Her alarmed father summoned the police, and when Shada walked out of the lingerie shop she was surrounded and arrested. At first, the police said that Shada was stalking the young woman and that she was going to be charged as a harasser, which is a serious crime in my country.

Unfortunately, by this time the Saudi beauty claimed to have fallen ill and vomited on the floor. At this point Shada, who was unsophisticated to the point of near stupidity, fell to the floor and tried to clean up the mess with a handkerchief she had in her hand, which had some embroidery stitches on it. Shada actually reached out to touch the beauty, trying to tell her that she was sorry but that she was so beautiful she could not take her eyes from her face, that she did not know that such beauty existed.

The beauty's mother then became hysterical and shouted to the police that Shada was holding a handkerchief with a chant embroidered on it, saying Shada was in reality a witch who was trying to gather her daughter's vomit so as to create a spell. The mother claimed that all women were jealous of her daughter's beauty and obviously this witch was planning to murder her daughter using a chant or a spell.

I really did not know what to say. For the past few years, I had learned much about this new and scary trend in Saudi Arabia, but this was the first occasion when someone working for our family had been trapped in the lunacy.

"Well, where is Shada now?" I asked Kareem.

"In prison. By the time her father was notified, she had already been arrested and charged."

"What is the charge?"

Kareem nearly shouted, "Witchcraft! The foolish girl is being charged as a witch!"

"What can we do?"

"I do not know, Sultana. This is a touchy subject."

"Yes."

Kareem slumped into a chair. I had not seen my husband so disturbed in a long time. He gazed at me with pain in his eyes.

"Shada's parents are inconsolable. Most troubling, they believe that I can make a telephone call and all will be well. I really do not know what I can do."

I glanced at the clock. "You can do nothing, tonight, husband. It is late."

Kareem sighed noisily. "I hate what is happening in our country. There is a madness that is surrounding us. I do not know what it will take to stop this slide into total lunacy. Witches and witchcraft! These wild men are casting a shadow over our country, and us!"

Although most believe that the royal family can make such problems go away with a snap of our fingers, this is not true. The religious authorities are so powerful in Saudi Arabia that even our king handles them delicately. Although he is more influential than they are, he still must choose his battles with care. Neither Kareem nor I could win such a confrontation with the men of religion, not even to save Shada's life.

Kareem instructed one of his managers to stay the night at Shada's home, so as to comfort her parents. He left word that he would do what he could the following morning.

Our sleep was fitful, and when morning came we were not rested.

When Kareem left our home, he was a man with a purpose. He was going to gather several of his most influential cousins to ask their advice. As it turned out, his cousins did not want to be associated with the case, as they too were aware that anything to do with witches and sorcery is a very offensive matter in Saudi Arabia, unless one is going to join in the madness and deliver new victims for the religious authorities to torture. In such a case, the men of religion would be solicitous and friendly.

Soon Kareem found it necessary to hire one of the most respected lawyers in our country to plead Shada's case—a man whose own safety was not assured, even with the backing of the royal family. He grew increasingly fearful for his own safety—the men of religion glared at him in the courtroom and the judge threatened him with a long prison sentence for representing a witch! It is horrendous for all Saudis that often lawyers representing victims are put into prison to join their clients.

A dreadful nightmare was upon us. Everything in our country moves unhurriedly—and nothing more so than the legal system. Kareem and I found ourselves trapped in a sludge of apprehension and torment. We were told by the attorney my husband had hired that Shada had been found guilty and was going to be executed by beheading.

Few people from the West are aware that most Muslims are very superstitious and believe in magicians, black magic, the evil eye, and jinns, which are supernatural beings that try to frighten, or even harm, good Muslims.

From the time I was a child, even I was warned about the evil eye and about supernatural beings, although my father would grow annoyed if anyone mentioned jinns in his presence. Even though he was not highly educated, he was intelligent, and he claimed that jinns existed only in the mind, not in the physical life.

I knew no real details about witchcraft and sorcery until I was married and discovered that my mother-in-law was an avid believer in the power of black magic. She, like many Saudi royal women who have too much time on their hands, obtains elation through the supernatural. My mother-in-law even influenced Maha, who went through a period of practicing black magic, but Kareem and I so discouraged her that she soon forgot about it.

There are occasions when stories about sorcery and black magic bring smiles, such as the time in the mid-1980s when an American friend who lived in my country shared an amusing story. She was an avid reader and followed the news more closely than most. She was told about a radio announcement in Jeddah regarding a harmful jinn that a Saudi man had identified as lurking in a specific Jeddah community. Many citizens in Jeddah became alarmed over the sighting, and soon those people were spreading gossip about personally catching a glimpse of a particularly vile jinn roaming about in their neighborhood. The paper said that the jinn had been seen by one of their reporters. According to the journalist, the jinn was so physically unsightly that there were no fitting words to describe it. In one of the articles, readers were told that one of the Saudi men in the "jinn obsessed" neighborhood had even obtained a photograph of the hideous jinn. The paper promised to run the photograph, although, for some unexplained reason, they were holding the image for a week. Meanwhile, Jeddah citizens were told to stay in their homes at night and to keep doors locked at all times. Mass hysteria was building as each day the editors ran stories about the various sightings of the jinn, which was becoming increasingly dangerous, or so the newspaper asserted.

All following the story waited with nervous excitement, desperate to see this image of the jinn for themselves.

When the day finally arrived, the newspaper ran the photograph. My American friend was one of the first to open the paper. She later confessed that she had laughed aloud. The scary "jinn" was none other than a photograph of E.T., the small alien featured in

Steven Spielberg's very popular movie *E.T. the Extra-Terrestrial*, which was released in 1982.

In those days, few Saudis were traveling abroad, and, with *E.T.* banned in our country, only limited numbers of Saudi citizens had seen the film.

I later saw that edition of the newspaper myself, and although I too laughed at the absurdity of the fear created by a fantasy produced in Hollywood, I also remember being slightly ashamed that so many of my countrymen had believed the story. We heard that true hysteria had broken out in Jeddah on seeing the image of such a creature. Many believed it was true, that E.T. was a real being stalking their neighborhood, waiting in the dark to attack them or their children.

Although Saudis have always had a dread of the dark side of life, for some reason, and I do not know why, for the past ten years this hidden side of life has swept through the nation, so now there is enormous paranoia in many Saudi minds. Authorities in Saudi Arabia even banned British writer J. K. Rowling's *Harry Potter* series, believing that the books and movies would lead Saudi citizens to practice sorcery and magic.

Fearfully for Saudi citizens and others living in our land, the Committee for the Promotion of Virtue and the Prevention of Vice (CPVPV)—or the religious police, the angry-eyed men often seen roaming our streets with their long beards and ankle-length gowns—has an obsessive focus on suppressing sorcery and hunting witches, which is weirdly entangled with their enthusiasm for upholding our conservative faith. Most alarmingly, this same committee has now created a special "Anti-Witchcraft Unit" to educate all living in Saudi Arabia about the evils of sorcery and witchcraft. The Anti-Witch Unit has an enormous government budget to pursue any and all who are casting spells against the innocent. They permeate our society with fear, as they pass out leaflets, operate hotlines, and set up sting operations to try to dupe some poor soul into making any kind of statement that will bring suspicion on his or her head. They encourage normal people to report any behavior they believe to be odd. Has someone stared at them for too long? Have they become ill after a neighbor came for a visit? Has a man become impotent? If so, he should remember which person he was with shortly before he lost his "manhood." Has anyone tried to buy a sheep or a camel and described specific features he would like the animal to have? If so, a person should call up the Anti-Witch hotline and provide authorities with the name of the guilty party. Based on such vague and nonsensical evidence, Saudi citizens or visitors to our country are in danger of possible arrest and serious charges.

These men, whom I personally consider to be as ignorant as a human being can be, are creating a fertile field for witch-hunting, for there have been a number of cases where those seeking revenge falsely claim sorcery or witchcraft against innocent people. Perhaps a maid reports a rape, or a driver reports nonpayment of his salary. Angry employers can and do make a counterclaim, charging such people with being witches or performing sorcery. If such accusations are made, their accusers are arrested, tried, and often executed, despite their innocence.

I find it impossible to believe that anyone even moderately educated, or partially rational, could accept as true such gibberish! But this is the reality of life in Saudi Arabia for some people in the year 2014.

Since 2012 there have been nearly one thousand cases of arrest, trial, imprisonment, and, for some, execution for sorcery and witchcraft.

Even as this book is being written, there are more than two hundred people who are imprisoned in Saudi Arabia for sorcery or for being a witch. Of this number, more than twenty have lost their appeals and are scheduled to be executed by beheading.

Here are some of the facts known about only a few specific cases, which have occurred in Saudi Arabia over the last several years:

1. A Sri Lankan domestic worker (male) was sentenced to one year in jail and one hundred lashes for practicing black magic, although no one ever showed any specific examples of what kind of black magic he had practiced.
2. A second Sri Lankan citizen, this time a woman, was arrested on suspicion of practicing witchcraft after she stared too long at a child in a shopping center. She was wearing a black cord around her wrist, which was found by the judge to imply that she must be a witch. Her punishment is unknown as of this writing.
3. A Saudi woman named Amina bint Abdul Halim bin Salem Nasser was executed for committing sorcery and witchcraft, although the specific deeds she committed have not been made public. Members of the committee made a simple statement that Ms. Nasser was a threat to Islam.
4. A Saudi man named Muree bin Ali bin Issa al-Asira was falsely reported as committing sorcery. When various books and talismans were found in his home, he was arrested, tried, and beheaded in the southern Najran province.

5. A Saudi woman, age sixty, was beheaded for witchcraft after "tricking people into giving her money" after she claimed she could heal them of sickness.

6. Mustafa Ibrahim, an Egyptian man, was beheaded after he was accused of casting spells to try to separate a married couple. The judge said he was convinced of Mustafa's guilt after the discovery in Mustafa's home of candles, foul-smelling herbs, and books.

7. A famous case involving a Muslim Lebanese citizen has been made known worldwide only because the Lebanese government fought for his release and his story made the news. The man, named Ali Hussain Sibat, was the TV host of a popular show in Lebanon called *The Hidden*. The show was in reality a psychic hotline. Mr. Sibat gave advice to members of the audience and sometimes cast a few spells. This show had obviously caught the attention of the Saudi religious police because when Mr. Sibat traveled to Saudi Arabia for pilgrimage he was arrested on charges of sorcery. Although he was not a Saudi citizen, and his "crimes" had occurred in another country, it did not stop the Anti-Witchcraft Unit. Feeling themselves the keepers of the faith not only in Saudi Arabia but also across the world, they took Mr. Sibat to trial and won a guilty verdict from the judge. Mr. Sibat was sentenced to beheading. The date was set several times over the course of several years, but each time the date arrived, the Lebanese government succeeded in stopping the execution. Although it is believed that Mr. Sibat has not been beheaded, the Saudi authorities will not say if he has been released, is still in prison, or is back home in

Lebanon. If he has been released, he has remained quiet publicly, although I am certain that in private he is speaking stridently about the barbarity of my country. Kareem promises to learn his fate, and the moment he does I will make it public.

8. An Eritrean man was arrested and imprisoned after his leather telephone address book was confiscated and presented to the court as a "talisman" because the religious police could not read the man's foreign writing and believed that the booklet was filled with chants that would cause men to leave their wives or wives to leave their husbands. The poor man must have been confused and terrified, for he was not given an attorney and all the proceedings were in a language he did not understand, although his telephone booklet was held up and pounded on the table and was the cause of his imprisonment and a punishment of hundreds of lashes.

9. Sudanese Abdul Hamid bin Hussein Moustafa al-Fakki was the victim of a sting operation, in which an undercover agent working for the committee asked him to create a spell that would make his father leave his second wife. The undercover agent swore that al-Fakki said he could do it, but for a charge of $1,500. No one knows, of course, if this is the case, as the religious authorities are so eager to arrest, flog, and even behead people. Who can trust their testimony?

10. Last, a poor woman was trapped by a female undercover agent who asked the woman if she might turn her husband into an obedient man. Supposedly, the woman said she could, and she was promptly arrested and later sentenced to death.

Faria and Shada—two innocent girls, both victims of barbaric rituals and superstitions that would blight their lives forever. I failed to get either girl out of my mind for several months. I was informed by Nadia that Faria had disappeared into the morass of her ultraconservative tribe when her parents appeared at the hospital and insisted that their daughter leave with them to return home. Nadia said that Faria was weeping bitter tears as she left her room.

I suffered nightmares that poor Faria was married against her will to a brute of a man, a man who would have no sympathy for her maimed condition and would rip anew her genital area many times, repeatedly bringing pain and anguish to that young woman.

And Shada? How was poor Shada coping with being locked in a prison in Riyadh? Was she capable of preparing herself psychologically for the terrible fate that awaited her? She was to lose her head for nothing more than admiring a woman of beauty?

I spent so many nights living through what I believed was happening to Faria and Shada that I felt myself on the brink of insanity. Indeed, it took months before their fates were finally determined.

I saw that my husband was suffering, too. His face was drawn and I noticed new wrinkles; his once dark hair was turning gray. I knew that my husband felt he was a prince without power, something very difficult for a proud and worthy man to come to terms with.

One long night Kareem paced through our quarters before sitting at his desk, taking his pen and writing words that poured from his heart. My husband is a poet and he captures pain and joy as I cannot. The following morning, after Kareem had slipped from our apartments to go for coffee, I sat in his chair and read the sorrowful words he had composed:

When I was born, my homeland was in my eyes.
The curls and curves of the Riyadh sand were there,
    waiting for a pair of sandals.
The mountains of Taif offered a lovely shade.
The blue waters of the Red Sea cooled my body.
But now I see my homeland through other eyes, and
    it is their vision that is destroying my dream.
The burning sands now burn through my sandals.
The floods of the mountains sweep away the trees of
    shade.
The Red Sea waters choke me until I cannot feel my
    breath.
Take away these angry men who claim to speak to
    Allah. They do not even know His language.
They babble in a foreign voice as they destroy my
    homeland.
And I sit helplessly, unable to save the land I love.

I have never loved Kareem more than I did at that moment.

# Chapter Twelve
# More Tears to Cry

To my despair, I suffer as many failures as successes when it comes to helping vulnerable women in Saudi Arabia. And so it came to pass that months after poor Faria was forcibly removed from the hospital she returned as a patient for a second time. Nadia was very upset when she telephoned Amani to give her the upsetting news that Faria had indeed been forced into a marriage she did not want.

Faria had never regained her full strength after the wounds and infection she had suffered from the female genital mutilation she'd had to endure. Sadly, her husband was a brute who was only interested in his sexual pleasure, and he became angry because Faria was not a willing partner. She hid from him when he ordered her to the marriage bed.

After her second hospital admission, she had recovered and returned to her husband. But the poor young woman was still desperately unhappy, and she wept and pleaded for someone to help her escape from a marriage and husband who repelled her.

Nadia had kept in touch with Faria as best she could, and the last time they spoke on the telephone she had confided that her husband had begun beating her despite the fact that she was pregnant. Faria was terrified at the thought of the pain she would endure delivering her child after the permanent injuries and scarring she had suffered as a result of FGM. But then, quite suddenly, there had been no further communication from Faria. She seemed to have disappeared.

Never again did Faria answer Nadia's calls, and never again was Faria admitted to the hospital. It is possible, although unlikely, that her family moved away, but we may never discover what happened to the poor girl and we all fear the worst.

Poor Amani sheds tears of grief each time she speaks of Faria, so at last my youngest daughter fully realizes that for the women of Saudi Arabia life is often cruel and brutal. Although Amani has a great passion for our work, I know now that my daughter is opening her eyes to the reality of our world.

As for Shada, the young innocent girl who was so severely punished for gazing innocently at another woman and accused of being a witch, her story has a much happier ending. This is because my husband did something he said he would never do. After being told by the barrister representing Shada that it was clear that the clerics in charge of the courts would never rule in favor of a woman accused of being a witch, for the religious establishment in Saudi Arabia is especially keen on punishing anyone charged with sorcery or witchcraft, Kareem bribed three clerics with large sums of money, men who were in charge of Shada's case. He is not proud to have adopted such tactics, but I have never been so proud of Kareem; it takes an exceptional person to go against everything he believes in, not for his own benefit but to help someone else. Kareem rationalized that it was merely a little sin to bribe someone, and a small price to pay compared with the much bigger sin of allowing an innocent young woman such as Shada to be executed for being naive. Her only sin was to be entranced by a beautiful woman and proclaim her admiration.

And so we suffered defeat and we enjoyed victory. But we got little pleasure from our triumph, for we mourned the loss of Faria.

It is my prayer and my hope that the day will come when women will not have to endure the torture of genital mutilation—or the agony of being forced to marry a man, young or old, who is a stranger to them.

Surely you know by now that I am a woman of passion—a woman who loves deeply. The intense emotion I feel produces a desire to protect those I love. When I was young, my need to protect had the negative side effect of my needing also to control. Such a need has an undesirable impact on everyone: the one who loves, and the one who is loved.

As I matured, I came to see that the love Saudi men say they feel for Saudi women is really about control. Many times I have heard Saudi men claim that their love means they must protect, while they deny their need to command, restrict, and control.

So I guard the love I feel, loving with gentleness and care, without trying to control.

I am a daughter who has intensely loved her mother from the moment of my birth. My love for her continues to grow with each passing year and will never depart so long as my beating heart pumps blood around my body. I wish I could say the same for my father. As a child, fear overwhelmed a yearning to love my father just as I loved my mother. It was with tremendous sadness that I long believed that even up until the moment a shroud is slipped over my body and I am lowered into a desert grave, I would never feel true love for my father. I could never forgive the way he favored my brother over my sisters and me, and this fueled the bad feeling between my brother and me that exists even today. But after reaching a certain age, love began to grow for the imperfect man who gave me life. Now, for the first time, I can say that I am a daughter who loves her father.

I am a sister who loves each of her nine sisters, although my love is strongest for my sister Sara. I cannot say the same about my brother, Ali. In the past, I have felt moments of affection for Ali, but my love diminished with each cruel act he committed against his wives, children, siblings, nieces, and nephews. Now when I think of Ali, my heart feels only sorrow.

I am a wife who loves her husband. Like most women from Saudi Arabia, my marriage was arranged. I was only a teenager when I was told I was to marry, but I was one of the lucky Saudi girls, for I was allowed a supervised meeting and telephone calls with my fiancé prior to the wedding. These meetings and calls served to reassure me that Kareem was a good man. Indeed, Kareem's handsome face brought happiness to me at our first meeting. My heart whispered a message of love from the first moment we looked into each other's eyes. I have loved him nearly every moment since that time. My love faltered only once, on the occasion when he expressed a wish to take a second wife. My violent reaction was not what he expected, and I succeeded in obstructing his devilish plans when I fled from him, out of our country. Thanks be to Allah, that terrible time was but a fleeting moment, and never again has my husband stirred the poison that a second wife would bring. I am a full partner in our marriage and I know that Kareem and I have one of the happiest marriages in Saudi Arabia. My husband expresses daily his love for me, and his gladness that we are a couple, feelings that are reciprocated.

Love for others is a great treasure for me. But there is no love that is as important as the love I feel for children.

I am a grandmother who intensely loves her grandchildren. I married young, and I gave birth to my children when I was young. So now I am a young grandmother who loves her three grandchildren as much as it is possible to love. Without hesitation, I would sacrifice my life for Little Princess Sultana, Prince Khalid, and Prince Faisal.

I am a mother who loves her three children with a passion I cannot name. Although I was a rebellious child who created many problems in our family life, the moment I became a young mother my entire focus was to shelter and protect my children. Despite this need to protect, however, I was always determined to raise strong and independent children who would grow into confident adults— people who would be free to express themselves and stand up for what they believed in.

I remember each child's birth as if it happened yesterday.

At Abdullah's birth, I was enthusiastic when the pangs of childbirth came to me, as I knew that if God was willing, I would soon have an infant in my arms. Although experiencing childhood as a Saudi girl in the Kingdom of Saudi Arabia had taught me that a male child would have an easier life, I was enamored of female children and my heart was set on having a little girl. All those around me, other than my sister Sara, expressed eagerness for a male child because in Saudi Arabia people celebrate the birth of sons and mourn the birth of daughters. The very idea maddened me. I deplored the injustice of this cultural tradition and, although writhing in pain with birth contractions, my rebellious streak flamed anew as I tried to will myself to give birth to a daughter.

But Allah had decided that my firstborn would be a boy; it was my fate, and my son's fate.

I was prepared to be sad at the sight of a male child but was astonished by the rising of tender emotions as I looked upon this beautiful infant. Here is the memory of my son Abdullah's birth as was written in the first book about my life:

*All thoughts of a daughter vanished when my yawning son was placed in my arms. A daughter would come later. This male child would be taught different and better ways than the generation before him. I felt the power of my intentions creating his future. He would not be backward in his thinking, his sisters would be given a place of honor and respect, and he would know and love his partner before he wed. The vast possibilities of his accomplishments glowed and glittered as a new start. I told myself that many times in history one man has created change that influenced millions. I swelled with pride as I considered the good to mankind that would flow from the tiny body in my arms. Without doubt, the new beginning of women in Arabia would start with my own blood.*

It is delightful to look back in time, seeing with the eyes of memory my beautiful baby boy, and to compare my dreams of his life with the reality that is today. I am astonished by the precision of my thoughts and wishes for my son, for indeed Abdullah the tiny infant grew into a man of impeccable character and impressive accomplishments. My son is an enlightened man who has always honored and respected his sisters, and later loved and honored his wife and daughter. He has been a perfect son to his mother and father. Abdullah is a very intelligent man, and he accomplishes miracles in business, according to my husband. He is also a humanitarian and has proven his devotion to goodness more times than I can count, as he always helps the needy, those who are less fortunate than he is.

If given the opportunity to wave a magic wand that produces instant change, I would not alter his looks, his personality, or his character.

As I remember Abdullah's birth, I also recall every moment of the day when my oldest daughter was born. I have not yet told the world what happened when Maha appeared to us before her time was due. Kareem and I were not yet prepared, as we believed we had several more weeks before our second child would join our family. But Maha has always been an impatient child, one who reacts unexpectedly to all things in life. Her arrival into this world was no different.

I remember longing for a quiet evening at our Riyadh palace with my husband, as I was big with child. But Kareem was eager to spend the evening with his brother, Assad, and despite my wishes spoke of his need to discuss some business matter relating to an important multinational company that was bidding for business in the kingdom. He knew this type of business meeting was of no interest to me, so I was unlikely to question it, and he also made it clear that he did not wish to leave me at home. Kareem said that while he and his brother discussed business, Sara and I could enjoy each other's company. Kareem mentioned that they would have come to us, but one of Sara's daughters had eaten some tainted fish and was feeling ill. Nothing makes a person so sick as spoiled seafood. Sara, of course, refused to leave her sick daughter, which was not a surprise, as my sister has been the most devoted mother to all her children.

And so I agreed to accompany my husband, although his persistence put me in a foul mood because I have always believed that when a woman is heavily pregnant she should be rewarded by having all her wishes granted.

The car ride to my sister's palace was uneventful, and it wasn't until we arrived that everything seemed to turn into some kind of comical sketch, a farce that went horribly wrong. It seems that the entire family had eaten the same bad seafood, for Assad became ill just as he was offering greetings to Kareem and me. With his hand held over his mouth, he ran away to find a bathroom so that he might vomit. Just then, as Sara invited us to join her in the sitting room, her sick daughter stumbled into the room looking for her mother. Rather sweetly, the child tried to greet me with kisses, until I gently told her, "Kisses are not needed, sweet child. Go and rest so that your body will heal."

Sara's daughter bravely smiled but then turned pale and began to be sick once again—this time all over me!

Sara caught her embarrassed daughter by her shoulders and gently moved her from me, saying, "Do not worry, darling. Return to bed. I will take care of Sultana."

I was stunned and unable to move. I could feel the wet vomit and smell the vile odor. Kareem gasped loudly and called out to the servants to bring towels. I felt myself feeling faint and I heaved once or twice before throwing up on one of my sister's priceless carpets. This was all turning into a nightmare!

Kareem panicked because he was very concerned for me. He picked me up and started spinning like a top, yelling, "Where shall I take her, where shall I take her?"

The spinning around made me feel even worse. I became dizzy and I began to feel sick again. By this time, my yet-to-be-born daughter had obviously picked up on the excitement—they say the unborn can hear all things around them, and can feel the emotions of their mother, who is carrying them in her body.

Maha began kicking inside me at the same time as I felt the first pangs of childbirth. Even as an unborn baby Maha was very serious and very strong, and her kicking feet, combined with the start of the pain, caused me to scream so loudly that a thoroughly alarmed Kareem lost his grip and I slipped from his arms and down to the floor, although I managed to land in a sitting position, thank goodness.

I was unharmed, but Kareem did not know this, so he became very agitated again, feeling that he had harmed his pregnant wife. He yelled for a wheelchair, and when no one came immediately, he ran past me, but slipped on the wet floor and fell heavily to the ground.

With powerful contractions taking my breath, I could do nothing but sit and call out for help as the pains came more closely spaced than they should have been. I knew enough from my first birth to realize that the closer the contractions, the sooner the birth. By this time Assad had recovered from his vomiting and, hearing my screams, he ran into the room. Startled to see his brother and his sister-in-law on the floor, he was confused. I have to say the confusion was made worse by Kareem, who, still panicking, insisted that I had been hurt when he'd dropped me.

I managed to speak, to tell them both, "No, I am unhurt, but I feel certain that our baby is coming soon. I need to go to the hospital."

Total terror washed across Kareem's face, for he knew our baby was not yet due for another month and he feared that he had damaged me and our unborn child. Assad appeared to be having difficulty moving his feet, but Kareem by this time was standing. He shook his brother and said, "We must go."

Sara and two servants came back into the room with towels, and all were perplexed by the scene, and my moans, which were growing in intensity. Kareem grabbed a few towels from Sara's hands and told her, "Sultana is having the baby."

"Sultana!" Sara shouted, but did not move, as she was in shock too.

My husband cleaned me as best he could, then brushed at his own clothing with a quick swipe before reaching down and once again gathering me in his arms.

Assad insisted on driving us to the hospital: my last impression was of Sara standing in her driveway, shocked and confused by the turn of events that had unfolded in her home.

I will never forget the wild car ride; Assad was excited and could not remember the correct turns to make. It did not help the situation that my husband was yelling at his nervous brother; at one point he even reached across the seat and lightly slapped the side of Assad's head with his open hand after his poor brother had missed the correct turn twice. "Pay attention, Assad," he yelled. "Do you want to deliver this baby in the car?"

Finally, we arrived. We were where we were supposed to be, and I was quickly helped into the delivery room. The nurses soon learned that my baby was in a hurry to come into the world. In fact, had Assad not finally made the correct turn, I fear what would have happened.

My suffering was short with Maha, but the evening was so frenzied that out of my three children her arrival is perhaps the most memorable and chaotic!

I felt quite unstable after the shock of the evening, but I was relieved when I was assured that our daughter was healthy. My emotions slowly calmed. And so I held my precious girl and gazed at her perfection and thanked Allah for the birth of a girl who would fill many family hours with her sweetness. Now, we all know that while she is a good and worthy person who helps many people, Maha does not have an easy personality like her brother Abdullah. Our daughter has brought more tension into our family than we could have ever imagined when we welcomed her as a beautiful, tiny infant into our lives. But I would never exchange my daughter for another, as I love and respect her for who she is.

Several years later our family was blessed with a second daughter, Amani. After the flurry of turmoil generated by Maha's birth, when I was seven months pregnant with our third child, my husband announced that we should keep close to home without any social visits out of the palace. I did not disagree. And so when we felt the urge to see family members, our families came to us, although with my third baby I felt sleepy, and even weary, nearly every moment of every day. I enjoyed little activity, spending most of my time lounging with a book or playing board games with Kareem and other close family members.

The week before Amani was due I felt a tightening through my body and I became concerned. That was when a nervous Kareem insisted that I go into the royal pregnancy ward of the hospital early and remain there until our child was born. I was not too pleased with this turn of events, but allowed Kareem his way, as his face grew long with worry and he became a pest about it. Once in the hospital, my sisters took turns to stay with me, and although I found peace with Nura, the oldest of my sisters, and with Sara, with whom I share a very close and loving relationship, my other sisters exhausted me because they tried to entertain me by continually telling family stories they found to be hilarious but which in reality were only moderately amusing. Endless loud laughter can become tiring, incredibly boring, and annoying when that is all one is hearing.

And so it came to be that the child who would create the most difficulties and tribulations in our lives would come nearly effortlessly into the world. While I was thrilled to have a second daughter, as I incorrectly believed that my two girls would become the closest of companions, most members of Kareem's family were miserable, as they could speak of nothing more than the importance of many sons. After I became frustrated to the point of anger, Kareem reprimanded those family members who had upset me and they said nothing more—other than to comment on Amani's unusually tiny size; she was only slightly larger than those the medical world terms premature babies. Of course, her small size brought criticism too, as Saudis favor robust girls, believing that a bigger female will one day birth a larger and stronger son. Everything of importance in Saudi society is wrapped around the well-being of males.

Although I had never given a lot of thought to the number of children Kareem and I would have, in my culture most women have children until they are physically incapable of having more. We are a country and a culture that puts great emphasis upon large families, and those with no children or with small families are pitied. Yet when I was diagnosed with breast cancer, my childbearing days came to an end and our little family grew no larger. Although that was one of the darkest times of my life, for I feared I might not live to raise my young children, leaving them motherless, as my own mother had left me, those days were long ago. Now with three adult children, I no longer suffer such nightmares.

And so my happiness is complete. The love I feel for my three children and my three grandchildren is so immense that a single smile from one of them can take my breath away. My eternal love for my children and grandchildren, and my knowledge of the innocence and sweetness of a child, is why I drop to my knees in a state of disbelief and complete misery when I hear about the cruelty that some Saudis inflict on their own flesh and blood. A second horrendous crime attaches itself to the first when government agencies created to follow up such stories and protect the helpless close their eyes to the abuse.

When the stories you have read in this book were compiled for this fourth volume about my life, the great cruelties inflicted upon some Saudi children tugged at my heartstrings. I knew that I must not forget them, that I must disclose their stories. I have so dreaded the moment that this topic must be raised: in fact, it is only in the final chapter of this fourth book that I can bring myself to re live the horror and misery others have visited upon innocent children.

I will no longer postpone the inevitable. I will tell you about only a few of these tortured and abused babies, for nothing is more tragic than the mistreatment and death of children. My only wish is for the entire world to come together to make adult brutality against children the most important topic of our time. A great movement should sweep the world, from Saudi Arabia to every country and society in existence, to ensure that every innocent child will live free of cruelty and abuse against its little body and mind.

And so I am asking you to join me on the most unsavory journey a feeling heart can make, as we enter the hearts and minds of the little children who have been tortured, and in some cases murdered, by the ones who should have protected them against all harm.

## The Saddest Stories of All

The Saudi Arabian coastal city of Jeddah is an ancient town of exotic beauty. The ageless city curls alongside the warm blue waters of the Red Sea, with seaside avenues bustling with people. The archaic section of Jeddah is composed of a warren of old buildings, with imaginative wooden window coverings in the Hejazi architectural style, specially built to allow the cool breezes in but still maintain the privacy of girls and women, who could not be seen by men walking on the streets below.

Anytime I am visiting Jeddah I make a point of asking my driver to take me to the oldest part of the city, and sometimes we stop for a time so that I can gaze at those window coverings, remembering the many stories told to me by my mother and older aunties of how some of the Jeddah-born women never left those old homes. There were women who entered those beautiful homes as young brides and left swathed in their shrouds, from the marriage bed to the cemetery, according to my mother.

At those times I relish the idea that so much has changed in my country and, most important, in only a few generations. But before I allow myself too much joy in my memories, I evoke the bleak lives of those same women who lived forever behind those walls, women hidden from the world, helpless against those who might abuse them.

Sadness grips my heart when I acknowledge that while the overwhelming majority of the abused in my country are female, there are occasions when boys too suffer horrific abuse.

The following story concerns a young boy from Jeddah who was kept isolated in his home, abused and forgotten. It is an important story to relate because it serves to demonstrate how, throughout the world, vulnerable young children are the victims of horrific abuse. We must not turn our heads away and ignore these harsh realities. It is our duty, for the sake of innocent children, to be vigilant and always be aware that these horrific crimes are happening around us. We must do our best to prevent them when we can.

The story came to my attention via a princess cousin who lives in Jeddah all year round. She was terribly distraught when telling me about this nine-year-old Saudi boy who had been abused for years. Here is his story, as told to my princess cousin by a social worker in Jeddah who had access to his medical file and who read the words of the young boy to this cousin:

"I have three brothers and one sister. My parents wanted my brothers and my sister, but for some reason they did not want me and told me so. In fact, they thought it best if I would die. I would not bother them anymore, if I was dead. I do not know why they did not love me. I was a good boy. I loved them. I wanted them to love me, too.

"I believe they stopped loving me after I wet my bed at night. My mother would go crazy and scream and beat me with her hands whenever I wet the bed. My father would hear her screams and he would add

310

to my misery by kicking me. When they beat me, I became afraid because I am only a little boy. I was so nervous that I began to wet my bed every night.

"My parents became so angry that they locked me in a small bedroom without any food. I became so hungry that I became dizzy in my head and stumbled when I tried to walk. I was so thirsty that my tongue grew too big for my mouth. I felt as if I was choking. My lips cracked. I thought I would die. There was a small room with a toilet, but they turned the water off to that toilet. But they forgot that some water was standing. So I drank that toilet water and saved my life.

"Once I pushed my ear flat against the door so that I could hear what was going on. I heard a little noise and realized that my mother was listening on the other side of the door. I was very quiet because I became very afraid. When she heard no noise coming from the room, I heard her tell my father that she thought I was dead and when night came they could take me out on Medina Road and bury me in the desert. No one would know, and no one would miss me. I believe I was already a forgotten child.

"But I refused to die, even though I was so badly treated and so afraid of the dark. I spent all my time quietly crying and begging to be freed from the room. I could hear my brothers playing and having some fun, but they were not allowed to talk to me.

"I wanted to go to school because my brothers went there and I knew that they had fun with their friends. My parents allowed my brothers to go to school, but they said I was too stupid to learn anything.

"I became very sick once and was so hot that my mother said I had a very high temperature. My parents laughed very loud and I remember my father saying that this might kill me. When I refused to die, they became even more angry at me. That is when they started boiling water in a big pot. My father held me down and my mother poured the boiling water over my body. I screamed and screamed because it hurt so much. I was screaming, too, because I thought I really was going to die and I did not want to die. I wanted to live.

"I learned later that my screams were heard by a good neighbor who knew that a child was being hurt. That neighbor called the police and made a report that his neighbors were killing a child. The caller was very alarmed and demanded help.

"That is when some nice people came and got me. They were shocked to see my body. Those people looked at me with big eyes and said I was too skinny and that I had been burned.

"I do not know what will happen to me now, but I am scared still. I do not know what will happen to my parents. I feel very sad. If only they had loved me and wanted me, I would have been better. I would have slept on the floor so that I did not wet the bed. I could be at home and live with my brothers and my sister if only I had not wet the bed."

The abuse inflicted on this child has given me many sleepless nights. I praise God that a neighbor heard the boy's screams and decided to take action. In Saudi Arabia, that neighbor should be celebrated as a hero. Unfortunately, few people will involve themselves in any family matter, even if they hear screams and cries. Most Saudi Arabians believe family privacy to be more precious and more important than human life.

The good people who work for the government-appointed committee to protect Saudi women and children are heroes, too. Tragically, most government organizations look the other way when a man is abusing his wife, or a father is abusing his child. In the little boy's case, the specialists were intelligent and brave to go against the system of protecting Saudi men from punishment for the most violent crimes against women and children.

I have been told that such dreadful incidents are becoming more widespread in my country. However, I am of the opinion that the number of abuse cases is not actually increasing; the statistics are climbing only because such cases are becoming public knowledge. There is more awareness of what is going on in some Saudi homes. In our recent past, all abuse was hidden. Nowadays, for the first time, some abuse cases reach Saudi eyes and ears—and I am glad of this.

Abuse against children happens all over the country. Even in places where you would think people live a calm and good life, places such as Abha.

If you leave Jeddah and drive to the south, you will come to Abha, which is an unusual city for a desert kingdom. There are approximately 500,000 citizens living in this beautiful place. Surrounded by fertile mountains, with a mild climate and more rainfall than one usually sees in Saudi Arabia, Abha has many gardens, parks, and streams, and over the years has become a favorite tourist spot for Saudis. Everywhere one looks in Abha, one sees ecological splendor, but sadly the physical beauty of the land is not reflected in human nature.

There is one home in Abha where nothing of beauty could survive. The shadow of evil cloaked an entire family living in that house, resulting in the hideous torture of three young girls, one of whom died as a result, thirteen-year-old Dalal. The three sisters were left at the mercy of their father after their parents separated.

Dalal's case brings us to the topic of child custody. In Saudi Arabia, which is guided by sharia law, fathers have sole legal custody of their children in the case of a divorce. During the separation, the fate of the children will depend upon the relationship between the parents or the character of the father. Although a fair-minded person will understand that a mother should not be kept from her children, during the separation stage the mother has no power over her children. Later on, after the divorce, sharia law says that mothers should have physical custody of young children, with girls up until they reach puberty (which is said to be age seven or age nine, according to the Muslim country in which one lives) and sons until age seven. Although this is the law, if the father objects and demands physical custody, it is almost impossible for the mother to see her children; few courts will favor a wife against her husband in this male-obsessed land of mine.

In the sad case of Dalal and her two sisters, the father refused any visitation by the mother of the children. So three girls were at the mercy of their father, a man whose heart overflowed with the most malevolent rage.

From the beginning of the separation, Dalal's father took his three daughters out of school and forced them to remain isolated at home. When the school administrators contacted the children's father and asked that they be allowed to return to school, his response was negative. He believed they did not benefit from their studies.

No one saw the three girls for many months. They did not attend school, they were not seen in the family garden, they were not seen peeking out of windows.

They were not seen because they were chained.

After Dalal's death, it was discovered that when the father left for work or to run errands, he chained his daughters, literally tethering them like animals in their home. Two of them were chained to windows, while Dalal was chained to the door. The girls were left hanging with chains around their arms and neck until the father saw fit to return home. While painfully held hostage in this way, they were not fed, they could not go to the bathroom, they could not sit.

Then the day came when the father lost his temper with Dalal and placed the chains in a particular way so that she would slowly choke to death. Upon the father's return later in the evening, thirteen-year-old Dalal was still hanging, but now she was dead.

This evil Saudi father at first lied, saying that Dalal was playing on a swing and choked to death on the ropes, but quickly he admitted that he had killed his daughter. He appeared proud of his deed. He had no fear of the government because in Saudi Arabia men can kill their wives and daughters without receiving serious punishment. Perhaps he will pay blood money to the mother, or perhaps not. Perhaps he will serve a few months in prison, or perhaps not. All a man has to do is to say that his daughter had dishonored the family name and he will not be punished, as it is believed that a man has the right to protect his family honor, which is priceless, while a female child has no value at all. A female child such as Dalal.

The phrase "*Ana Amal*—I am Amal," concerning a little girl named Amal, has become a catchword in our household and serves to remind us of both the danger that stalks many children and the difficulty female victims have in receiving justice.

Of all the tragic cases in Saudi Arabia, none is more horrifying than the nightmare of torture and abuse suffered by little Amal, a five-year-old child said to be a happy spirit who, like most children of her age, delighted in playtime. She was also a little girl who greatly loved her mother and her father.

Amal's tragic story demonstrates that a five-year-old girl is more vulnerable than most. In the case of divorce, the mother cannot be with her children at all times. Most children of divorced parents will by necessity spend periods alone with their father. While most Saudi fathers love and protect their children, there are men who are sadists and brutes, such as Amal's father. When a man such as this beats and rapes his daughter, it is impossible for that small child to defend herself. At only five years of age, little Amal was too young and too small to protect herself against a grown man.

Amal's mother was married to Fahim, a Saudi man who had spent much of his life as a drug addict.

He was a big man, and so violent and brutal that Amal's mother filed for divorce in a court in Dammam in the Eastern Province. Amal's mother was granted a divorce, which in itself is a minor miracle in my country. Although Amal's father retained guardianship over his daughter, as well as legal custody, which is routine in Saudi Arabia, the mother was allowed physical custody up until Amal reached her seventh birthday.

According to sharia law, girls should remain with their mothers until they are seven years old, although there are many cases where the father refuses to relinquish custody, even to infants, and the courts generally do not pursue him for justice for the mother or the child.

Amal's father was given generous visitation, being allowed two weeks each visit during the years prior to Amal's reaching seven years old, when her father would assume full physical custody. Tragically, little Amal did not live to celebrate her seventh birthday.

After a time, Fahim repented his drug addiction and persuaded Amal's mother to remarry him. His rash talk of becoming a new man, someone who had changed, was a ruse. And once again Amal's mother filed for divorce, gaining the same physical custody, while Amal's father was her guardian and had legal custody.

Before long Fahim was appearing on various Muslim television networks, claiming to be an Islamic cleric and giving emotional testimony on how he had left his drug life behind him and was a reformed man. He had a devoted following of people who thought that, indeed, Fahim was a man to believe, trust, and admire.

Although he expressed little desire to see his daughter, Amal's mother is a law-abiding woman and she arranged for her child to meet the visitation agreement requirements and spend time with her father and his new wife, Amal's stepmother.

Three visits came and went without incident. According to Amal's mother, the girl felt safe with her father and his new family, and looked forward to her time with him.

After Amal's father moved to Riyadh, there was no communication for a long time. So when the time came for Amal's visitation of two weeks with her father, Amal's mother followed the court agreement and took her daughter to Riyadh to see her father.

But something went terribly wrong during the visit to Riyadh. Perhaps Fahim succumbed to his previous drug habit, or perhaps his evil nature simply overpowered him. At the end of the two-week visit, when Amal's mother contacted her ex-husband to arrange to pick up her child, Fahim said no, she could not have her daughter back. He told her that he would make Amal forget her mother. Little Amal came on the phone and, in her sweet little voice, told her mother, "I love you, Mummy. I love you and I will always pray for you."

Amal's mother could not know that her ex-husband had entered a dangerous state of paranoia—believing that, among other things, his five-year-old daughter had lost her virginity! The most dishonorable thing that can happen to a Saudi father is for his daughter to lose her virginity, so Amal's father felt compelled to punish Amal for the crime. And so he began torturing the girl, raping her in every body orifice. He whipped her with cables. He crushed her skull. He broke her ribs. He broke her arm. He ripped open her rectum during a violent rape, and to stop the bleeding, he attempted to burn her rectal tissue so that the rectum would close.

While raping tiny Amal over and over, Fahim broke her back. And still Amal lived.

And where was Amal's stepmother during this crime? Was she watching? Was she joining Fahim in torturing the little girl? Why didn't she call the police and save the child? These are all unanswered questions.

The torture continued until finally it was clear that Amal was dying.

Her father took her to a hospital in Riyadh, where he showed no remorse or shame for what he had done to his daughter, despite the horror expressed by the medical staff. He knew that there was no court in Saudi Arabia that would issue an appropriate punishment, for he was the father of the girl, and rulings in such crimes are routinely based on Saudi laws that say a father cannot be executed for murdering his children, nor can husbands be executed for murdering their wives.

Amal would be of no value in the eyes of Saudi courts—she was only a girl.

Little Amal remained in a coma for months before she finally expired from a torture so hideous that there is no word in any language to describe it.

There were twists and turns in the court proceedings. The case was so heinous that the Saudi public expressed outrage over the child's torture and death and, most tellingly, the court's reaction to the father's trial and subsequent sentencing.

Fahim was sentenced to pay blood money to the mother after serving a very short jail term of a few months. The judge in the case ruled that blood money was the proper punishment and that the months served awaiting trial were punishment enough for Fahim's crime of raping and killing his daughter. The judge made an outrageous statement, saying that in his view Fahim did not intend to kill his daughter, which in essence meant that the brutal rapes and beatings were not a crime in the eyes of the judiciary!

There was an outcry in the kingdom, as most realized that such a light sentence would encourage some fathers to abuse their children. Without proper laws to deter such domestic violence, those with common sense knew it would increase.

Due to public pressure, Fahim returned to court to face yet another judge; this court, in Hawtat Bani Tamim, to the south of Riyadh, took a different and more serious stance. At this hearing, the judge ruled that the earlier sentence had been too lenient, and Fahim received eight years in prison and 800 lashes for torturing his daughter to death. Amal's stepmother received a sentence of ten months in prison and 150 lashes because she did not report the rapes and the torture of little Amal.

After this ruling, Amal's mother decided to accept blood money. The courts then ruled that the blood money and the four months Fahim had served were enough punishment for the crime.

Due to a second outcry from the Saudi public, the courts are revisiting the case. We do not yet know the final outcome, although most believe that the father will be quietly released from prison to live his life without appropriate punishment for this most heinous of crimes.

If so, we will know that the injustice that is set like the hardest granite stone against Saudi Arabian women and girls persists, even when Saudi citizens demand change.

Like so many women in Saudi Arabia, I will never forget little Amal or the abuses that can happen to a female in my country. There is an Egyptian saying, "To speak the name of the dead makes them live again." Every day of my life I look into the mirror and I think of Amal and the sweet little girl she was, and the wonderful woman I am sure she would have become, and I say, "*Ana Amal*—I am Amal."

I ask that you do the same.

"*Ana Amal*—I am Amal."

I will speak Amal's name every day of my life, and she will live in my mind and heart so long as I live.

With such crimes committed against women and children—crimes which remain unpunished in our society—it is little wonder that I sometimes feel despair and sorrow for the fate of many vulnerable people in Saudi Arabia. My efforts to help others can sometimes feel so small, so insignificant, no matter how hard I try. As I have said before, I suffer as many failures as successes.

A change in our laws and in the cultural traditions that tether us to medieval practices is desperately needed and always welcomed—even if such changes are often ineffective and frustratingly slow to come about. But this is why I refuse to give up the fight for justice and equality.

There remains so much to do—and it is why, dear reader, I still have more tears to cry.

# Jean Sasson Remembers

My personal journey into the closed and private world of Saudi women began in 1978, when I was employed at the King Faisal Specialist Hospital and Research Centre in Riyadh, the Saudi capital. The hospital was a dream brought to life by Saudi Arabia's third king, King Faisal. Tragically, he was assassinated by a nephew prior to the official opening of the facility in 1975. The hospital had been open only three years when I arrived. I was fortunate to work as medical affairs coordinator to the head of the hospital, Dr. Nizar Feteih. My position meant that I was privy to confidential information about the most influential members of the Saudi royal family, including King Khalid and Crown Prince Fahd and their wives and children.

Although I signed a two-year contract, and could have left the kingdom in 1980, I chose to stay on and work for a total of four years. After leaving the hospital, I continued to live in Saudi Arabia for another eight years, until 1990.

The first thing I had noticed upon my arrival in the kingdom in 1978 was that women there lived as second-class citizens. As an American expatriate, I enjoyed more personal freedom than most women and because of my job I came in contact with women from all walks of society. In fact, I met Saudi women from the Bedouin class, from the professional class, and from the royal family. And everywhere I looked I could see blatant discrimination against women. Women were veiled. Women walked silently behind men. Women were forbidden to drive, or even to ride bicycles. All marriages were arranged. At the time, I saw little hope for progress in the lives of women. In fact, it was forbidden to even discuss the plight of Saudi women.

Yet during those early days, excitement was in the air, for the royal government of Saudi Arabia was pouring billions of dollars of oil money into the infrastructure and advancement of the kingdom. Although decidedly backward when I first arrived, Saudi Arabia advanced rapidly; within ten years, large desert cities had magically become modern cities. Many thousands of expatriates lived and worked in Saudi Arabia in those days, and most Saudis seemed pleased to welcome these foreign workers among them. Yet the Saudis' embrace of "modernization" did not mean "Westernization." Despite the enormous and rapid progress, many Saudi women continued to live in purdah, hidden behind the veil and beneath the unquestioned rule of the men of their family.

In 1983, five years after arriving in the kingdom, I met Princess Sultana Al Sa'ud. Young, beautiful, and bold, she was determined to bring change to the women of her country. We met at an Italian Embassy dinner party. I was there with my British husband, Peter Sasson, and she was there with her husband, Kareem Al Sa'ud, a prince in the royal family, although Sultana was born a princess in her own right.

We liked each other instantly and our friendship slowly strengthened. Over time we grew to trust each other completely. Before long I was attending women's parties in her home and even accompanying her on trips to southern France and other exciting places.

I had become familiar with the tragedy of the lives of many Saudi women since I'd arrived in the country, but with Princess Sultana now alongside as my guide I saw more deeply than ever the true extent of the problem. And certainly I had been unaware that the lives of the royal women, too, could be extremely bleak and stripped of personal freedoms.

I was surprised when Princess Sultana asked me to write the story of her life. I could not imagine that such a privileged person would risk everything to tell the truth about the hardships of women in her country. After all, she was a high-ranking princess, the daughter of one of the sons of the first king, Abdul Aziz bin Abdul Rahman Al Sa'ud, and through her arranged marriage the wife of one of the Al Sa'ud royal princes.

Although Sultana had impeccable royal credentials and unimaginable wealth, she had never known true freedom. She had always been rebellious, defying her ancient culture, which dictated virtual slavery for women—all women, even those of the royal family.

I was content with my privileged life in the kingdom, so I resisted sharing the princess's revelations until the day came when I was prepared to leave the country. I knew that I could not have written a revealing book about a Saudi princess and remained in the country. I would have been imprisoned, or worse.

Although Sultana was disappointed by my refusal to write her story initially, our friendship flourished and I continued to enjoy her company. I had been fortunate to receive a multiple exit/reentry visa to the kingdom from a member of the royal family, so I returned in 1991 and 1992. When in Saudi Arabia, I socialized only with female members of her family, but when we met in Europe male members were often in attendance, too.

After I published *The Rape of Kuwait* in 1990, which detailed atrocities committed after the invasion of the country, the princess became even more determined that I write her story. And I did.

*Princess: A True Story of Life Behind the Veil in Saudi Arabia* was a shocking exposé embraced by not only English-speaking readers but also those in Europe, Asia, Africa, and many other parts of the world. In fact, my book on Princess Sultana was the first of its genre, revealing untold secrets of Saudi Arabian society and Saudi culture. Due to popular demand, the first book was followed by two sequels, both of which were also highly successful.

For years, my readers have pleaded with me to give them an update on how Princess Sultana and her family are doing. These fans longed for a fourth book and often surprised me with tears if I told them that no follow-up was in the works. (Since *Princess* was first published twenty years ago, I have written ten other books, all but one focusing on women's lives. These books are set in Iraq, Kurdistan, Afghanistan, and Kuwait.)

Another reason I was resisting writing a further installment was that I was wary of returning to the kingdom again. After the first *Princess* book was published, I had been warned that I would be arrested if I went back under my own name. The Saudi authorities will punish anyone they can get their hands on who is critical of their country.

In addition, I had always said I would *not* do a fourth book with Princess Sultana about the women of Saudi Arabia until favorable change in women's lives came about. Princess Sultana had told me over the years that the kingdom was changing dramatically, in terms of both its infrastructure and its people, and although some women still face terrible discrimination, and the pace of change remains grudgingly slow, life for most women there is gradually taking a turn for the better. Therefore, during 2013, we felt that the time had come for us to reveal what is happening in Saudi women's lives today.

And so the princess and I have continued our unique journey. Princess Sultana has been the perfect guide to lead me into the complexities of female life in Saudi Arabia. She is unusual in her society—an educated woman determined to expose the brutalities so common in her country. Few women in the Western world can rival Princess Sultana for her outspokenness, and no woman I have met in Saudi Arabia could—or can—match her exceptional courage.

Princess Sultana is one of many thousands of Saudi royals—a class estimated at fifteen thousand people in 2013. Yet only a few thousand royals wield true power in the kingdom; Princess Sultana and her family are an important arm of the dominant ruling Al Sa'ud clan. Her father is a powerful prince of the first-generation sons of the first ruler, King Abdul Aziz. Her brother and her husband are both second-generation leading Al Sa'ud princes. Her son has taken his place in the family as an influential third-generation prince. Therefore, through Princess Sultana I am kept apprised of the inner workings of the ruling family.

Princess Sultana is an extremely wealthy and influential princess in her own right. She and her husband own many businesses around the world. They have fabulous palaces in Saudi Arabia, Egypt, France, and Spain. Yet Princess Sultana is not one of the royals who care only for money, clothes, and jewels. Instead, she has devoted her life to the advancement of women. Her charities help girls and women in many countries. In fact, she supports more than seven hundred Muslim families, ensuring that all of their children can obtain education, if that is their wish.

Princess Sultana is the mother of three children—a son and two daughters. She is the grandmother to three—two boys and a girl. She has raised her children with great care, attempting to instill in them a sense of obligation to use their enormous wealth to help others.

Princess Sultana is a unique royal, and it is for this reason perhaps that all three books about her have been a huge success all over the world. Published in more than forty countries, they have been bestsellers in many lands. The books have never been out of print in most countries.

The first book focused on Princess Sultana, her childhood and her early years of marriage and motherhood. It shared a number of gripping stories about the princess and other women she knew. The second book told the story of Princess Sultana's three children and looked at Saudi social expectations of motherhood. The third book broadened its lens to provide readers with an intimate perspective on the princess's life and the lives of her sisters, their children, and other women in the kingdom, including low-paid workers who faced dire struggles.

All of the stories were true. Some of them involved young girls forced to marry men three times their age, while others told of women so badly brutalized that their tragic lives were shortened by untimely death. All were enthralling and drew readers into the lives of women in Saudi Arabia to such an intimate degree that girls and women from all over the world still write to tell me how the books altered their lives in a very positive manner. Many women today are working on behalf of human rights because they were inspired by Princess Sultana.

Although the books flowed from my pen, all the information in them came from the princess. I wrote the book in the voice of the princess because hers is so compelling and because readers are drawn into her world through her appealing personality.

As I have said, the princess and I believed that now is the right time to share new stories about women in Saudi Arabia. This is because of a great desire for change rising within the Saudi people. For the first time in the country's history, there is open debate about women's lives—even in the national Saudi Arabian newspapers, an airing that would have been unheard of when I lived there.

The political atmosphere in Saudi Arabia is also undergoing change, largely thanks to the current king, Abdullah. Abdullah was understood to be highly conservative, but upon his accession to the throne he surprised everyone by instigating change for women. The princess and I believe this development is due in part to two very bold and forceful women in King Abdullah's life: his daughters. They urged him to use his powerful influence to assist Saudi females. For example, when a young Saudi woman videotaped herself driving a car and posted the proof on YouTube, she was promptly arrested. Her young son was taken away, and she was jailed and sentenced to a flogging. In the past, the king would not have stood in the way of this type of ruling, but King Abdullah, at the urging of the women in his life, stepped in and freed the woman, rebuking the clerics by tossing out the sentence of her flogging. Although the woman had to sign an agreement pledging she would never drive again, most in Saudi Arabia breathed a sigh of relief that the harshest punishments were prevented.

So, positive change in women's lives is definitely taking place, spurred on largely by the fact that Saudi Arabia now provides schooling for all Saudis, including females. Although there are some women whose fathers will not allow them to be educated, most girls and women seek higher education. The heightened confidence and ability among the women of Saudi Arabia is now convincing the nation's men that a free woman with intelligence and education is a good thing for the family, and for society overall.

There is no doubt that a fascination with Saudi Arabia and the progress of its women has captured the world's conscience. But before we get too carried away by the positive changes that have been made, it is important to remember that Saudi Arabia is one of the last places on earth today where women are not truly free. For this reason, we must not forget that, while there is progress, there are still many heartbreaking stories to be told. Saudi women remain wholly accountable to men, who go unpunished even if they murder their wives or daughters. Shockingly, few laws are in place to protect women from violence. In this book, some of the tragic stories are revealed. It is because of these women that Princess Sultana told me: "I have more tears to cry."

The princess and I speak several times a year, and we try to see each other in person at least every twelve to eighteen months. Of course, our conversations focus on the plight of women worldwide, but chiefly the women of Saudi Arabia. I was waiting for some kind of change to come within the kingdom and it now appears that change is happening.

When Princess Sultana and I discussed the possibility of a new volume, she thought for only a moment and then responded with enthusiasm. She agreed with me that we should continue to tell this story in her voice. She agreed that we should focus on ordinary Saudi women who are still struggling but who now are achieving genuine victories in their personal lives.

The book you just read also revealed the details of Princess Sultana's current life—what is happening with her children, grandchildren, siblings, and other relatives. Readers who love Princess Sultana and her family will delight in these updates.

Many young women in the world have not yet known the joy of meeting this unique Saudi woman, who shows determined courage against the most daunting odds: she fights against the men who are fighting to keep women in servitude.

This book was written not only for the millions of Princess Sultana supporters; it was also written for a new generation of readers eager to gain insight into a new generation of Saudi women.

I would like to personally thank everyone who reads my books and supports the women I write about.

*With warmest wishes,*

*Jean Sasson*

## GO TO THE BACK OF THIS BOOK FOR TWO EXCERPTS OF JEAN SASSON'S BOOKS

# List of Characters

**The Al Sa'ud Royal Family**

**King Abdul Aziz** *First king of Saudi Arabia and Princess Sultana's grandfather*

**King Fahd** (deceased) *Fifth king of Saudi Arabia and Princess Sultana's uncle*

**King Khalid** (deceased) *Fourth king of Saudi Arabia and Princess Sultana's uncle*

**Prince Abdul Aziz bin Fahd** *Youngest son of King Fahd and Princess Jawhara, Princess Sultana's cousin*

**Prince Abdullah** *Prince Kareem and Princess Sultana's eldest child and only son*

**Princess Aisha** *Cousin to Princess Maha and Princess Amani*

**Prince Ali** *Princess Sultana's full brother*

**Prince Assad** *Princess Sara's husband, and Prince Kareem's brother*

**Prince Hadi**  *Husband of Princess Munira, deceased*

**Prince Kareem**  *Princess Sultana's husband*

**Prince Mohammed**  *Princess Sultana's nephew, son of her deceased sister Princess Reema*

**Prince Salman**  *Princess Sultana's nephew, son of her brother, Prince Ali*

**Princess Amani**  *Prince Kareem and Princess Sultana's youngest daughter*

**Princess Dunia**  *Princess Sultana's sister*

**Princess Haifa**  *Princess Sultana's sister*

**Princess Jawhara**  *King Fahd's favorite wife*

**Princess Maha**  *Prince Kareem and Princess Sultana's eldest daughter*

**Princess Medina**  *Princess Sultana's niece, Prince Ali's daughter*

**Princess Medina**  *Princess Sultana's older cousin who suffered severe hair loss*

**Princess Munira**  *Princess Sultana's niece, Prince Ali's daughter*

**Princess Nashwa**  *Prince Assad and Princess Sara's daughter*

**Princess Nora bint**  *Sister of Princess Sultana's grandfather,*

**Princess Nura** (deceased)  *Princess Sultana's eldest sister*

**Princess Rana**  *Princess Sultana's niece, daughter of Princess Nura*

**Princess Sara**  *Princess Sultana's sister*

**Princess Sita**  *Princess Sultana's sister-in-law*

**Princess Tahani**  *Princess Sultana's sister*

**Princess Zain**  *Princess Sultana's daughter-in-law, wife of Prince Abdullah*

**Little Sultana**  *Princess Sultana's first grandchild, daughter of her son Abdullah*

**Little Prince Faisal**  *Princess Sultana's second grandchild, son of her son Abdullah*

**Little Prince Khalid**  *Princess Sultana's third grandchild (second grandson) and son of her daughter Amani*


**Other Notable Characters**

**Sheikh Abdul Aziz bin Baz** (deceased)  *Saudi cleric, once the Grand Mufti of Saudi Arabia, and Princess Amani's favorite cleric*

**Batara**  *Princess Sultana's Indonesian driver*

**Laila** *Young Saudi woman who avoided an early marriage when her brother assisted her in owning and running her own beauty salon, something very difficult for a woman in Saudi Arabia*

**Fatima** *Abused Saudi wife and mother of twin girls*

**Dr. Meena** *A Saudi woman, and highly respected physician, from a poor background*

**Nadia** *A young Saudi woman who is a social worker*

**Noor** *Bedouin woman who was involved in a case of domestic abuse*

**Sabeen** *Princess Sultana's Indonesian housemaid*

**Faria** *A young Saudi woman who was the victim of female genital mutilation*

**Shada** *A young woman accused of being a witch*

**Dalal** *A thirteen-year-old girl who suffered abuse and died at the hands of her father*

**Amal** *A five-year-old girl who was raped and killed by her father*

# Appendix A
# Facts about Saudi Arabia

## General Information

Head of State: HM King Abdullah ibn Abdul Aziz Al
   Sa'ud
Official Title: Custodian of the Two Holy Mosques


## Main Cities

Riyadh – capital
Jeddah – port city
Mecca – holiest city of Islam, toward which Muslims
   pray
Medina – burial place of Prophet Muhammad
Taif – summer capital and summer resort area
Dammam – port city and commercial center
Dhahran – oil industry center
Al Khobar – commercial center
Yanbu – natural gas shipping terminal
Hail – trading center
Jubail – industrial city
Ras Tanura – refinery center
Hofuf – principal city of the Al Hasa Oasis

## Religion

Islam: It is a crime to practice other religions in Saudi Arabia.

## Public Holidays

Eid al-Fitr – five days
Eid ul-Adha – eight days

## Short History

Saudi Arabia is a nation of tribes that can trace their roots back to the earliest civilizations of the Arabian Peninsula. The ancestors of modern-day Saudis lived on ancient and important trade routes, and much of their income was realized by raiding parties. Divided into regions and ruled by independent tribal chiefs, the various warring tribes were unified under one religion, Islam, led by the Prophet Muhammad, in the seventh century. Before the Prophet died, age sixty-three, most of Arabia was Muslim.

The ancestors of the present rulers of Saudi Arabia reigned over much of Arabia during the nineteenth century. After losing most of Saudi territory to the Turks, they were driven from Riyadh and sought refuge in Kuwait. King Abdul Aziz Al Sa'ud, father of the present-day king, returned to Riyadh and fought to regain the country. He succeeded and founded modern Saudi Arabia in 1932. Oil was discovered in 1938, and Saudi Arabia rapidly became one of the world's wealthiest and most influential nations.

## Geography

Saudi Arabia, with an area of 864,866 square miles, is one third the size of the United States and is the same size as Western Europe. The country lies at the crossroads of three continents: Africa, Asia, and Europe. Extending from the Red Sea in the west to the Persian Gulf in the east, it borders Jordan, Iraq, and Kuwait to the north, and Yemen and Oman to the south. The United Arab Emirates, Qatar, and Bahrain lie to the east.

A harsh desert land, with no rivers and few permanent streams, Saudi Arabia is home to the Rub al Khali (Empty Quarter), which is the largest sand desert in the world. The mountain ranges of Asir Province rise to more than nine thousand feet in the southwest.

## Calendar

Saudi Arabia uses the Islamic calendar, which is based on a lunar year, rather than the Gregorian calendar, which is based on a solar year. A lunar month is the time between two successive new moons. A lunar year contains twelve months but is eleven days shorter than the solar year. For this reason, the holy days gradually shift from one season to another.

Lunar year dates are derived from AD 622, the year of the Prophet's emigration, or Hejira, from Mecca to Medina. The Islamic holy day is Friday. The working week in Saudi Arabia begins on Saturday and ends on Thursday.

## Economy

More than one quarter of the world's known oil reserves lie beneath the sands of Saudi Arabia. In 1933, Standard Oil Company of California won the rights to prospect for oil in Saudi Arabia. In 1938, oil was discovered at Dammam Oil Well No. 7, which is still producing oil today. The Arabian American Oil Company (Aramco) was founded in 1944 and held the right to continue to search for oil in the kingdom. In 1980, the Saudi government assumed ownership of Aramco.

The kingdom's oil wealth has ensured that the citizens of Saudi Arabia live the kind of opulent lifestyle enjoyed by few. With free education and interest-free loans, most Saudis prosper. All Saudi citizens, as well as Muslim pilgrims, receive free health care. Government programs provide support for Saudi Arabians in the case of disability, death, or retirement. The entire country is an impressive socialist state. Economically, Saudi Arabia has developed into a modern, technologically advanced nation.

## Currency

The Saudi riyal is the basic monetary unit in Saudi Arabia. The riyal consists of 100 halalas and is issued in notes and coins of various denominations. The riyal is 3.7450 to the U.S. dollar.

## Law and Government

Saudi Arabia is an Islamic state and the law is based on sharia, the Islamic code of law taken from the pages of the Koran, and the Sunna, which are the traditions addressed by Prophet Muhammad. The Koran is the constitution of the country and provides guidance for legal judgments.

Executive and legislative authority is exercised by the king and the Council of Ministers. Their decisions are based on sharia law. All ministries and government agencies are responsible to the king.

## Religion

Saudi Arabia is home to Islam, one of the three monotheistic religions. Muslims believe in one God and that Muhammad is his Prophet. As the heartland of Islam, Saudi Arabia occupies a special place in the Muslim world. Each year, millions of Muslim pilgrims journey to Mecca in Saudi Arabia to pay homage to God. For this reason, Saudi Arabia is one of the most traditional Muslim countries and its citizens adhere to a strict interpretation of the Koran.

A Muslim has five obligations, called the Five Pillars of Islam. These obligations are:

1. Profession of faith: "There is no god but God; Muhammad is the messenger of God."
2. A Muslim should pray five times a day, facing the city of Mecca.
3. A Muslim must pay a fixed proportion of his income, called *zakat*, to the poor.
4. During the ninth month of the Islamic calendar, a Muslim must fast. During this time, called Ramadan,

Muslims must abstain from food and drink from dawn to sunset.

5. A Muslim must perform the hajj, or pilgrimage, at least once during his lifetime (if he has the economic means).

# Appendix B
# Glossary

**abaya**: a black, full-length outer garment worn by Saudi women

*abu*: father

**Al Sa'ud**: ruling family of Saudi Arabia

**Bedouin**: a nomadic desert people, the original Arabs

**Dhu al Hijjah**: the twelfth month of the Hejira calendar

**Dhu al Qi'dah**: the eleventh month of the Hejira calendar

**haji**: person who makes the pilgrimage to Mecca (a title that denotes honor)

**hajj**: annual pilgrimage to Mecca made by those of the Islamic faith

**Hejira**: Islamic calendar, which started on the date that the Prophet Muhammad fled Mecca and escaped to Medina (622)

**ibn**: means "son of" (e.g., Khalid ibn Faisal, son of Faisal)

*ihram*: special time during hajj when all Muslims refrain from normal life and dwell on nothing but religious matters

**imam**: person who leads communal prayers and/or delivers the sermon on Fridays

**infanticide**: practice of killing an infant. In pre-Islamic times, a common practice in Arabia, thereby ridding the family of unwanted female children.

**Islam**: religious faith of Muslims of which Muhammad was the Prophet. Islam was the last of the three great monotheistic religions to appear.

**Kaaba**: Islam's holiest shrine, a sacred sanctuary for all Muslims. The Kaaba is a small building in the Holy Mosque of Mecca, nearly cubic in shape, built to enclose the Black Stone, which is the most venerated Muslim object.

**kohl**: a black powder used as eye makeup by Saudi Arabian women

**Koran**: the Holy Book of all Muslims, containing the words of God as they were given to the Prophet Muhammad

*la*: Arabic word meaning "no"

*Mahram*: males to whom a woman cannot be married, such as her father, brother, or uncle, who are allowed to be a woman's escort when traveling. Must be a close relative.

**Mecca**: holiest city of Islam. Each year, millions of Muslims travel to Mecca to perform the annual pilgrimage.

**Medina**: second holiest city of Islam. The burial place of the Prophet Muhammad.

**monotheism**: belief that there is only one god

**Morals Police, also known as Committee for the Promotion of Virtue and the Prevention of Vice (CPVPV)**: religious authorities in Saudi Arabia who have the power to arrest those they believe commit moral wrongs or crimes against Islam or go against the teachings of Islam

344

**muezzin**: the crier who calls the faithful to pray five times a day

**Muslim**: adherent of the religion founded by the Prophet Muhammad in the year 610

*mut'a*: temporary marriage allowed to those of the Islamic faith

*mutawa*: the religious police, also known as the Morals Police. Men who seek out, arrest, and punish those who do not abide by Saudi religious law.

**Najd**: the traditional name for central Arabia. The inhabitants of this area are known for their conservative behavior. The ruling family of Saudi Arabia are Najdis.

**polygamy**: marriage to more than one spouse at the same time. Men of the Muslim faith are legally allowed four wives at one time.

**purdah**: a practice of confining women to their homes. This total seclusion of females can occur in some Muslim countries.

**purification**: the ritual of cleansing prior to offering prayers to God practiced by Muslims

**riyal**: Saudi Arabian currency

**secular**: not religious

**Shiite**: the branch of Islam that split from the Sunni majority over the issue of Prophet Muhammad's successor. One of two main sects.

**Sunna**: traditions of the Islamic faith, as addressed by the Prophet Muhammad

**Sunni**: the majority orthodox branch of Islam. Saudi Arabia is 95 percent populated by those of the Sunni sect. The word means "traditionalists." One of two main sects.

*thobe*: a long shirtlike dress that is worn by Saudi men. It is usually made of white cotton but can be made of heavier, darker-colored fabric for the winter months.

**Umm Al Qura:** "Mother of Cities" or "the Blessed City," that is, Mecca

*umrah:* a short pilgrimage (to Mecca) undertaken by those of the Muslim faith that can be made any time of the year

**woman's room:** room in a man's house used to confine Saudi Arabian women who go against the wishes of their husbands, fathers, or brothers. The punishment can be for a short period or a life sentence.

*zakat:* obligatory alms giving required of all Muslims that is the third pillar of Islam

# Appendix C
# Saudi Arabia Timeline

**570** *19 January.* Prophet Muhammad, the founder of Islam, is born in Mecca.

**632** *8 June.* Prophet Muhammad dies in Medina. After his death, his companions compile his words and deeds in a work called the Sunna, which contains the rules for Islam. The most basic are the Five Pillars of Islam, which are 1) profession of faith; 2) daily prayer; 3) giving alms; 4) ritual fast during Ramadan; 5) hajj, the pilgrimage to Mecca.

**1400s** The Sa'ud dynasty is founded near Riyadh.

**1703** Muhammad ibn Abd al-Wahhab (d. 1792), Islamic theologian and founder of Wahhabism, is born in Arabia.

**1710** Muhammad ibn Al Sa'ud is born.

**1742–65** Muhammad bin Sa'ud Al Sa'ud joins the Wahhabists.

**1744** Muhammad ibn Al Sa'ud forges a political and family alliance with Muslim scholar and reformer Muhammad ibn Abd al-Wahhab. The son of Ibn Sa'ud marries the daughter of Imam Muhammad.

**1804** The Wahhabis capture Medina.

**1811** Egyptian ruler Muhammad Ali overthrows the Wahhabis and reinstates Ottoman sovereignty in Arabia.

**1813** The Wahhabis are driven from Mecca.

**1824** The Al Sa'ud family establishes a new capital at Riyadh.

**1860s–90s** The Al Sa'ud family moves to exile in Kuwait when the Ottoman Empire conquers their territory in Arabia.

**1876** Sultana's grandfather, Abdul Aziz ibn Sa'ud, founder of the kingdom, is born.

**1883** *20 May.* Faisal ibn Hussein is born in Mecca. He later becomes the first king of Syria (1920) and Iraq (1921).

**1901** Muhammad bin Rasheed captures Riyadh, forcing the Al Sa'ud family out of the area. Abdul Aziz leaves Kuwait to return to Arabia with family and friends with plans to attack Riyadh.

**1902** *January.* Abdul Aziz attacks Mismaak fort and recaptures Riyadh. Sa'ud ibn Abdul Aziz, son of Ibn

Sa'ud, is born. At his father's death, he will rule Saudi
Arabia from 1953 to 1964.

**1904** Faisal ibn Abd al-Aziz, who one day will be a
king of Saudi Arabia, is born.

**1906** Abdul Aziz Al Sa'ud regains total control of the
Nejd region.

**1906–26** Abdul Aziz Al Sa'ud and his forces capture
vast areas and unify much of Arabia.

**1916** Mecca, under control of the Turks, falls to the
Arabs during the Great Arab Revolt. British officer T.
E. Lawrence meets Arab prince Faisal Hussein, forging
a friendship. T. E. Lawrence is assigned as the British
liaison to Faisal Hussein.

**1917** *6 July.* Arab forces led by T. E. Lawrence and
Abu Tayi capture the port of Aqaba from the Turks.

**1918** *1 October.* Prince Faisal takes control of Syria
when the main Arab force enters Damascus.
Lawrence of Arabia blows up the Hejaz railway line
in Saudi Arabia.

**1921** At the Cairo Conference, Britain and France
carve up Arabia and create Jordan and Iraq, making
brothers Faisal and Abdullah kings. France is given
influence over what is now Syria and Lebanon.

**1923** Abdul Aziz's son Fahd is born in Riyadh. He will
one day reign as king of Saudi Arabia.

**1924** Ibn Sa'ud, king of the Nejd, conquers Hussein's kingdom of Hejaz. He rules over Saudi Arabia, later taking Mecca and Medina.

**1926** *January.* Abdul Aziz is declared King of Hejaz and Sultan of Nejd.

**1927** Saudi Arabia signs the Treaty of Jeddah and becomes independent of Great Britain.

**1927–28** King Abdul Aziz crushes the fanatical Islamist tribes of central Arabia.

**1931** Mohammed bin Laden (who one day will be the father of Osama bin Laden) emigrates to Saudi Arabia from Yemen. He works hard to establish his business, later building a close relationship with King Abdul Aziz and King Faisal.

**1932** The kingdoms of Nejd and Hejaz are unified to create the Kingdom of Saudi Arabia under King Abdul Aziz ibn Sa'ud. Saudi Arabia was named after King Ibn Sa'ud, founder of the Saudi dynasty, a man who fathered forty-four sons, who continue to rule the oil-rich kingdom.

**1933** Saudi Arabia gives Standard Oil of California exclusive rights to explore for oil.

**1938** Standard Oil of California strikes oil at Dammam No 7.

**1945** *14 February.* Saudi king Abdul al-Aziz and American president Franklin D. Roosevelt meet on a ship in the Suez Canal, where they reach an understanding whereby the United States will protect the Saudi royal family in return for access to Saudi oil.

*22 March.* The Arab League is formed in Cairo, Egypt. Saudi Arabia becomes a founding member of the United Nations and the Arab League.

**1953** King Abdul Aziz, Sultana's grandfather, dies, age seventy-seven. He is succeeded by his son Sa'ud.

**1953–64** King Sa'ud rules.

**1957** *Friday, 15 February.* Osama bin Laden is born in the early hours in Riyadh, Saudi Arabia. His parents are Yemen-born Mohammed Awad bin Laden and Syrian Alia Ghanem.

**1962** Saudi Arabia abolishes slavery.

**1964** *2 November.* Faisal ibn Abdul Aziz Al Sa'ud (1904–75) succeeds his older brother, Sa'ud bin Abdul Aziz, as king of Saudi Arabia.

**1964–75** King Faisal rules.

**1965** King Faisal defies Islamist opposition when he introduces television and later women's education. Riots ensue. Later senior clerics are convinced by the government that television could be used to promote the faith.

**1967** *6 June.* An Arab oil embargo is put into effect after the beginning of the Arab-Israeli Six-Day War.

*3 September.* Mohammed bin Laden, the wealthy father of Osama bin Laden, dies in a plane crash, leaving the well-being of his children to King Faisal.

**1973** An oil embargo against Western nations is announced, lasting until 1974. Gasoline prices soar from 25 cents per gallon to $1. As a result, s t o c k s o n the New York Stock Exchange fall.

**1975** *25 March.* King Faisal of Saudi Arabia is assassinated by his nephew. Crown Prince Khalid becomes king.

*18 June.* Saudi Prince Faisal ibn Musaid is beheaded in Riyadh for killing his uncle, King Faisal. Crown Prince Khalid is declared king.

*November.* Armed men and women seize the Grand Mosque in Mecca. They denounce the Al Sa'ud rulers, demanding an end to foreign ways. The radicals are led by Saudi preacher Juhayman al Utaybi. The siege goes on until French special forces are flown to Mecca to assist. The extremists are shot and killed or captured, later to be beheaded.

**1980** Osama bin Laden starts his struggle of fighting against the Soviets in Afghanistan. This is where he will later found his Al Qaeda network.

Saudi Arabia executes the remaining radicals for the siege of the Grand Mosque. The radicals are beheaded in various towns across the country.

**1982** *13 June.* King Khalid dies. He is succeeded by his half-brother Crown Prince Fahd.

**1983–2005** Prince Bandar bin Sultan Al Sa'ud, one of King Fahd's favorite nephews, serves as Saudi Arabia's ambassador to Washington.

**1985** Great Britain signs an $80 billion contract with Saudi Arabia to provide 120 fighter jets and other military equipment over a period of twenty years.

**1987** *31 July.* Iranian pilgrims and riot police clash in the holy city of Mecca. The Iranians are blamed for the deaths of 402 people.

**1988** Saudi-born Osama bin Laden founds Al Qaeda ("the base"), a Sunni fundamentalist group with a goal of establishing an Islamic caliphate throughout the world.

**1990** *July.* The worst tragedy in modern Saudi Arabia occurs at the hajj in Mecca, when 1,402 Muslim pilgrims are killed in a stampede inside a pedestrian tunnel.

*6 November.* A group of Saudi women drive cars in the streets of Riyadh in defiance of a government ban. The protest creates enormous problems for the women drivers: they are arrested and fired from their jobs, banned from traveling, and named as prostitutes. This event leads to a formal ban on driving for women.

Saudi Arabia and Kuwait expel a million Yemeni workers as the government of Yemen sides with Saddam Hussein in the first Gulf War.

**1991** *January.* U.S.-led forces attack the Iraqi military in Kuwait. The ground war begins between Iraq and the Coalition forces. Iraqi forces are routed from Kuwait and are no longer a danger to Saudi Arabia.

**1992** King Fahd outlines an institutional structure for the country. A law is passed that allows the king to name his brothers or nephews as successors and to replace his successor at will.

**1994** *23 May.* 270 pilgrims are killed in a stampede in Mecca, as worshippers gather for the symbolic ritual of "stoning the devil."

Osama bin Laden is disowned by his Saudi family and stripped of his Saudi citizenship. His fortune is estimated at $250 million.

**1995** 192 people are beheaded in Saudi Arabia over the year—a record number.

**1996** Osama bin Laden is asked to leave Sudan after the Clinton administration puts pressure on the Sudanese government. Osama takes his son Omar with him to return to Afghanistan. The rest of his family and close associates soon follow.

A nephew of King Fahd falsely accuses one of his employees of witchcraft. The employee, Abdul-Karim Naqshabandi, is executed.

An ailing King Fahd cedes power to his half-brother Crown Prince Abdullah.

**1997** 343 Muslim pilgrims die in a fire outside the holy city of Mecca. More than a thousand others are injured.

**1998** 150 pilgrims die at the "stoning of the devil" ritual during a stampede that occurs on the last day of the annual pilgrimage to the holy city of Mecca.

**1999** The Saudi Arabian government claims it will issue travel visas into the kingdom to upscale travel groups.

*21 August.* Members of the royal family are shocked when Prince Faisal bin Fahd, the eldest son of King Fahd, dies of a heart attack, age fifty-four. As head of the Arab Sports Federation, he had just returned from the Arab Games in Jordan.

*17 November.* A car bomb in Riyadh kills Christopher Rodway, a British technician. In 2001, three Westerners are charged with the bombing.

**2001** *26 January.* A UN panel angers the Saudi government and citizens when it criticizes Saudi Arabia for discriminating against women, harassing minors, and for punishments that include flogging and stoning.

*5 March.* 35 Muslim pilgrims suffocate to death during the "stoning of the devil" ritual at the annual hajj in Mecca.

*March.* The Higher Committee for Scientific Research and Islamic Law in Saudi Arabia says that Pokémon games and cards have "possessed the minds" of Saudi children.

*September.* After 9/11, six chartered flights carrying Saudi nationals depart from the USA. A few days later, another chartered flight carrying twenty-six members of the bin Laden family leaves the USA.

**2002** *17 February.* Saudi Crown Prince Abdullah presents a Middle East peace plan to *New York Times* columnist Thomas Friedman. The plan includes Arab recognition of Israel's right to exist if Israel pulls back from lands that were once part of Jordan, including East Jerusalem and the West Bank.

*March.* There is a fire at a girls' school in Mecca, but the police block the girls from fleeing the building because they are not wearing the veil. A surge of anger spreads across Saudi Arabia when fifteen students burn to death.

*13 April.* Saudi Arabian poet Ghazi Al-Gosaibi, Saudi ambassador to Britain, publishes the poem "The Martyrs" in the Saudi daily *Al Hayat,* praising a Palestinian suicide bomber.

*25 April.* American president George W. Bush meets with Crown Prince Abdullah, who tells Bush that the United States must reconsider its total support of Israel. Abdullah gives Bush his eight-point proposal for Middle East peace.

*April.* The Saudi Arabian government closes several factories that produce women's veils and abayas that are said to violate religious rules. Some of the cloaks are considered too luxurious, with jewels sewn on the shoulders.

*May.* There is a disagreement between Saudi diplomats and members of the UN Committee Against Torture over whether flogging and the amputation of limbs are violations of the 1987 Convention Against Torture.

*December.* Saudi dissidents report the launch of a new radio station, Sawt al-Islah (the Voice of Reform), broadcasting from Europe. The new station is formed with the explicit purpose of pushing for reforms in Saudi Arabia.

**2003** *February.* In Mina, Saudi Arabia, fourteen Muslim pilgrims are trampled to death when a worshipper trips during the annual hajj pilgrimage.

*29 April.* The United States government announces the withdrawal of all combat forces from Saudi Arabia.

*12 May.* Multiple and simultaneous suicide car bombings at three foreign compounds in Riyadh, Saudi Arabia, kill twenty-six people, including nine U.S. citizens.

*14 September.* Saudi national and marijuana trafficker Dhaher bin Thamer al-Shimry is beheaded; forty-one people have been beheaded by September.

*14 October.* Hundreds of Saudi Arabians take to the streets, demanding reform. This is the first large-scale protest in the country, as demonstrations are illegal.

Indonesian maid Ati Bt Abeh Inan is accused by her Saudi employer of casting a spell on him and his family and is sentenced to death. After serving ten years in prison, she is pardoned and sent back to West Java.

It is discovered that Libya planned a covert operation to assassinate Crown Prince Abdullah.

**2004** *1 February.* During the hajj, 251 Muslim worshippers die in a stampede.

*10 April.* Popular Saudi Arabian TV host Rania al-Baz is severely beaten by her husband, who thought he had killed her. She survived, suffering severe facial fractures that required twelve operations. She allowed photos to be broadcast and opened discussions about ongoing violence against women in Saudi Arabia. She traveled to France, where she wrote her story. It was reported that she lost custody of her children after her book was published.

*May.* In Yanbu, Saudi Arabia, suspected militants spray gunfire inside the offices of an oil contractor, the Houston-based ABB Ltd. Six people are killed. Many are wounded. Police kill four brothers in a shoot-out after a car chase in which the attackers reportedly dragged the naked body of one victim behind their getaway car.

*6 June.* Simon Chambers, thirty-six, an Irish cameraman working for the BBC, is killed in a shooting in Riyadh. A BBC correspondent is injured.

*8 June.* An American citizen working for a U.S. defense contractor is shot and killed in Riyadh.

*12 June.* An American is kidnapped in Riyadh. Al Qaeda posts the man's picture on an Islamic Web site. He is identified as Lockheed Martin businessman Paul M. Johnson Jr. Islamic militants shoot and kill American Kenneth Scroggs in his garage in Riyadh.

*13 June.* Saudi Arabia holds a three-day "national dialogue" in Medina on how women's lives could be improved and the recommendations are passed on to Crown Prince Abdullah.

*15 June.* Al Qaeda threatens to execute Paul M. Johnson Jr. within seventy-two hours unless fellow jihadists are released from Saudi prisons.

*18 June.* Al Qaeda claims to have killed American hostage Paul M. Johnson Jr. They post photos on the Internet showing his body and severed head.

*June.* The Saudi parliament passes legislation overturning a law banning girls and women from participating in physical education and sports. In August, the Ministry of Education announces that it will not honor the legislation.

*20 July.* The head of slain American hostage Paul M. Johnson Jr. is found during a raid by Saudi security forces.

*30 July.* In the United States, in a Virginia court, Abdurahman Alamoudi pleads guilty to moving cash from Libya to pay expenses in the plot to assassinate Saudi Prince Abdullah.

*28 September.* The use of mobile phones with built-in cameras is banned by Saudi Arabia's highest religious authority. The edict claims that the phones are "spreading obscenity" throughout Saudi Arabia.

*6 December.* Nine people are killed at the U.S. Consulate in Jeddah when Islamic militants throw explosives at the gate of the heavily guarded building. They force their way into the building and a gun battle ensues.

**2005** *13 January.* Saudi judicial officials say a religious court has sentenced fifteen Saudis, including a woman, to as many as 250 lashes each and up to six months in prison for participating in a protest against the monarchy.

*10 February.* While women are banned from casting ballots, Saudi male voters converge at polling stations in the Riyadh region to participate in city elections. This is the first time in the country's history that Saudis are taking part in a vote that conforms to international standards.

*3 March.* Men in eastern and southern Saudi Arabia turn out in the thousands to vote in municipal elections. It is their first opportunity to have a say in decision making in Saudi's absolute monarchy.

*1 April.* Saudi Arabia beheads three men in public in the northern city of al-Jawf; in 2003 the three men killed a deputy governor, a religious court judge, and a police lieutenant.

*8 May.* A Pakistani man is beheaded for attempting to smuggle heroin into the kingdom.

*15 May.* Three reform advocates are sentenced to terms ranging from six to nine years in prison. Human rights activists call the trial "a farce."

*15 May.* Saudi author and poet Ali al-Dimeeni is sentenced to nine years in prison for sowing dissent, disobeying his rulers, and sedition. His 1998 novel *A Gray Cloud* centers on a dissident jailed for years in a desert nation prison where many others have served time for their political views.

*27 May.* King Fahd, Saudi Arabia's monarch for twenty-three years, is hospitalized for unspecified reasons.

*1 August.* King Fahd dies at the King Faisal Specialist Hospital in Riyadh. His half-brother Crown Prince Abdullah is named to replace him.

*8 August.* Hope rises in Saudi Arabia after the new king, Abdullah, pardons four prominent activists who were jailed after criticizing the country's strict religious environment and the slow pace of democratic reform.

*15 September.* The Saudi government orders a Jeddah chamber of commerce to allow female voters and candidates.

*21 September.* Two men are beheaded in Riyadh after being convicted of kidnapping and raping a woman.

*17 November.* A Saudi high school chemistry teacher, accused of discussing religion with his students, is sentenced to 750 lashes and forty months in prison for blasphemy following a trial on 12 November.

*27 November.* To the delight of Saudi women, two females are elected to a chamber of commerce in Jeddah. This is the first occasion when women have won any such post in the country, as they are largely barred from political life.

*8 December.* Leaders from fifty Muslim countries promise to fight extremist ideology. The leaders say they will reform textbooks, restrict religious edicts, and crack down on terror financing.

Saudi Arabia enacts a law that bans state employees from making any statements in public that conflict with official policy.

**2006** *12 January.* Thousands of Muslim pilgrims trip over luggage during the hajj, causing a crush in which 363 people are killed.

*26 January.* Saudi Arabia recalls its ambassador to Denmark in protest at a series of caricatures of the Prophet Muhammad published in the Danish *Jyllands-Posten* newspaper. Discontent spreads across the Muslim world for weeks, resulting in dozens of deaths.

*19 February.* Following the publication of the twelve cartoons of the Prophet—highlighting what it describes as self- censorship—the *Jyllands-Posten* newspaper prints a full-page apology in a Saudi-owned newspaper.

*6 April.* Cheese and butter from the Danish company Arla are returned to Saudi Arabian supermarket shelves following a boycott sparked by the country's publication of offensive cartoons.

*April.* The Saudi Arabian government announces plans to build an electrified fence along its 560-mile border with Iraq.

*16 May.* Newspapers in Saudi Arabia report that they have received an order from King Abdullah telling editors to stop publishing pictures of women. The king claims that such photographs will make young Saudi men go astray.

*18 August.* According to the *Financial Times*, Great Britain has agreed to a multibillion-dollar defense deal to supply seventy-two Eurofighter Typhoon aircraft to Saudi Arabia.

*20 October.* In an attempt to defuse internal power struggles, King Abdullah gives new powers to his brothers and nephews. In the future, a council of thirty princes will meet to choose the crown prince.

The kingdom beheaded eighty-three people in 2005 and thirty-five people in 2004.

**2007** *4 February.* A Saudi Arabian judge sentences twenty foreigners to receive lashes and prison terms after convicting them of attending a mixed party where alcohol was served and men and women danced.

*17 February.* A report published by a U.S. human rights group reveals that the Saudi government detains thousands of prisoners in jail without charge, sentences children to death, and oppresses women.

*19 February.* A Saudi court orders the bodies of four Sri Lankans to be displayed in a public square after being beheaded for armed robbery.

*26 February.* Four Frenchmen are killed by gunmen on the side of a desert road leading to the holy city of Medina in an area restricted to Muslims only.

*February.* Ten Saudi intellectuals are arrested for signing a polite petition suggesting it is time for the kingdom to consider a transition to constitutional monarchy.

*27 April.* In one of the largest sweeps against terror cells in Saudi Arabia, the Interior Ministry says police arrested 172 Islamic militants. The militants had trained abroad as pilots so they could duplicate 9/11 and fly aircraft in attacks on Saudi Arabia's oil fields.

*5 May.* Prince Abdul-Majid bin Abdul-Aziz, the governor of Mecca, dies, age sixty-five, after a long illness.

*9 May.* An Ethiopian woman convicted of killing an Egyptian man over a dispute is beheaded. Khadija bint Ibrahim Moussa is the second woman to be executed this year. Beheadings are carried out with a sword in a public square.

Nayef al-Shaalan, a Saudi prince, is sentenced in absentia in France to ten years in prison on charges of involvement in a cocaine smuggling gang.

*23 June.* A Saudi judge postpones the trial of three members of the religious police for their involvement in the death of a man arrested after being seen with a woman who was not his relative.

*9 November.* Saudi authorities behead Saudi citizen Khalaf al-Anzi in Riyadh for kidnapping and raping a teenager.

Saudi authorities behead a Pakistani for drug trafficking. This execution brings to 131 the number of people beheaded in the kingdom in 2007.

*14 November.* A Saudi court sentences a nine-year-old girl who had been gang-raped to six months in prison and two hundred lashes. The court also bans her lawyer from defending her, confiscating his license to practice law and summoning him to a disciplinary hearing.

*17 December.* A gang-rape victim who was sentenced to six months in prison and two hundred lashes for being alone with a man not related to her is pardoned by the Saudi king after the case sparks rare criticism from the United States.

**2008** *21 January.* The newspaper *Al-Watan* reports that the Interior Ministry issued a circular to hotels asking them to accept lone women as long as their information was sent to a local police station.

*14 February.* A leading human rights group appeals to Saudi Arabia's King Abdullah to stop the execution of a woman accused of witchcraft and performing supernatural acts.

*19 May.* Teacher Matrook al-Faleh is arrested at King Saud University in Riyadh after he publicly criticized conditions in a prison where two other human rights activists are serving jail terms.

*24 May.* Saudi authorities behead a local man convicted of armed robbery and raping a woman. The execution brings the number of people beheaded in 2008 to fifty-five.

*20 June.* Religious police arrest twenty-one allegedly homosexual men and confiscate large amounts of alcohol at a large gathering of young men at a rest house in Qatif.

*8 July.* A human rights group says domestic workers in Saudi Arabia often suffer abuse that in some cases amounts to slavery, as well as sexual violence and lashings for spurious allegations of theft or witchcraft.

*30 July.* The country's Islamic religious police ban the sale of dogs and cats as pets. They also ban owners from walking their pets in public because men use cats and dogs to make passes at women.

*11 September.* Sheikh Saleh al-Lihedan, Saudi Arabia's top judiciary official, issues a religious decree saying it is permissible to kill the owners of satellite TV networks who broadcast immoral content. He later adjusts his comments, saying owners who broadcast immoral content should be brought to trial and sentenced to death if other penalties do not deter them.

*November.* A U.S. diplomatic cable says donors in Saudi Arabia and the United Arab Emirates send an estimated $100 million annually to radical Islamic schools in Pakistan that back militancy.

*10 December.* The European Commission awards the first Chaillot Prize to the Al-Nahda Philanthropic Society for Women, a Saudi charity that helps divorced and underprivileged women.

**2009** *14 January.* Saudi Arabia's most senior cleric is quoted as saying it is permissible for ten-year-old girls to marry. He adds that anyone who thinks ten-year-old girls are too young to marry is doing those girls an injustice.

*14 February.* King Abdullah dismisses Sheikh Saleh al-Lihedan. King Abdullah also appoints Nora al-Fayez as deputy minister of women's education, the first female in the history of Saudi Arabia to hold a ministerial post.

*3 March.* Khamisa Sawadi, a seventy-five-year-old widow, is sentenced to forty lashes and four months in jail for talking with two young men who are not close relatives.

*22 March.* A group of Saudi clerics urges the kingdom's new information minister to ban women from appearing on TV or in newspapers and magazines.

*27 March.* King Abdullah appoints his half-brother Prince Naif as his second deputy prime minister.

*30 April.* An eight-year-old girl divorces her middle-aged husband after her father forces her to marry him in exchange for $13,000. Saudi Arabia permits such child marriages.

*29 May.* A man is beheaded and crucified for slaying an eleven-year-old boy and his father.

*6 June.* The Saudi film *Menahi* is screened in Riyadh more than thirty years after the government began shutting down theaters. No women were allowed, only men and children, including girls up to ten.

*15 July.* Saudi citizen Mazen Abdul-Jawad appears on Lebanon's LBC satellite TV station's *Bold Red Line* program and shocks Saudis by publicly confessing to sexual exploits. More than two hundred Saudi Arabians file legal complaints against Abdul-Jawad, dubbed a "sex braggart" by the media, and many Saudis say he should be severely punished. Abdul-Jawad is convicted by a Saudi court in October 2009 and sentenced to five years in jail and one thousand lashes.

*9 August.* Italian news agencies report that burglars have stolen jewels and cash worth 11 million euros from the hotel room of a Saudi princess in Sardinia, sparking a diplomatic incident.

*27 August.* A suicide bomber targets the assistant interior minister Prince Mohammed bin Naif and blows himself up just before going into a gathering of well-wishers for the Muslim holy month of Ramadan in Jeddah. His target, Prince Naif, is only slightly wounded.

*23 September.* A new multibillion-dollar co-ed university opens outside the coastal city of Jeddah. The King Abdullah Science and Technology University, or KAUST, boasts state-of-the-art labs, the world's fourteenth-fastest supercomputer, and one of the biggest endowments worldwide. Currently enrolled are 817 students representing 61 different countries, with 314 beginning classes in September 2009.

*24 October.* Rozanna al-Yami, age twenty-two, is tried and convicted for her involvement in the *Bold*

*Red Line* program featuring Mazen Abdul-Jawad. She is sentenced to sixty lashes and is thought to be the first female Saudi journalist to be given such a punishment. King Abdullah waived the flogging sentence, the second such pardon in a high-profile case by the monarch in recent years. He ordered al-Yami's case to be referred to a committee in the ministry.

*October.* The bin Laden family goes under the spotlight in *Growing Up Bin Laden: Osama's Wife and Son Take Us Inside Their Secret World*, written by American author Jean Sasson. The book is based on interviews with Sasson conducted with Omar bin Laden and his mother, Najwa bin Laden.

*9 November.* A Lebanese psychic, Ali Sibat, who made predictions on a satellite TV channel from his home in Beirut, is sentenced to death for practicing witchcraft. When he traveled to Medina for a pilgrimage in May 2008, he was arrested and threatened with beheading. The following year a three-judge panel said that there was not enough evidence that Sibat's actions had harmed others. They ordered the case to be retried in a Medina court and recommended that the sentence be commuted and that Sibat be deported.

**2010** *19 January.* A thirteen-year-old girl is sentenced to a ninety-lash flogging and two months in prison as punishment for assaulting a teacher who tried to take the girl's mobile phone away from her.

*11 February.* Religious police launch a nationwide crackdown on shops selling items that are red, as they say the color alludes to the banned celebration of Valentine's Day.

*6 March.* The Saudi Civil and Political Rights Association says that Saudi security officers stormed a book stall at the Riyadh International Book Fair and confiscated all work by Abdellah Al-Hamid, a well-known reformer and critic of the royal family.

*20 April.* When Ahmed bin Qassin al-Ghamidi suggests that men and women should be allowed to mingle freely, the head of the powerful religious police has him fired.

*10 June.* After a Saudi man kisses a woman in a mall, he is arrested, convicted, and sentenced to four months in prison and ninety lashes.

*22 June.* Four women and eleven men are arrested, tried, and convicted for mixing at a party. They are sentenced to flogging and prison terms.

*15 August.* Ghazi Al-Gosaibi, a Saudi statesman and poet, dies after a long illness. Al-Gosaibi was close to the ruling family, although his writings were banned in the kingdom for most of his life. The Saudi Culture Ministry lifted the ban on his writings the month before his death, citing his contribution to the nation.

*26 August.* T. Ariyawathi, a housemaid from Sri Lanka working in Saudi Arabia, is admitted to hospital for surgery to remove twenty-four nails embedded in her body. Her Saudi employer hammered the nails into her body as punishment.

*17 November.* King Abdullah steps down as head of the country's National Guard. His son assumes the position.

*20 November.* A young woman in her twenties defies the kingdom's driving ban and accidentally overturns her car. She dies, along with three female friends who were passengers.

*22 November.* King Abdullah visits New York for medical treatment and temporarily hands control to Crown Prince Sultan, his half-brother.

*23 November.* Saudi media announce that a Saudi woman accused of torturing her Indonesian maid has been sent to jail, while the maid, Sumiati Binti Salan Mustapa, is receiving hospital treatment for burns and broken bones.

An estimated 4 million Saudi women over the age of twenty are unmarried in a country of 24.6 million. It is reported that some male guardians forcibly keep women single, a practice known as *adhl.* Saudi feminist Wajeha al-Huwaider describes male guardianship as "a form of slavery."

**2011** *16 January.* A group of Saudi activists launches "My Country," a campaign to push the kingdom to allow women to run in municipal elections scheduled for spring 2011.

*24 January.* New York–based Human Rights Watch says in its World Report 2011 that Saudi Arabia's government is harassing and jailing activists, often without trial, for speaking out in favor of expanding religious tolerance, and that new restrictions on electronic communication in the kingdom are severe.

*9 February.* Ten moderate Saudi scholars ask the king for recognition of their Uma Islamic Party, the kingdom's first political party.

*15 February.* The Education Ministry says the kingdom plans to remove books that encourage terrorism or defame religion from school libraries.

*24 February.* Influential intellectuals say in a statement that Arab rulers should derive a lesson from the uprisings in Tunisia, Egypt, and Libya, and listen to the voice of disenchanted young people.

*5 March.* Saudi Arabia's Interior Ministry says demonstrations won't be tolerated and its security forces will act against anyone taking part in them.

*11 March.* Hundreds of police are deployed in the capital to prevent protests calling for democratic reforms inspired by the wave of unrest sweeping the Arab world.

*18 March.* King Abdullah promises Saudi citizens a multibillion-dollar package of reforms, raises cash, loans, and apartments in what appears to be the Arab world's most expensive attempt to appease residents inspired by the unrest that has swept two regional leaders from power.

*2 May.* Osama bin Laden, the founder and head of the Islamic militant group Al Qaeda, is killed in Pakistan shortly after 1:00 a.m. PKT by U.S. Navy SEALs.

*22 May.* Saudi authorities rearrest activist Manal al-Sharif, who defied a ban on female drivers. She had been detained for several hours a day by the country's religious police and released after she'd signed a pledge agreeing not to drive. Saudi Arabia is the only country in the world that bans women, both Saudi and foreign, from driving.

*18 June.* Ruyati binti Satubi, an Indonesian grandmother, is beheaded for killing an allegedly abusive Saudi employer.

*28 June.* Saudi police detain one woman driving in Jeddah on the Red Sea coast. Four other women accused of driving are later detained in the city.

*25 September.* King Abdullah announces that the nation's women will gain the right to vote and run as candidates in local elections to be held in 2015 in a major advance for the rights of women in the deeply conservative Muslim kingdom.

*27 September.* Saudi female Shaima Jastaina is sentenced to be lashed ten times with a whip for defying the kingdom's prohibition on driving. King Abdullah quickly overturns the court ruling.

*29 September.* Saudi Arabian men cast ballots in local council elections, the second-ever nationwide vote in the oil-rich kingdom. Women are not allowed to vote in the election. The councils are one of the few elected bodies in the country, but have no real power, mandated to offer advice to provincial authorities.

Manssor Arbabsiar, a U.S. citizen holding an Iranian passport, is arrested when he arrives at New York's Kennedy International Airport. Mexico worked closely with U.S. authorities to help foil an alleged $1.5 million plot to kill the Saudi Arabian ambassador to Washington. On 11 October Arbabsiar is charged in the U.S. District Court in New York with conspiring to kill Saudi diplomat Adel Al-Jubeir.

*22 October.* Saudi Crown Prince Sultan bin Abdul Aziz, heir to the Saudi throne, dies in the United States. He had been receiving treatment for colon cancer, first diagnosed in 2009.

*27 October.* Saudi Arabia's powerful interior minister, Prince Naif bin Abdul Aziz, is named the new heir to the throne in a royal decree read out on Saudi state television.

*30 November.* Amnesty International publishes a new report accusing Saudi Arabia of conducting a campaign of repression against protesters and reformists since the Arab Spring erupted.

*6 December.* Saudi Arabia sentences an Australian man to five hundred lashes and a year in prison after he is found guilty of blasphemy. Mansor Almaribe was detained in Medina on 14 November while making the hajj pilgrimage and accused of insulting companions of the Prophet Muhammad.

*10 December.* Saudi Arabia's *Okaz* newspaper reports that a man convicted of raping his daughter has been sentenced to receive 2,080 lashes over the course of a thirteen-year prison term. A court in Mecca found the man guilty of raping his teenage daughter for seven years while under the influence of drugs.

*12 December.* Saudi authorities execute a woman convicted of practicing magic and sorcery. Court records state that she had tricked people into thinking she could treat illnesses, charging them $800 per session.

*15 December.* Police raid a private prayer gathering, arresting thirty-five Ethiopian Christians, twenty-nine of them women. They later face deportation for "illicit mingling."

Seventy-six death row inmates are executed in Saudi Arabia in 2011.

Indonesian maid Satinah Binti Jumad Ahmad is sentenced to death for murdering her employer's wife in 2007 and stealing money. In 2014, the Indonesian government agree to pay $1.8 million to free her.

**2012** *2 January.* Saudi Arabia announces that on 5 December, it will begin enforcing a law that allows female workers only in women's lingerie and apparel stores.

*12 February.* Malaysian authorities deport Hamza Kashgari, a young Saudi journalist wanted in his home country over a Twitter post about the Prophet Muhammad, defying pleas from human rights groups who say he faces execution. His tweet read: "I have loved things about you and I have hated things about you and there is a lot I don't understand about you."

*February.* A royal order stipulates that women who drive should not be prosecuted by the courts.

*22 March.* Saudi Arabian media reports say single men in Riyadh will be able to visit shopping malls during peak hours after restrictions aimed at stopping harassment of women are eased.

*4 April.* A Saudi official reiterates that Saudi Arabia will be fielding only male athletes at the London Olympics. However, Prince Nawaf bin Faisal announces that Saudi women taking part on their own are free to do so, but the kingdom's Olympic authority would "only help in ensuring that their participation does not violate the Islamic sharia law."

A man found guilty of shooting dead a fellow Saudi is beheaded. His execution in Riyadh brings the total number of beheadings to seventeen for 2012.

*23 May.* An outspoken and brave Saudi woman defies orders by the notorious religious police to leave a mall because she is wearing nail polish and records the interaction on her camera. Her video goes viral, attracting more than a million hits in just five days.

*16 June.* Saudi Crown Prince Naif bin Abdul Aziz, a half-brother of King Abdullah, dies. Naif is the second crown prince to die under King Abdullah's rule.

*18 June.* Saudi Arabia's defense minister, Prince Salman bin Abdul-Aziz, a half-brother to the king, is named the country's new crown prince.

*24 June.* In Saudi Arabia, a man dies from severe pneumonia complicated by renal failure. He had arrived at a Jihad hospital eleven days earlier with symptoms similar to a severe case of influenza or SARS. In September, an Egyptian virologist says it was caused by a new coronavirus. Months later the illness is named MERS (Middle Eastern respiratory syndrome).

*June.* Blogger Raif Badawi is jailed for ridiculing Islamic religious figures.

*20 July.* Saudi authorities warn non-Muslim expatriates against eating, drinking, or smoking in public during Ramadan, or face expulsion.

*30 July.* Saudi Arabia implements a ban on smoking in government offices and most public places, including restaurants, coffee shops, supermarkets, and shopping malls.

**2013** *9 January.* Saudi authorities behead a Sri Lankan domestic worker for killing a Saudi baby in her care. Rizana Nafeek was only seventeen at the time of the baby's death and proclaimed her innocence, denying strangling the four-month-old boy. Many agencies and individuals worldwide pleaded with the boy's family, and with the Saudi government, to pardon the girl.

*11 January.* King Abdullah issues two royal decrees granting women 30 seats on the Shura Council. The council has 150 members. Although the council reviews laws and questions ministers, it does not have legislative powers.

*15 January.* Dozens of conservative clerics picket the royal court to condemn the recent appointment of 30 women to the 150-member Shura Council.

*1 April.* A Saudi newspaper reports that the kingdom's religious police are now allowing women to ride motorbikes and bicycles, but only in restricted recreational areas. They also have to be accompanied by a male relative and be dressed in the full Islamic abaya.

*16 May.* Riyadh vegetable seller Muhammad Harissi sets himself on fire after police confiscate his goods after he was found to be standing in an unauthorized area. He died the next day.

*29 July.* Raif Badawi, editor of the Free Saudi Liberals Web site, is sentenced to seven years in prison and six hundred lashes for founding an Internet forum that violates Islamic values and propagates liberal thought. Badawi has been held since June 2012 on charges of cyber crime and disobeying his father.

*20 September.* U.S. prosecutors drop charges against Meshael Alayban, a Saudi princess accused of enslaving a Kenyan woman as a housemaid, forcing her to work in abusive conditions, and withholding her passport. Lawyers for the Saudi royal accused the thirty-year-old Kenyan, who has not been named, of lying in an attempt to obtain a visa to stay in the United States.

*8 October.* A Saudi court sentences a well-known cleric convicted of raping his five-year-old daughter and torturing her to death to eight years in prison and 800 lashes. The court also orders the cleric to pay his ex-wife, the girl's mother, one million riyals ($270,000) in "blood money." A second wife, accused of taking part in the crime, is sentenced to ten months in prison and 150 lashes.

*18 October.* Angered by the failure of the international community to end the war in Syria and act on other Middle East issues, Saudi Arabia says it will not take up its seat on the UN Security Council.

*22 October.* A source says that Saudi Arabia's intelligence chief revealed that the kingdom will make a "major shift" in relations with the United States in protest at its perceived inaction over the Syria war and its overtures to Iran.

*24 October.* Saudi women are warned that the government will take measures against activists who go ahead with a planned weekend campaign to defy a ban on women drivers in the conservative Muslim kingdom.

*26 October.* Saudi activists say more than sixty women claimed to have answered their call to get behind the wheel in a rare show of defiance against a ban on female driving. At least sixteen Saudi women received fines for defying the ban on female driving.

*27 October.* Saudi police detain Tariq al-Mubarak, a columnist who supported ending Saudi Arabia's ban on women driving.

*3 November.* A Kuwaiti newspaper reports that a Kuwaiti woman has been arrested in Saudi Arabia for trying to drive her father to a hospital.

*12 December.* Saudi Arabia's Grand Mufti, the highest religious authority in the birthplace of Islam, condemns suicide bombings as grave crimes, reiterating his stance in unusually strong language in the Saudi-owned *Al Hayat* newspaper.

*20 December.* Saudi Arabia beheads a drug trafficker. So far in 2013, seventy-seven people have been executed, according to an AFP count.

*22 December.* Saudi Arabia's official news agency says King Abdullah has appointed his son, Prince Mishaal, as the new governor of Mecca.

**2014** *20 February.* Human rights groups criticize an agreement between Indonesia and Saudi Arabia aimed at giving Indonesian maids more protection in the kingdom, with one saying "justice is still far away."

*16 March.* The local *Okaz* daily reports that organizers at the Riyadh International Book Fair have confiscated "more than 10,000 copies of 420 books" during the exhibition, which began on 4 March. Organizers had announced ahead of the event that any book deemed "against Islam" or "undermining security" in the kingdom would be confiscated.

*8 April.* Saudi Arabia's Shura Council recommends that a long-standing ban on sports in girls' state schools, which was relaxed in private schools in 2013, be ended altogether.

# About the Author

Jean Sasson has traveled widely in the Middle East and lived in Saudi Arabia for more than twelve years. She has spent much of her career as a writer and lecturer sharing the personal stories of courageous Middle Eastern women. Her book *Princess: The True Story of Life Behind the Veil in Saudi Arabia* became a classic, an international bestseller, and formed the basis of a compelling series. *Princess, More Tears to Cry* is Jean's twelfth book. She currently makes her home in Atlanta, Georgia.

# The Princess Series

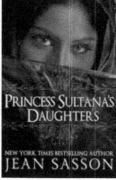
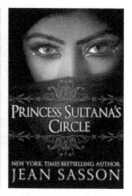

"Absolutely riveting and profoundly sad..."
–*People* magazine

"Must-reading for anyone interested in human rights."
–*USA Today*

"A chilling story...a vivid account of an air-conditioned nightmare..." –*Entertainment Weekly*

"Shocking...candid...sad, sobering, and compassionate..."
–*San Francisco Chronicle*

In Jean Sasson's international best sellers, the books about Princess Sultana Al Sa'ud vividly depict the harsh reality of life lived behind the black veil. Through Sasson, Princess Sultana tells the world about the lives of women who live in a society where they have few rights, little control over their own lives or bodies, and have no choice but to endure the atrocities perpetrated against them. Years have passed, and despite the Arab Spring and the call for new freedom for men and women, too little has changed for the women of Saudi Arabia.

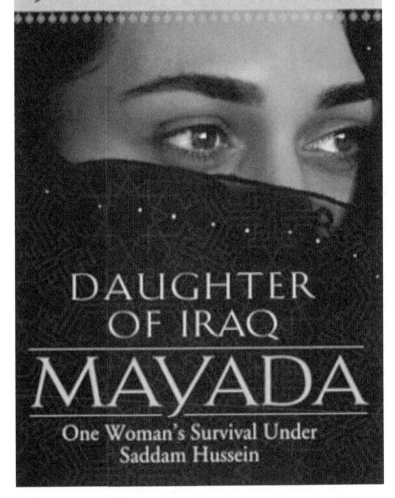

NEW YORK TIMES BESTSELLING AUTHOR OF
*Princess: A True Story of Life Behind the Veil in Saudi Arabia*

# JEAN SASSON

## DAUGHTER OF IRAQ

# MAYADA

### One Woman's Survival Under Saddam Hussein

"Sasson's candid, straightforward account of Mayada's
time...gives readers a glimpse of the cruelty and
hardship endured by generations of Iraqis."
–*Publishers Weekly*

# YASMEENA'S CHOICE

## A TRUE STORY

*of war, rape, courage and survival*

NEW YORK TIMES
BESTSELLING AUTHOR

# JEAN SASSON

This is the true story of Yasmeena, a bright and beautiful young
Lebanese woman who was imprisoned in Kuwait during the first
Gulf War. Yasmeena's shocking journey is a tale of the madness of
war, of the sexual brutality unleashed by chaos, and of one
woman's courage to stand in danger's way to aid her fellow
sufferers. This is an explicit, graphic, and honest book. It is for
mature audiences only.

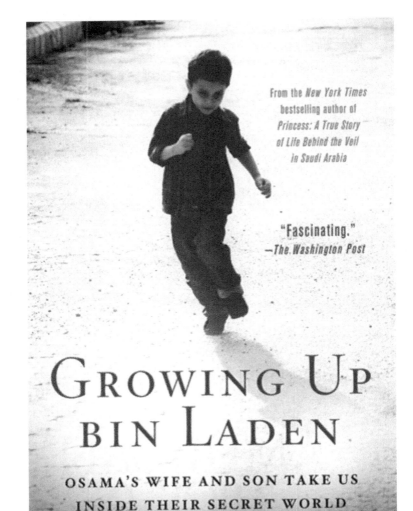

From the *New York Times*
bestselling author of
*Princess: A True Story
of Life Behind the Veil
in Saudi Arabia*

"Fascinating."
—*The Washington Post*

# Growing Up bin Laden

## OSAMA'S WIFE AND SON TAKE US INSIDE THEIR SECRET WORLD

Najwa bin Laden | Omar bin Laden | Jean Sasson

"The most vivid look the American public has had at Bin
Laden's family life...The most complete account
available."
—*New York Times*

"Fascinating." —*The Washington Post*

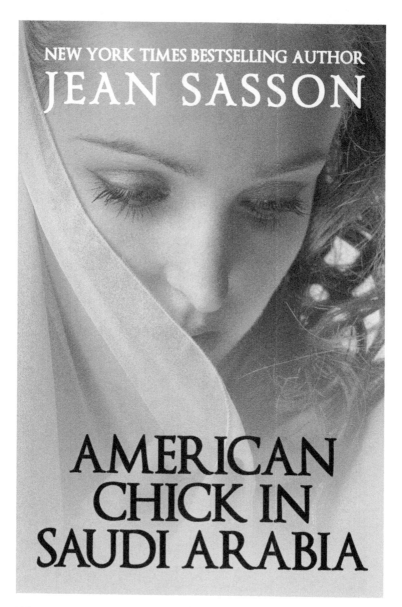

# JEAN SASSON

# AMERICAN CHICK IN SAUDI ARABIA

When Jean Sasson, a young Southern woman living in Jacksonville Beach, Florida, answers a call to work in the royal hospital in Saudi Arabia, what should have been a 2-year stay turns into a life-changing adventure spanning over a decade.

# JEAN SASSON

# FOR THE LOVE
# OF A SON

One Afghan woman's quest
for her stolen child

"I thank you for sharing your extraordinary and
heartbreaking story with the world."
–Hillary Rodham Clinton,
former US Secretary of State

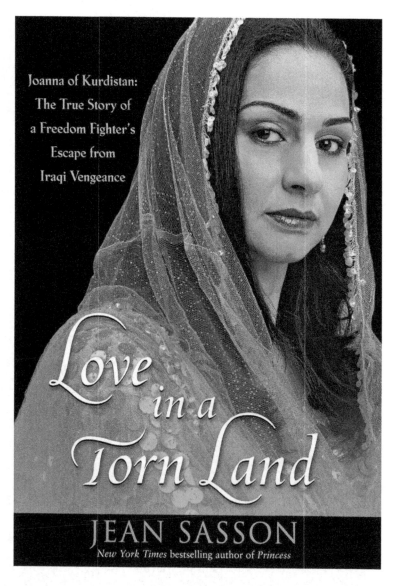

Joanna of Kurdistan:
The True Story of
a Freedom Fighter's
Escape from
Iraqi Vengeance

*Love*
*in a*
*Torn Land*

JEAN SASSON
*New York Times* bestselling author of *Princess*

"A very human look at the struggle of the Kurds in Iraq
and one woman's heroism"
—*Booklist*

# Read an excerpt from Jean Sasson's *Princess: A True Story of Life Behind the Veil in Saudi Arabia*

Jean Sasson has spent her career sharing the personal stories of courageous Middle Eastern women. *PRINCESS: A True Story of Life Behind the Veil in Saudi Arabia* was an international bestseller. It has become a classic, taught in colleges and high schools and devoured by anyone who aspires to understand the Middle East.

The series of books about Princess Sultana Al-Sa'ud first began with *Princess: A True Story of Life Behind the Veil in Saudi Arabia*, first published in 1992 by William Morrow. The book was a huge bestseller around the world and was named as one of the Great Books by Women since the year 1300. It was also an Alternate Selection of the Literary Guild and Doubleday Book Club and a Reader's Digest Selection. The book has never been out of print and has sold millions of copies worldwide, from North American to Europe to Asia to Africa and to the Middle East. Over twenty years after the world first learned about Princess Sultana, readers clamor for more stories from this beloved princess. Here is a chapter excerpt from the book that so captivated readers worldwide.

# Princess: A True Story of Life Behind the Veil in Saudi Arabia

## Chapter Fourteen: Birth

The most complete and powerful expression of life is birth. The acts of conceiving and birthing are more profound and beautiful than any miracle of art. This I learned as I waited for our first child with such great joy and happiness.

Kareem and I had meticulously planned the birth. No detail was too small to take into account. We made reservations to travel to Europe four months before the expected date of arrival. I would give birth at Guy's Hospital in London.

As with so many carefully laid plans, minor occurrences prevented our departure. Kareem's mother, blinded by a new veil made of thicker fabric than usual, sprained her ankle when she stumbled over an old Bedouin woman sitting in the souq; a close cousin on the verge of signing an important contract requested that

Kareem postpone his departure; and my sister Nura frightened the family with what the doctor thought was an appendicitis attack. Once we were past these crises, false labor pains began. My physician forbade me to travel. Kareem and I accepted the inevitable and set about making arrangements for our child to be born in Riyadh.

Unfortunately, the King Faisal Specialist Hospital and Research Centre that would offer us royals the latest medical care had yet to open. I would give birth at a smaller institution in the city, best known for harboring germs and for its lackadaisical staff.

Since we were of the Royal Family, we had options not available to other Saudis. Kareem arranged for three rooms in the maternity ward to be converted into a royal suite. He hired local carpenters and painters. Interior decorators from London were flown in, tape measures and fabric samples in hand.

My sisters and I were guided through the unit by the proud hospital administrator. The suite glowed a heavenly blue with silk bed covers and drapes. An elaborate baby bed with matching silk coverlets was fastened with heavy bolts to the floor, in the event that a member of the negligent staff might carelessly tip the bed and toss our precious child to the floor! Nura bent double with laughter when told of the precaution and warned me that Kareem would drive the family insane with his schemes to protect our child.

I sat speechless when Kareem advised me that a staff of six would soon arrive from London to assist me in the birth. A well-known London obstetrician, along with five highly skilled nurses, had been paid an enormous fee to travel to Riyadh three weeks prior to the estimated delivery date.

Since I was a motherless child, Sara moved into

the palace toward the end of my pregnancy. She watched me as I watched her. I observed her carefully, absorbing the sad changes in my dear sister. I told Kareem I feared she would never recover from her abhorrent marriage; her quiet moods were now a permanent component of what had once been a thoroughly cheerful and joyous character.

How unfair life could be! I, by my very aggressiveness, could have better dealt with an abusive husband, for bullies tend to be less forceful in the face of someone who will stand up to them. Sara, with her peaceful soul and gentle spirit, had been an easy target for the arrogance of her untamed husband.

But I was thankful for her smooth presence. As my body swelled, I became jittery and unpredictable. Kareem, in his excitement over fatherhood, had lost all his good sense.

Due to the presence of Kareem's brother Asad and various cousins who came and went at will, Sara had been careful to veil when she left our apartments on the second floor. The single men of the family were housed in another wing, but they roamed the palace at all hours. After Sara's third day in our home, Noorah sent word through Kareem that there was no need for her to veil when she entered the main living areas of the villa or the gardens. I was pleased for any loosening of the tight restraints on women that so encumbered our lives. Sara was apprehensive in the beginning, but soon shed the excess covering of black with ease.

One late evening Sara and I were reclining in wicker lounges, enjoying the cool night air of the common garden. (There are women's gardens and common, or family, gardens on most Saudi palace grounds.) Unexpectedly, Asad and four acquaintances returned from a late-night appointment.

When she heard the men approaching, Sara turned her face to the wall, for she had no desire to bring disgrace on the family by showing herself to strangers. I felt no inclination to emulate her movement, so I loudly proclaimed our presence by shouting to Asad that there were unveiled women in the garden. The men with Asad hurriedly passed our way without a glance and entered one of the side doors to the men's sitting room. As a courtesy, Asad casually walked our way to speak and inquire of Kareem's whereabouts when his eyes happened to rest on Sara's face.

His physical reaction was so sudden that I feared he had been stricken with a heart attack. His body jerked so grotesquely that I moved as rapidly as my belly allowed and shook his arm to get his attention. I was genuinely concerned. Was he ill? Asad's face was flushed and he seemed unable to move without direction; I led him to a chair and called out loudly for one of the servants to bring water.

When no one responded, Sara jumped to her feet and rushed inside to get the water herself. Asad, embarrassed, tried to leave, but I was convinced that he was about to faint. I insisted he stay. He said he felt no pain, yet he could not explain his sudden loss of movement.

Sara returned with a glass and a bottle of cold mineral water. Without looking at him, she poured a drink and raised the glass to his lips. Asad's hand brushed Sara's fingers. Their eyes locked. The glass slipped from her grasp and crashed to the ground. Sara swept past me as she ran into the villa.

I left Asad to his friends, who had become impatient and begun to empty into the garden. They were more flustered upon viewing my face than my huge, protruding belly. I defiantly waddled by them, and made a point of greeting them full in the face. They responded with embarrassed mumbles.

Kareem awoke me at midnight. When he arrived at the palace, he had been intercepted by Asad. Kareem wanted to know from me what had happened in the garden. I sleepily related the evening's occurrence and inquired about Asad's health.

I sat up with a start when Kareem replied that Asad was insisting on marrying Sara. He had announced to Kareem that he would never know happiness if Sara were not his wife. This, from the playboy of all playboys! A man who had, only a few short weeks earlier, saddened his mother when he vehemently swore never to marry.

I was astonished. I told Kareem that it was easy to surmise Asad's attraction to Sara by his behavior in the garden, but that this insistence on marriage was unbelievable! After a few moments of visual pleasure? I dismissed it as nonsense and turned back on my side.

While Kareem was showering, I rethought the event and left our bed. I knocked on Sara's door. Since there was no answer, I slowly pushed the door open. My sister was sitting on the balcony staring at a star-filled sky.

With great difficulty, I maneuvered myself into a corner of the balcony and sat in a silent stupor at this turn of events. Without looking in my direction, Sara spoke with certainty.

"He wishes to marry me."

"Yes," I agreed in a small voice.

With a burning look in her eye Sara continued. "Sultana, I saw my life ahead of me when I looked into his soul. This is the man Huda saw when she said I would know love. She also said that as a result of this love, I would bring six little ones into the world."

I closed my eyes in an attempt to bring to mind the comments made by Huda on that day long ago in our parents' home. I remembered talk of Sara's unrealized ambitions and the mention of marriage, but little else of the conversation remained fresh in my mind. I shivered when I realized that much of what Huda had predicted had come true.

I felt compelled to dismiss the idea of love at first sight. But I suddenly recalled my charged emotions the day I first met Kareem. I bit my tongue and made no sound.

Sara patted my belly. "Go to bed, Sultana. Your child needs rest. My destiny will come to me." She turned her gaze back to the stars. "Tell Kareem that Asad should go and speak with Father of this matter."

When I returned to the bed, Kareem was awake. I repeated Sara's words, and he shook his head in wonder and muttered that life was indeed strange, then wrapped his arms around my belly. Sleep came easily to us, for our lives were fixed on a carefully charted course, and neither of us expected unknowns. The following morning I left Kareem to his shaving and moved heavily down the staircase. I heard Noorah before I saw her. She, as was her favorite pastime, was quoting a proverb. I cursed under my breath but listened quietly at the doorway.

" 'The man who marries a woman for her beauty will be deceived; he who marries a woman for good sense can truly say he is married.' "

I had no feeling left to fight so I thought to cough to announce my presence. When Noorah began to speak again I changed my mind. I held my breath and strained my ears to hear her words.

"Asad, the girl has been married before. She was quickly divorced. Who knows the reason? Reconsider, my son, you can wed whom you wish. You will be wise to start with a woman that is fresh, not one that is wilted from use! Besides, my son, you see the ball of fire that is Sultana. Can her sister be of a different substance?"

I followed my stomach into the room, my heart aflutter. She was cautioning Asad against Sara. Not only that, the leopard had not changed its spots; in secret Noorah still hated me. I was a bitter potion for her to swallow.

Aware of Asad's carefree character, I had not been in favor of his and Sara's love. Now I would be a resolute supporter of their wishes. Relieved, I could easily see by Asad's expression that nothing would alter his plans. He was a man possessed.

The conversation folded when they saw my face, for I have difficulty in clothing anger; I was furious that Noorah assumed that grief would arise from her son's union with my sister. Surely, I could not argue against my own rebellious nature. I had assumed the role at an early age and had no inclination to alter. But for Sara to be labeled with my reputation was maddening!

In my youth, I had heard many old women say: "If you stand near a blacksmith, you will get covered in soot, but if you stand near a perfume seller, you will carry an aroma of scent with you." I realized that as far as Noorah was concerned, Sara was carrying the soot of her younger sister. My feeling was now bottomless rage at my mother-in-law.

Sara's beauty had sparked jealousy in many of our sex. I knew that her appearance closed the possibility of any consideration given to her gentle character and blazing intellect. Poor Sara! Asad stood up and nodded slightly in my direction. He excused himself from our company. Noorah looked like someone suffering from a dagger wound when he turned back to her and said, "The decision is made. If I am acceptable to her and her family, no one can delay me."

Noorah yelled at his back about the insolence of youth and tried to layer him with guilt when she exclaimed that she was not long for the world; her heart was weakening by the day. When Asad ignored her obvious ploy, she shook her head in sorrow. Brows knitted, she thoughtfully sipped at a cup of coffee. No doubt she was plotting against Sara as she had against the Lebanese woman.

In a state of high emotion, I rang the bell for the cook and ordered yogurt and fruit for breakfast. Marci came into the room and relieved the pain of my swollen feet with her skilled fingers. Noorah attempted conversation, but I was too angry to respond. As I began to nibble fresh strawberries—flown in daily from Europe—a labor pain took me to the floor. I was frightened and screamed in agony, for this crushing pain was too soon, and far too severe. I knew the pain should begin as a twinge, as the false labor that had nudged me in the past.

Chaos erupted as Noorah called out in one breath for Kareem, for Sara, for the special nurses, and for the servants. In moments, Kareem lifted me in his arms and bundled me into the back of an extra-long limousine, which had been especially converted for this event. The seats had been ripped out and a bed built in on one side. Three small seats had been made ready to accommodate Kareem, Sara, and a nurse. The physician from London and the other four nurses had been alerted and were following in a separate limousine.

I clutched my back while the nurse tried in vain to monitor my heartbeat. Kareem yelled at the driver to go faster; then he reversed his orders and screamed for him to go slower, declaring in a loud voice that his reckless driving would kill us all. He thumped the poor man on the back of the head when he allowed another driver to cut in front of our car.

Kareem began to curse himself for not arranging a police escort. Sara did her best to calm Kareem, but he was like an unleashed storm. Finally, the British nurse spoke loudly in his face; she advised him that his conduct was harmful to his wife and child. She threatened to remove him from the vehicle if he did not quiet himself.

Kareem, a prominent royal prince who had known no criticism in his life from a woman, entered a state of shock and was speechless. We all breathed a sigh of relief.

The hospital administrator and a large staff that had been alerted by the household were waiting at the side door. The administrator was delighted that our child would be born in his institution, for in those days many of the young royals traveled abroad for the event of birth.

My labor was long and difficult, for I was young and small in size and my baby was stubborn and large. I recall little of the birth itself; my mind was seduced with drugs and my memory is hazy. The nervous tension of the staff inflated the mood of the room, and I heard the physician insult his staff time and again. Without doubt, they were, as were my husband and family, praying for the birth of a son. Their reward would be great if a male child appeared; if a female child was born, there would be great disappointment. As far I was concerned, a female child was my desire. My land was bound to change, and I felt myself smile with anticipation of the agreeable life my baby daughter would know.

The cheering of the physician and his staff awoke me from a shadowy hollow. A son was born! I was sure I had heard the physician whisper to his head nurse, "The rag-head in the dress will fill my pockets for this prize!" My mind protested at this insult to my husband, but a deep slumber took me from the room and the remark was not recalled for many weeks. By that time, Kareem had awarded the physician a Jaguar and fifty thousand English pounds. His nurses were presented with gold jewelry from the Souks along with five thousand English pounds each. The jubilant hospital administrator from Egypt received a substantial contribution to be used for the maternity wing. He was overjoyed with a bonus of three months' salary.

All thoughts of a daughter vanished when my yawning son was placed in my arms. A daughter would come later. This male child would be taught different and better ways than the generation before him. I felt the power of my intentions creating his future. He would not be backward in his thinking, his sisters would be given a place of honor and respect, and he would know and love his partner before he wed. The vast possibilities of his accomplishments glowed and glittered as a new star. I told myself that many times in history, one man has created change that influenced millions. I swelled with pride as I considered the good to mankind that would flow from the tiny body in my arms. Without doubt, the new beginning of women in Arabia could start with my own blood.

Kareem gave little thought to the future of his son. He was enamored of fatherhood and quite rash with foolish statements regarding the number of sons we would produce together. We were mindless with joy!

# You are about to read an excerpt chapter from *Yasmeena' Choice* by Jean Sasson

This is the true story of Yasmeena, a bright and beautiful young Lebanese woman who was imprisoned in Kuwait during the first Gulf War. Yasmeena's shocking journey is a tale of the madness of war, of the sexual brutality unleashed by chaos, and of one woman's courage to stand in danger's way to aid her fellow sufferers. This is an explicit, graphic, and honest book. It is for mature audiences only.

Yasmeena was quite literally an innocent abroad. She was college educated, an English-speaking flight attendant graced with an unusual amount of confidence and sophistication. She was also a virgin and a conservative Muslim daughter and sister.

When Yasmeena's flight out of Kuwait was delayed, it was because Saddam Hussein had just invaded Kuwait. Iraqi soldiers threw her into a woman's prison where the guards committed ghastly sexual attacks and tortured the women in excruciating ways.

After Yasmeena was brutalized by the captain of the prison, she thought she was the most unfortunate woman on earth. But that was before she befriended Lana, whose brutal rapist took glee in inflicting hurt. Yasmeena used her position as the captain's favorite to protect her friend, though she also was forced into a wrenching decision.

*Yasmeena's Choice* reads like a thriller. As the Americans and other allies march into Kuwait and the Iraqis flee, Yasmeena escapes. Eventually she finds a safe harbor where Jean Sasson interviews her and records every horrific element of her experience.

Jean Sasson has wanted to write this story for many years. But she knew that the sexual explicitness and the violence would make the tale difficult to publish. A year ago, Yasmeena's story and the choices she was forced to make invaded Sasson's dreams. She realized that now was the right time to share the story. And so here it is, Sasson's testament to an articulate, angry, brave young woman who not only survived but who was eager to share her story with the world.

# Yasmeena's Choice

## Chapter Two: Captured!

### Iraq Remaps Kuwait as Province 19:

Baghdad, Iraq – This nation redrew the world map Tuesday, erasing Kuwait from the face of the globe and making the former emirate its new, and clearly its richest, southernmost province. In a decree from President Saddam Hussein, Iraq spared no effort in removing every reference to the name of the nation that was its southern neighbor for more than a century, officially designating Kuwait as Province 19. The same decree ordered that the nation's capital of Kuwait City will now be known as the provincial capital of Kadhima, an ancient Arabic name for the region.
-*Los Angeles Times,* August 29, 1990

Kuwaitis stumbled in shock for the first few weeks of the Iraqi occupation. The Kuwaiti government had fled the country on the first day of the invasion. They were now operating out of the mountain city of Taif, Saudi Arabia. The Kuwaiti military had been quickly overrun. Civilians were left to deal with an aggressive Iraqi army with no good deeds in their minds.

By nature, Kuwaitis were not a war-minded people. Those left to contend with the Iraqi military were mainly civilians of a small rich nation who had never in their lives known violence. The ordinary Kuwaiti citizen minded his own business, accumulated wealth, and didn't think much about the routine disorder that too often visited the rest of the Arab world. At least that was Yasmeena's opinion.

After the invasion, though, everything changed. The Kuwaitis, whom Yasmeena had once considered soft from so much wealth, soon proved to Yasmeena that the gentleness cloaked men of resolve and strength. Kuwaiti men rose up like angry lions to defend their country.

Yasmeena methodically noted the activities of the family that had offered her sanctuary. She soon recognized that the members were of one mind and that they would struggle against the invaders in any way possible. The two sons, both in their twenties, were deeply involved in the new Kuwaiti underground. The men bravely contested the Iraqi fighters, even after the Kuwaiti military was overpowered.

As for the Iraqi soldiers, they appeared stupefied to discover that Kuwaitis had no desire to be made a part of Iraq. Kuwait City was renamed Kadhima and declared the 19th province of Iraq, but the Kuwaitis rebuffed the claim and organized a hardy resistance. But Kuwaiti tenacity against foreign rule triggered a fiercer counteraction from the Iraqi soldiers.

Before long, the Iraqis assumed that all young Kuwaiti men were a part of the resistance, and targeted all Kuwaiti men of a certain age. When free travel in the country became difficult for the Kuwaiti men, the men tapped their sisters or cousins to transport weapons and important documents. For a time, the Iraqis didn't suspect women as resistance fighters, so the plan initially met with great success, at least in the beginning.

Although the nighttime belonged to the Kuwaiti resistance, the Kuwait's cities were calm during daylight hours. In monotony of the tedious days, jaded Iraqi soldiers sought distraction. There was little entertainment available because the entire country had been gutted, including the amusement parks, which were now stacked in colorful metal piles all around Baghdad.

The Iraqi soldiers imagined perhaps that the "silent Kuwaitis" who had not yet joined the resistance might issue invitations for dinner or parties. But they were wrong. Although the Palestinians and some other nationalities working in the kingdom cooperated with the Iraqis, Kuwaitis scorned the invaders. The bored Iraqis were easily offended, developing quick-trigger tempers that erupted when Kuwaitis spurned their offers of friendship.

As the days passed, the Iraqi soldiers grew even nastier. Far from home, they did what so many soldiers of war have done since the beginning of human civilization: They began raping women.

From Kuwaiti neighbors, Yasmeena heard whispers that Iraqi soldiers were attacking women in their homes. Yasmeena and the other women of the household listened anxiously when it was reported that the soldiers had established a routine. They would break down doors, truss the men with ropes and secure them in separate areas. Then they would force the women to strip and would take turns raping any and all females from the ages of twelve to forty...or even fifty if the older woman had maintained a youthful appearance.

Other accounts reported that soldiers sometimes eyed the women at established roadblocks. If the soldiers found any of the female passengers physically desirable, they would hold the Kuwaiti men at gunpoint and quickly take the women away to be raped.

Several gun battles broke out at roadblocks when armed Kuwaiti men defended their women.

Due to these stories, the women of the household didn't protest when the men of the house told them to hide if they heard unknown male voices.

\*\*\*

"After Iraq's invasion, Kuwaitis are being subjected to looting, rape, torture, and executions. Based on scores of interviews with refugees, we have found a horrifying picture of widespread arrests, torture under interrogation, summary executions, mass rapes, and extrajudicial killings."
-*Amnesty International,* September 1990

But after a few weeks, talk of sexual attacks diminished. Everyone believed that the worst had passed when they heard the erroneous report that Baghdad had ordered such lawlessness to cease. The truth was that Iraqi soldiers had recently devised a different scheme to seize females to rape.

After living a few weeks with her Kuwaiti hosts, one of the sons of the household asked Yasmeena if she would consider driving a bundle of leaflets to a different section of the city. She agreed, instantly eager to support the family that had welcomed her into their home. She knew that the resistance was growing more powerful, and that the Iraqis were on heightened alert for hidden weapons and other resistance materials, but at the time she believed that their focus was still solely on men. Just the day before, Yasmeena and her Kuwaiti friend had driven through a roadblock at which the Iraqi soldiers merely smiled and waved.

While getting dressed for the assignment, Yasmeena was excited. She was finally going to do something worthwhile.

Several hours later, Yasmeena was happy to be driving alone, feeling almost normal, free and happy. She was humming along to the memorable tune *"Ya Habayeb,"* or *"My Loved Ones,"* by Najwa Karam, an-up-and coming Lebanese singing star. Music had always lifted Yasmeena's spirits and today was no different. Also, she was pleased to help her friends in the important cause of resistance.

She had no way of knowing that on that very day, Iraqi soldiers were implementing a new order from Baghdad. The Iraqi command in Kuwait had been told that all adults living in Kuwait, regardless of their nationality, sex or age, were now suspected of criminal behavior. All were to be halted and their vehicles searched. There were to be no exceptions.

Ignorant of the new orders, Yasmeena confidently went on her way. She felt no danger. She was familiar with most of the roadblocks in the area, and she had her documents ready to show, although she doubted she would need them.

Her mood changed quickly when she arrived at the first roadblock on Athilali Street, which was one of the most important streets in the capital. She smiled at the young soldier who stood by her window. The soldier did not return her smile. Unmoved by her youth and beauty, his expression was unwavering as he regarded her in a cold, brisk manner. After staring impersonally at her for a few moments, he demanded that she step out of, and away from, the vehicle while they conducted their search.

Everything quickly fell apart. Three soldiers attacked the automobile as though it were their dedicated enemy. They ripped apart the seat leather with a sharp instrument. They worked like robots, moving on to examine the underside of the automobile with a mirror attached to a long reed-like stick. They then lifted the hood, examining the engine as though they had never seen one before.

Yasmeena was numb with fear, for she knew that the brothers had hidden the flyers in the trunk of the automobile. Those flyers were tucked into the backs of ten large picture frames, each depicting a London landmark. Other items were scattered in the trunk, put there to divert the attention of any soldier conducting a search. There were several dolls and stuffed animals, all of which were quickly ripped to bits with a sharp knife. There was a bag of women's clothing, which was examined before being brusquely tossed to the side of the road. The soldiers at first dismissed the picture frames, until one sharp-eyed soldier noticed that the frames were without glass, and that the London photographs bulged from the frames.

Yasmeena gasped for air when the soldier tore open the frame and flyers showered out. Yasmeena stared helplessly at the floating debris, whispering to herself, "I am doomed. I am doomed. God help me, I am doomed."

Despite her fear, she kept her composure while showing the soldiers her Lebanese identity papers. "I am not even Kuwaiti," she said. "I have no fight with you Iraqis. Why would I break any laws?" She gestured at the automobile. "Just yesterday I found this car. It had keys in the ignition. It was left with the doors open. I waited for an hour and no one claimed it." She gazed meaningfully at the oldest of the men, the one with the most medals on his uniform, telling him, "You know that many foolish Kuwaitis are discarding their automobiles. I took an abandoned car. I have not even looked into the trunk of this car, believe me."

The older soldier gave her a shrewd look, trying to decide if she was telling the truth. He knew that what Yasmeena said about the Kuwaitis and their automobiles was accurate. Soon after invading the country, the Iraqis announced that Kuwait no longer existed. All Kuwaiti documents and registrations were no longer valid. All Kuwaiti vehicle registrations were invalid. Everyone must register as an Iraqi because there was no such thing as a Kuwaiti. According to the Iraqis, Kuwaitis had vanished from the earth, just like the dinosaurs.

But Kuwaitis were outraged by the order. They were Kuwaiti and proud of it. They would not so easily discard their Kuwaiti identification papers and registrations. Rather than submit to Iraqi orders, they hid their automobiles, determined not to drive them until the Iraqis were driven from their country. If they were driving their automobiles and saw an unexpected roadblock ahead, they stopped and abandoned their vehicles and walked, instead. Some Kuwaitis burned their expensive vehicles, saying they preferred to do so than submit to Iraqi orders. It would be good for their health to take up walking, they agreed.

Soon the Iraqi soldiers realized that the ordinary Kuwaiti was bolder than the average Iraqi. Long ago Saddam had beaten the spirit out of the Iraqis. Of course, this happened after Iraqis learned the hard way how Saddam Hussein responded to disobedience.

The Kuwaitis still had a lot of spirit and plenty of pride.

Yasmeena was not worried that her exposure would endanger her Kuwaiti hosts. The automobile could not be traced to the family. She knew that the resistance employed automobiles abandoned by fleeing Palestinians or Indians or other nationalities so that the vehicle could not be tracked back to any Kuwaiti family still living in the country.

Yasmeena felt a brief flicker of hope. Perhaps the soldiers would believe her lie that she had found the automobile and decided to take it. How could she know that the resistance had stuffed some of their flyers in the picture frames? She knew that there was no date stamped on the flyers so the timeliness of her travel could not be gauged.

The old soldier could not make up his mind. Had the moment not been so grave, Yasmeena would have seen the humor in his indecision. He pursed his lips and sighed and stared at Yasmeena, then his eyes crossed two or three times, for what reason she did not know. But caution overcame his desire to release her, for finally he motioned for Yasmeena to be handcuffed. She was then pushed into a military vehicle where she sat and listened to four soldiers discuss where to take her.

The soldiers briefly debated before one of the younger men determined her future. Rather than deliver her to the prison especially for resistance members, the soldier said that he knew of a special prison suitable for her. After a long pause, the old soldier agreed for him to take her. Yasmeena stared at the man, her eyes pleading, but the old soldier turned away to question another driver.

Yasmeena's fate was set from that moment. She was too numb to protest further when the soldier ordered her to move from that vehicle and follow him to another. Yasmeena was thinking, remembering that she had recently heard that Kuwaiti men discovered transporting items for the rebellion were always tortured before being executed. Was she being taken to be tortured and executed?

Never had she felt so helpless. Rescue would be impossible because no one had any idea what was happening to her.

She was relieved not to be blindfolded and thus observed everything around her. Her thoughts were whirling, her mind moving as fast as a spinning propeller. Perhaps she would get an opportunity to escape and if she did, she wanted to know which direction to run. Soon the soldier turned into a side street and drove to an unfamiliar area of the city. By this time, Yasmeena was certain that she was being taken for torture and execution. Or perhaps they executed prisoners on the outskirts of the city, perhaps in the desert? But before they left the city, the soldier stopped at a squat, nondescript beige building that was clearly a neighborhood prison.

Ordered to leave the vehicle and go into the prison, Yasmeena did as she was told. As she was walking toward the prison entrance, two Iraqi soldiers were leaving. It took her a confused moment to realize that the two men were pulling a young Arab woman by her hair. The girl was weeping.

Yasmeena gasped. Weakness went through her entire body until her legs sagged like soft wax, making it nearly impossible to stand. She paused, trying to gather her strength as she attempted to learn what was going on with the young woman. Her guard shouted at her and pushed her into the building. Quickly she heard a barrage of gunshots and knew that she was being taken to a prison where executions did occur.

At that realization she yearned that her arms might sprout propellers so that she might soar over the building and fly like a bird with powerful wings away from those sounds of death, but her all-too-human body grounded her.

Her unsmiling guard warned her that girls who did not cooperate were eliminated. That menacing man used his finger to slice across his own neck. A second guard appeared. He looked at Yasmeena and grinned, then hissed like a cobra, bringing to mind the shocking time a real cobra snake carelessly handled at a street fair in Bombay was flashed near to her face. As the snake passed inches away, its head got even larger and its cavernous mouth opened wide and it hissed loudly. Yasmeena had nearly fainted at the sight. Now the hissing man caused a similar shock. She stood without moving until an unseen hand pushed her into an empty cell. A gravelly voiced man curtly ordered to stand to attention, "Don't move!"

There she stood with her brown eyes shining with tears, her hair gleaming, and her face frozen in panic. A dozen men walked back and forth, all looking at her with alert eyes, their heads moving like automated robots, scanning every inch of her from her head to her toe, with protruding eyes lingering longest on her chest area.

For the first time in her life her breasts felt like enemies who imperiled her life. For a menacing moment she thought they might burst from her bra and entice the eager men to come after her. Yasmeena resembled her mother, who had large perky breasts and now those inherited breasts were prompting grown men to scheme what they might do if they could clutch them in their hands or use them as a pillow for their faces. The scene of eager men plotting assault on her body was like watching a perverted movie. She could barely think, although her head pounded with the knowledge that she was in the worst predicament of her life.

Then a muted but deep voice was heard and the men quieted. A tall Iraqi with a look of stern command suddenly loomed before her, his unexpressive gaze so unlike the other men. After a few moments, he nodded and said, "This one is mine." The other men scattered, their interest vanishing for a woman they knew that they would never possess. Their Captain had spoken.

The man they called Captain meandered down the long hallway, leaving Yasmeena's vision without once speaking directly to her.

Made in the USA
Columbia, SC
04 January 2021